# SAMUEL TAYLOR COLERIDGE
## A NARRATIVE OF
## THE EVENTS OF HIS LIFE

# Samuel Taylor Coleridge

## a narrative of

## the events of his life

*by*

## JAMES DYKES CAMPBELL

**HIGHGATE**

*Lime Tree Bower Press*

1970

First edition: London and New York
Macmillan & Co. 1894
Second Edition: 1896
This edition: published by Basil Savage
46 Brookfield, Highgate West Hill,
London N6

This copy has been printed from the British
Museum copy of the first edition by courtesy
of the Trustees

The frontispiece portrait of Coleridge is
by Peter Vandyke and is reproduced by
courtesy of The National Portrait
Gallery, London

SBN 902441 01 9

Reproduced and Printed in Great Britain by
Redwood Press Limited Trowbridge & London

# SAMUEL TAYLOR COLERIDGE

## A NARRATIVE OF THE EVENTS
## OF HIS LIFE

BY

JAMES DYKES CAMPBELL

London

MACMILLAN AND CO.

AND NEW YORK

1894

# PREFACE

THIS Memoir is mainly a reproduction of the biographical sketch prefixed to the one-volume edition of Coleridge's *Poetical Works*[1] published last spring. Such an Introduction generally and properly consists of a brief summary of some authoritative biography. As, however, no authoritative biography of Coleridge existed, I was obliged to construct a narrative for my own purpose. With this view, I carefully sifted all the old printed biographical materials, and as far as possible collated them with the original documents; I searched all books of Memoirs, etc., likely to contain incidental information regarding Coleridge; and, further, I was privileged by being permitted to make use of much important matter, either absolutely new, or previously unavailable.

My aim had been, not to add to the ever-lengthening array of estimates of Coleridge as a poet and philosopher, but to provide something

[1] *The Poetical Works of Samuel Taylor Coleridge.* Edited, with a Biographical Introduction, by James Dykes Campbell. London : Macmillan and Co. 1893.

which appeared to be wanting—a plain, and as far as possible, an accurate narrative of the events of his life; something which might serve until the appearance of the full biography which is expected from the hands of the poet's grandson, Mr. Ernest Hartley Coleridge.

In preparing the present reprint of the ' Biographical Introduction ' I have spared no effort towards making it worthy of separate publication, and of its new title. It has been carefully revised; and though neither form nor scale has been materially altered, I have not hesitated to expand the narrative wherever a fuller or clearer statement appeared to be desirable, or new facts which had come to light in the interval required to be mentioned.

Although in the footnotes I have found frequent opportunity of offering thanks for help rendered in the preparation of this work, I am indebted to many others who are not there mentioned; and to each of them I now tender my sincere thanks. To the generous sympathy and assistance of Mr. Ernest Hartley Coleridge my work owes more than I can adequately express; and in no less measure am I grateful to two other friends, Canon Ainger and Mr. Leslie Stephen, whose help in every direction has been invaluable to me.

The portrait which forms the frontispiece has been reproduced directly from the original, now in the National Portrait Gallery. This belonged to Cottle, and was admirably engraved in his *Early Recollections*, where he thus writes of it: 'This portrait of Mr. Coleridge was taken in oils by a Mr. [Peter] Vandyke (a descendant of the great Vandyke). He was invited over from Holland by the late Sir Joshua Reynolds, to assist him in his portraits, particularly in the drapery department; in which capacity he remained with him many years. Mr. Vandyke afterwards settled in Bristol, and obtained great and just celebrity for his likenesses. His portrait of Mr. Coleridge did him great credit, as a better likeness was never taken, and it has the additional advantage of exhibiting Mr. C. in one of his animated conversations, the expression of which the painter has in good degree preserved.' Hancock's portrait of the following year has been more frequently engraved, and is therefore more familiar. Cottle says it 'was much admired at the time, and has an additional interest from having been drawn when Mr. C.'s spirits were in a state of depression, on account of the failure of the *Watchman*.' Several later portraits are mentioned in the text.

J. D. C.

# PRINTED AUTHORITIES CHIEFLY CITED

1. Letters, Conversations, and Recollections of S. T. Coleridge. With a Preface by the editor, Thomas Allsop. Third edition, 1864. (The first edition was published anonymously. Moxon. 1836. 2 vols.)
2. Early Years and Late Reflections. By Clement Carlyon, M.D. 4 vols. 1856-1858.
3. Biographia Literaria : or Biographical Sketches of my Literary Life and Opinions. By S. T. Coleridge, Esq. 2 vols. 1817.
4. Biographia Literaria [etc.] By S. T. Coleridge. Second edition, prepared for publication in part by the late H. N. Coleridge : completed and published by his widow. 2 vols. 1847.
5. Memoir and Letters of Sara Coleridge [Mrs. H. N. Coleridge]. Edited by her daughter. 2 vols. 1873.
6. Memorials of Coleorton : being Letters from Coleridge, Wordsworth and his sister, Southey, and Sir Walter Scott, to Sir George and Lady Beaumont of Coleorton, Leicestershire, 1803-1834. Edited by William Knight, University of St. Andrews. 2 vols. Edinburgh, 1887.
7. Early Recollections : chiefly relating to the late S. T. Coleridge, during his long residence in Bristol. By Joseph Cottle. 2 vols. 1837.
8. Reminiscences of S. T. Coleridge and R. Southey. By Joseph Cottle. 1847. (A recast of ' 7 ' with additions.)
9. Fragmentary Remains, literary and scientific, of Sir Humphry Davy, Bart. [etc.] Edited by his brother, John Davy, M.D. 1858.
10. Unpublished Letters from S. T. Coleridge to the Rev. John Prior Estlin. Communicated by Henry A. Bright (to the PHILOBIBLON SOCIETY). N.D.
11. The Life of S. T. Coleridge, by James Gillman. In 2 vols. ('Vol. I.' only was published.) 1838.
12. The Letters of Charles Lamb. Edited by Alfred Ainger. 2 vols. 1888.
13. A Group of Englishmen (1795-1815) : being records of the younger Wedgwoods and their Friends. By Eliza Meteyard. 1871.
14. Diary, Reminiscences, and Correspondence of Henry Crabb Robinson. Third edition. 2 vols. 1872.
15. Thomas Poole and his Friends. By Mrs. Henry Sandford. 2 vols. 1888.
16. The Life and Correspondence of R. Southey. 6 vols. 1849-1850.
17. Selections from the Letters of R. Southey. 4 vols. 1856.
18. Letters from the Lake Poets—S. T. Coleridge, William Wordsworth, Robert Southey—to Daniel Stuart, editor of *The Morning Post* and *The Courier*. 1800-1838. *Printed for private circulation.* 1889. Edited by Mr. Ernest Hartley Coleridge, in whom the copyright of the contents is vested.
19. Coleridge. By H. D. Traill. ' English Men of Letters ' series. 1884.
20. Memoirs of William Wordsworth. By Christopher Wordsworth, D.D., Canon of Westminster [afterwards Bishop of Lincoln]. 2 vols. 1851.
21. The Life of William Wordsworth. By William Knight, LL.D. 3 vols. 1889.

# CONTENTS

# CHAPTER I

## CHILDHOOD—CHRIST'S HOSPITAL

### A.D. 1772–1791

SAMUEL TAYLOR COLERIDGE was born at the Vicarage
of Ottery St. Mary, in Devonshire, on the 21st October
1772. His father was the Rev. John Coleridge, Vicar
of the Parish, and Chaplain-Priest and Master of its
Free Grammar School (commonly called the 'King's
School'), founded by Henry VIII. His mother was
the Vicar's second wife, and her maiden name was
Anne Bowdon. By his first wife, Mary Lendon, the
Vicar had three daughters, who were all alive in 1797 ;
and by his second, nine sons (of whom Samuel Taylor
was the youngest) and one daughter. The poet's
paternal grandfather, who had been 'a considerable
woollen trader in South Molton,' fell into poor circumstances when his son was about sixteen (c. 1735), and
John was then supported at school by a friend of the
family. When, in 1748,[1] he matriculated at Sidney
Sussex College, Cambridge, he was already married,
and on leaving the University, without a degree, he
settled as a schoolmaster at South Molton,[2] where his

---

[1] When about twenty-nine years of age, not 'twenty,' as misprinted in *Biog.
Lit.* 1847, ii. 314.

[2] Not 'Southampton,' as misprinted in *Biog. Lit.* 1847, ii. 314.

wife died in June 1751.   Having remarried *circa* 1754, he
removed in 1760 to Ottery St. Mary, on being appointed
to the living and the mastership of the school.   At that
time there were, besides a son who died in infancy,
two children of his second marriage—John, who died
in 1786, a captain H.E.I.C.S. ; and William, who died
in 1780, both unmarried.   In 1760 was born James,
who entered the army and married one of the co-
heiresses of Robert Duke, of Otterton, Esquire.
James's second son became Sir John Taylor Coleridge
(better known as ' Mr. Justice Coleridge'), the father
of the present Lord Chief-Justice.   James's fourth son
was Henry Nelson Coleridge, who married his cousin
Sara, the poet's only daughter.   The Vicar's next two
sons, Edward and George, both took orders.   The
latter succeeded (though not immediately) to the
Grammar School, and to the private boarding-school
which his father had carried on.   The seventh son,
Luke Herman, became a surgeon, but died at an early
age, in 1790, leaving but one child, a son, who became
in 1824 the first Bishop of Barbadoes.   Next came
Ann ('Nancy'), whose early death, swiftly following
on that of Luke, deeply affected the young poet.   The
eighth son was Francis Syndercombe, who died in
1792, a lieutenant H.E.I.C.S.   The ninth son, and
latest born of the Vicar's thirteen children, was the
poet, baptized 'Samuel Taylor,' after one of his god-
fathers.   Of all the thirteen, four alone have living
descendants—James, Edward, Luke, and Samuel
Taylor.   Descendants of James are numerous ; of
Edward there is a daughter ; of Luke there are a
grandson and great-grandson ; and of the poet, a grandson with his four children, and two grand-daughters.

   The Vicar is said to have been an amiable, simple-

minded, and somewhat eccentric scholar, sound in
Greek and Latin, and profound in Hebrew. Many
stories of his absent-mindedness were told in the
neighbourhood,[1] some of them probably true. His
famous son thus describes him to Poole : ' In learning,
good-heartedness, absentness of mind, and excessive
ignorance of the world, he was a perfect Parson
Adams.'[2] He printed several books[3] by subscription.
In *A Critical Latin Grammar*, he proposed (among
other innovations) to substitute for the vulgar names
of the cases ('for which antiquity pleads in opposition
to reason') 'prior, possessive, attributive, posterior,
interjective, and quale-quare-quidditive.'

The Vicar's wife was fortunately of a more practical
turn than himself. She was comparatively an uneducated woman, and unemotional ; but was an admirable
wife, mother, and housekeeper ; and although she
disliked 'your harpsichord ladies,' determined to make

[1] See Gillman's *Life of S. T. C.* chap. i., and De Quincey in his *Works* (1863),
ii. 70.

[2] *Biog. Lit.* 1847, ii. 315.

[3] (I) *Miscellaneous Dissertations* arising from the XVIIth and XVIIIth
chapters of the Book of Judges. 1768. 8vo, pp. 275.

(II) *A Critical Latin Grammar*, containing clear and distinct rules for boys
just initiated ; and Notes explanatory of almost every antiquity and obscurity in
the Language, for youth somewhat advanced in Latin learning. 1772. 12mo,
pp. xiv. ; 161.

(III) Also, ' For the use of Schools,' price 2s. bound, *Sententiæ Excerptæ*,
explaining the Rules of Grammar, and the various signification of all the Pre-
positions, etc. [Advertisement in II.]

(IV) *Government not originally proceeding from Human Agency, but Divine
Institution*, shewn in a Sermon preached at Ottery St. Mary, Devon, December
13, 1776, on the Fast Day, appointed by reason of our much-to-be-lamented
American War, and published at the request of the hearers. By John Coleridge,
Vicar of and Schoolmaster at Ottery St. Mary, Devon. London : printed for the
Author, 1777. 4to, pp. 15.

To No. I. is appended a long school prospectus, setting forth the method of
teaching, etc., and to No. II. an advertisement referring to the prospectus. From
these we learn that the Vicar took about twenty boys, who paid two guineas
entrance-fee, and sixteen guineas a year for board and the teaching of Latin,
Greek, and Mathematics. ' A Writing-Master attends, for those who chuse it,
at sixteen shillings per year ; and a Dancing Master (at present *Mr. Louis*, of
*Exeter*) once a week, at two guineas per year.'

gentlemen of her sons—an ambition in which their father was deficient.

Our knowledge of Coleridge's childhood is derived entirely from his letters to Poole [1] written in 1797— compositions which as fully as any of his poems are instinct with the writer's extraordinary genius. Even remembering the best successes of Charles Dickens and George Eliot, it may be affirmed that no more vivid and essentially truthful picture of a solitary and imaginative childhood has ever been drawn.

Coleridge describes himself as a precocious and imaginative child, never mixing with other boys. At the age of three he was sent to a dame's school, where he remained till he was six. 'My Father was very fond of me, and I was my Mother's darling; in consequence whereof, I was very miserable. For Molly, who had nursed my brother Francis, and was immoderately fond of him, hated me because my Mother took more notice of me than of Frank; and Frank hated me because my Mother gave me now and then a bit of cake when he had none'— Frank enjoying many titbits from Molly, who had only 'thumps and ill-names' for 'Sam,' which through life was the family abbreviation of the poet's name. 'So I became fretful and timorous, and a tell-tale; and the schoolboys drove me from play and were always tormenting me. And hence I took no pleasure in boyish sports, but read incessantly.' He read all the children's books he could find—*Jack the Giant-Killer*, and the like.

And I used to lie by the wall and mope; and my spirits used to come upon me suddenly, and in a flood; and I then was accustomed to run up and down the churchyard and act over again all I had been reading, on the docks and the nettles and the rank

---

[1] 'Biog. Supplement' to *Biog. Lit.* 1847, ii. 315–330.

grass. At six years of age, I remember to have read *Belisarius*, *Robinson Crusoe*, and Philip Quarll [*The Hermit*]; and then I found the *Arabian Nights' Entertainments*, one tale of which (the tale of a man who was compelled to seek for a pure virgin) made so deep an impression on me (I had read it in the evening while my Mother was at her needle) that I was haunted by spectres whenever I was in the dark; and I distinctly recollect the anxious and fearful eagerness with which I used to watch the window where the book lay, and when the sun came upon it, I would seize it, carry it by the wall, and bask and read.[1] My father found out the effect which these books had produced, and burned them.

So I became a dreamer, and acquired an indisposition to all bodily activity. I was fretful, and inordinately passionate; and as I could not play at anything, and was slothful, I was despised and hated by the boys; and because I could read and spell, and had, I may truly say, a memory and understanding forced into almost unnatural ripeness, I was flattered and wondered at by all the old women. And so I became very vain, and despised most of the boys that were at all near my own age, and before I was eight years old I was a *character*. Sensibility, imagination, vanity, sloth, and feelings of deep and bitter contempt for almost all who traversed the orbit of my understanding, were even then prominent and manifest.

That which I began to be from three to six, I continued to be from six to nine. In this year [1778] I was admitted into the Grammar School, and soon outstripped all of my age.

About this time the child had a fever. His nightly prayer was the old rhyme, beginning 'Matthew, Mark, Luke, John,' and 'frequently,' he adds, 'have I (half-awake and half-asleep, my body diseased, and fevered by imagination) seen armies of ugly things bursting in upon me, and then four angels ["Four good angels round me spread"] keeping them off.'

And so the child went on, living by himself in a fairy world of nursery tales, and Arabian Nights, 'cutting down weeds and nettles, as one of the Seven Champions of Christendom.' 'Alas!' he exclaims, 'I had all the simplicity, all the docility of the little

[1] See this reminiscence repeated, with some others, in *The Friend*, 1818, i. 251 *et seq.*

child, but none of the child's habits.   I never thought
as a child, never had the language of a child.'
Happily, wandering in Fairy Land is one of the
habits of most children, but in Coleridge's case the
usual correctives were wanting.   One adventure of
those days is worth recalling, as it is not improbable
that its effects on his constitution were never entirely
got rid of.   One evening, fearing punishment for a
somewhat serious fault, he ran away, not stopping
until he was a mile from home.   Both rage and
fear passed off, but he felt 'a gloomy satisfaction
in making his Mother miserable,' and determined
not to return.   He fell asleep, and in his slumber
rolled down to the unfenced bank of the Otter.
The night had become stormy, and he awoke about
five o'clock, wet, and so cold and stiff that he
could not move.   The Sir Stafford Northcote of
the period, who, with the Vicar and many of the
neighbours, had been searching all night for the
lost child, found him, and he was carried home.

I remember, and never shall forget, my Father's face as he
looked upon me while I lay in the servant's arms—so calm, and the
tears stealing down his face ; for I was the child of his old age.   My
Mother, as you may suppose, was outrageous with joy. . . . I
was put to bed, and recovered in a day or so.   But I was
certainly injured ; for I was weakly and subject to ague for many
years after.

Apparently, when Coleridge was no more than
eight, a career was marked out for him.

My Father (he writes), who had so little parental ambition in
him, that but for my Mother's pride and spirit, he would certainly
have brought up his other sons to trades, had nevertheless resolved
that I should be a parson.   I read every book that came in my way
without distinction ; and my Father was fond of me, and used to
take me on his knee, and hold long conversations with me.   I

remember, when eight years old, walking with him one winter evening from a farmer's house, a mile from Ottery; and he then told me the names of the stars, and how Jupiter was a thousand times larger than our world, and that the other twinkling stars were suns that had worlds rolling round them; and when I came home, he showed me how they rolled round. I heard him with a profound delight and admiration, but without the least mixture of wonder or incredulity. For, from my early reading of fairy tales and about genii, and the like, my mind had been habituated to the Vast; and I never regarded my senses in any way as the *criteria* of my belief. I regulated all my creeds by my conceptions, not by my sight, even at that age.

The few glimpses of his childhood afforded by the poems are invariably pleasant.[1]

The child seems to have been petted, not only by his parents, but by his brother George, whom he describes as his 'earliest friend.' All this, or the best of it, came to an end when the boy had hardly completed his ninth year. His father died suddenly on the 4th October 1781, and was succeeded, both as vicar and as schoolmaster, by Mr. Smerdon, with

[1] Dear native Brook! wild Streamlet of the West!
   How many various-fated years have past,
     What happy, and what mournful hours, since last
I skimmed the smooth thin stone along thy breast,
Numbering its light leaps! yet so deep imprest
Sink the sweet scenes of childhood, that mine eyes
   I never shut amid the sunny ray,
But straight with all their tints thy waters rise,
   Thy crossing plank, thy marge with willows grey,
And bedded sand that veined with various dyes
Gleamed through thy bright transparence! On my way
   Visions of Childhood! oft have ye beguiled
Lone manhood's cares, yet waking fondest sighs:
   Ah! that once more I were a careless Child!

This sonnet was addressed *To the River Otter*, about 1792-93. Six years later, in *Lines composed in a Concert-room*, Coleridge exclaimed—

O give me, from this heartless scene released,
   To hear our old musician, blind and grey,
   (Whom stretching from my nurse's arms I kissed,)
     His Scottish tunes and warlike marches play,
By moonshine, on the balmy summer-night,
   The while I dance amid the tedded hay
With merry maids, whose ringlets toss in light!

Further reminiscences of youthful Ottery days are to be found in *Frost at Midnight* and in *Lines to a beautiful Spring in a Village*.

whom Coleridge remained as a day-scholar until the
following April, when a presentation to Christ's Hospital was obtained for him from a Mr. John Way,
through the interest of Mr. Francis Buller (afterwards
the famous judge), who had been a pupil of the late
Vicar.   Thus 'too soon transplanted, ere his soul had
fixed its first domestic loves,' Coleridge entered the great
school on the 18th July 1782, an intervening period of
about ten weeks having been spent in London with
his mother's brother, Mr. John Bowdon, who had a
shop in Threadneedle Street.   This affectionate but
injudicious uncle, he relates, 'used to carry me from
coffee-house to coffee-house, and tavern to tavern,
where I drank, and talked, and disputed as if I had
been a man.'

After six weeks of the Junior School at Hertford
—'where I was very happy on the whole, for I had
plenty to eat and drink'—he was removed, in September, to the great London school, being placed in
the second, or 'Jefferies' Ward, and in the Under
Grammar School.   Christ's Hospital, he says, then
contained about seven hundred boys, about one-third
being the sons of clergymen.   The school and the
Coleridge of those days have been described for all
time in Lamb's essays — 'Recollections of Christ's
Hospital' (1813), and 'Christ's Hospital five-and-
thirty years ago' (1820).   The former is a serious
historical account of the Foundation and its advantages ; the latter presents the reverse of the medal—
the side which impressed itself most indelibly on the
Blue-coat boys of the essayist's time.   Although
Lamb was Coleridge's junior by a little more than
two years, he entered Christ's Hospital a few
months earlier.   His parents lived close at hand,

and Coleridge was the 'poor friendless boy' for
whom he speaks—

> My parents and those who should care for me were far away.
> Those few acquaintances of theirs which they could reckon upon as
> being kind to me in the great city, after a little forced notice, which
> they had the grace to take of me on my first arrival in town, soon
> grew tired of my holiday visits.   They seemed to them to recur too
> often, though I thought them few enough ; and, one after another,
> they all failed me, and I felt myself alone among six hundred
> playmates. . . . How, in my dreams, would my native town (far in
> the west) come back, with its church, and trees, and faces ! How
> I would wake weeping, and in the anguish of my heart exclaim
> upon sweet Calne in Wiltshire !

'Calne,' of course, is only Lamb's device for con-
cealing his friend's identity, and was selected, doubtless, partly for its cadence, and partly because Coleridge resided there shortly before going to Highgate.
The words about the boy's dreams are but a reflection
of Coleridge's own lines in *Frost at Midnight*—

> How oft, at school, with most believing mind,
> Presageful, have I gazed upon the bars,
> To watch that fluttering *stranger !* and as oft
> With unclosed lids, already had I dreamt
> Of my sweet birth-place, and the old church-tower,
> Whose bells, the poor man's only music, rang
> From morn to evening, all the hot Fair-day,
> So sweetly, that they stirred and haunted me
> With a wild pleasure, falling on mine ear
> Most like articulate sounds of things to come !
> So gazed I, till the soothing things, I dreamt,
> Lulled me to sleep, and sleep prolonged my dreams !
> And so I brooded all the following morn,
> Awed by the stern preceptor's face, mine eye
> Fixed with mock study on my swimming book :
> Save if the door half opened, and I snatched
> A hasty glance, and still my heart leaped up,
> For still I hoped to see the *stranger's* face,
> Townsman, or aunt, or sister more beloved,
> My play-mate when we both were clothed alike !

It is the same poem, written in the Stowey cottage
in February 1798, which contains the remarkable

prophecy how his beloved Hartley should wander like
a breeze by lakes and mountains, unlike his father,
who was

> reared
> In the great city, pent 'mid cloisters dim,
> And saw nought lovely but the sky and stars,

—sky and stars seen from the roof of Christ's Hospital, as we learn through Wordsworth—

> Of rivers, fields,
> And groves I speak to thee, my Friend ! to thee
> Who, yet a liveried schoolboy, in the depths
> Of the huge city, on the leaded roof
> Of that wide edifice, thy school and home,
> Wert used to lie and gaze upon the clouds
> Moving in heaven ; or, of that pleasure tired,
> To shut thine eyes, and by internal light
> See trees, and meadows, and thy native stream,
> Far distant, thus beheld from year to year
> Of a long exile.[1]

A long exile it proved, for it seems probable that
the boy did not return to Ottery until the summer of
1789. But Coleridge's school-days were not a mono-
tony of weeping and day-dreaming. Such, in some
measure, they may have been, perhaps, at first ; but
the clouds broke. A few of his letters from Christ's
Hospital have been preserved.[2] The earliest is dated
February 4, 1785, when the writer was in his twelfth
year, and was addressed to his mother. He acknow-
ledges 'with gratitude' 'two handkerchiefs, and the
half-crown from Mr. Badcock,' another half-crown and
the prospect of 'a plumb-cake' from Mrs. Smerdon ;
and he promises to take great care of the tips, 'as I
now consider that were it not for my kind friends I
should be as destitute of many little necessaries as

---

[1] *Prelude*, Book VI.
[2] *Unpublished Letters of S. T. Coleridge.* Edited by his Grandson, Ernest
Hartley Coleridge. *Illustrated London News*, April 1, 1893.

some of my school-fellows are; and Thank God and
my relations for them!' The letter ends with affectionate messages, in which he is joined by his Bowdon
'uncle, aunt, and cousins.' The many acknowledgments of kindnesses received from the Bowdons
incline one to believe that there is a touch of artistic
exaggeration in Lamb's words quoted above. 'Miss
Calerica,'[?] Coleridge writes, May 12, 1787, 'and my
cousin Bowdon behave more kindly to me than I can
express. I dine there every Saturday.' 'But, above
all,' he continues, 'I can never sufficiently express
my gratitude to my brother George. *He* is father,
brother, and everything to me.' About two years
before this, George had taken a situation as master in
Newcome's Academy at Hackney, where he remained
until he took up his permanent residence at Ottery
in 1794. He was probably the 'Dear Brother' to
whom the following request was addressed in a letter
described as 'undated, from Christ's Hospital, before
1790': 'You will excuse me for reminding you that,
as our holidays commence next week, and I shall go
out a good deal, a good pair of breeches will be no
inconsiderable accession to my appearance,' his present
pair being 'not altogether well adapted for a female eye.'

From the first Coleridge was full of 'natural glad-
ness,' and possessed in an extraordinary degree the
invaluable faculty of making friends. As close companions, he had Lamb, and a little host beside;
for protector and encourager, Middleton (afterwards
Bishop of Calcutta); and as tolerable substitutes
for a home, the house of his Bowdon uncle, and,
later, that of Mrs. Evans, the mother of Mary and
other daughters. Boyer (whose floggings did his
pupil no serious harm that we know of) took a

paternal headmaster's interest in him, and brought
him up in the way a good scholar, and even a good
poet, should go;[1] so that Coleridge, in spite of his
persistent waywardness, was enabled to carry off the
best honours the school afforded. In the letter of
May 12, 1787, already quoted from, he informs his
brother Luke: 'I suppose I shall be a Grecian in
about a year. Mr. Boyer says that if I take particular care of my exercises, etc., I may find myself
rewarded sooner than I expected. I know not exactly
what he means; but I believe it is something concerning putting me in the first form.' These anticipations
of promotion were not belied, for it was in 1788 that
he entered the ranks of the 'Grecians'—the small
band selected by the headmaster for special training
under his own eye for the University Exhibitions of
the school,[2] one of which Coleridge gained in due time.

But there were interruptions. When about fifteen
he took a fancy to be apprenticed to a friendly
cobbler in the neighbourhood of the school, and
induced the cobbler to make formal application to
Boyer. This was more than Boyer could stand, and
with assault and battery he drove the astonished
applicant from his sanctum. Coleridge himself seems
to have escaped unhurt from the fray. It was soon
after this that his brother Luke came up to walk the
London Hospital, and Coleridge then thought of
nothing but how he too might become a doctor.
He read all the medical and surgical books he
could procure, went round the hospital-wards with
Luke, and thought it bliss if he were permitted
to hold a plaster. 'Briefly' (he says) 'it was a

---

[1] *Biographia Literaria*, chap. i.

[2] See Lamb's account of the group—'seldom above two or three at a time
were inaugurated into that high order'—in *Recollections of Christ's Hospital*.

wild dream, which gradually blending with, gradually
gave way to, a rage for metaphysics, occasioned
by the essays on " Liberty " and " Necessity " in
*Cato's Letters*,[1] and more by theology. After I had
read Voltaire's *Philosophical Dictionary* I sported
infidel! but my infidel vanity never touched my
heart.'[2]  Boyer took his 'short way,' and reconverted
his pupil by means of a sound flogging—'the only
just one,' Coleridge was pleased in after-life to say,
he ever received from his master.  This was doubtless but a fond and passing conceit, for elsewhere he
blesses the floggings which saved him from being
emasculated into a 'juvenile prodigy.' Yet prodigy
he must have been, if his own and Lamb's reminiscences are to be accepted—accepted even with a sub-
stantial grain of salt; how he read straight through a
whole circulating library, of which he was made free
by a singular incident (his account of which is need-
lessly romantic); and how he invaded the murky
caves of the third-century Neo-Platonists[3] with his
boyish rush-light.

Truth there must be, and even something of fact,
in Lamb's famous passage—

Come back into memory, like as thou wert in the dayspring of
thy fancies, with hope like a fiery column before thee—the dark
pillar not yet turned—Samuel Taylor Coleridge—Logician, Metaphysician, Bard !—How have I seen the casual passer through the
Cloisters stand still, entranced with admiration (while he weighed
the disproportion between the *speech* and the *garb* of the young

---

[1] By John Trenchard and Thomas Gordon.    4 vols. 12mo, 1755.
[2] Gillman's *Life*, p. 23.
[3] In these adventures he was doubtless aided by the Latin translations usually
supplied with the original Greek, and by Thomas Taylor's, which appeared about
that time (translations which he once described as ' difficult Greek transmuted into
incomprehensible English '), though he asserts (*Biog. Lit.* i. 249) that he had
translated the eight hymns of Synesius from the Greek into English Anacreontics
before his fifteenth year !

Mirandula), to hear thee unfold, in thy deep and sweet intonations, the mysteries of Jamblichus, or Plotinus (for even in those years thou waxedst not pale at such philosophic draughts), or reciting Homer in his Greek, or Pindar—while the walls of the old Grey Friars re-echoed to the accents of the *inspired charity boy !* [1]

We hear nothing of games, but Coleridge enjoyed bathing excursions in the summer holidays. Once, as he told Gillman, he swam across the New River in his clothes, and let them dry on his back, with the consequence, apparently, that 'full half his time from seventeen to eighteen was passed in the sick-ward of Christ's Hospital, afflicted with jaundice and rheumatic fever.' [2] Coleridge was doubtless rendered the more susceptible by the effects of his runaway adventure eight years before. If the tradition [3] be true, that *Genevieve* was addressed to the daughter of his school 'nurse,' the attachment may have been formed during this illness—

> When sinking low the suff'rer wan
> Beholds no hand stretcht out to save,
>
> .     .     .     .     .
>
> I've seen thy breast with pity heave,
> And therefore love I thee, sweet Genevieve !

He has dated the poem '*æt*. 14,' and the illness ' 17-18,' but Coleridge was never sure of his own age, and such figures of his are, as a rule, untrustworthy. According, however, to his own statement, [4] he was about sixteen (1788) when he made the acquaintance of the Evans family—a connection destined to exercise an important influence on his career. It is Gillman who thus reports :—

[1] 'Christ's Hospital five-and-thirty years ago,' in *Essays of Elia.*
[2] Gillman's *Life*, p. 33.
[3] There was a tradition in Christ's Hospital that *Genevieve* was addressed to the daughter of Coleridge's school 'nurse.' For the head boys to be in love with these young persons was an institution of long standing. The lines quoted are taken from the earliest MS. text of the poem.
[4] Gillman's *Life*, p. 28.

About this time he became acquainted with a widow lady, 'whose son,'[1] says he, 'I, as upper boy, had protected, and who therefore looked up to me, and taught me what it was to have a mother. I loved her as such. She had three daughters, and, of course, I fell in love with the eldest. From this time to my nineteenth year, when I quitted school for Jesus, Cambridge, was the era of poetry and love.'

In 1822 he said in a letter to Allsop[2]—

And oh! from sixteen to nineteen what hours of paradise had Allen and I in escorting the Miss Evanses home on a Saturday, who were then at a milliner's, . . . and we used to carry thither, of a summer morning, the pillage of the flower-gardens within six miles of town, with sonnet or love-rhyme wrapped round the nose-gay. To be feminine, kind, and genteelly (what I should now call neatly) dressed, these were the only things to which my head, heart, or imagination had any polarity, and what I was then, I still am.

The latter reminiscence reflects more accurately than the former the earlier relations between Coleridge and the Evans sisters. Of the letters he wrote to the family from Cambridge—which doubtless were numerous—five have been preserved,[3] the latest being dated February 10, 1793. They are all strictly family letters, such as a son and brother would write—he seems to have been called 'Brother Coly' by the family—and are addressed indifferently to Mrs. Evans, and to her daughters. The only exception noticeable is that it is to Mary he addresses all his rhymes.[4] But there have been preserved also two letters addressed to Mary towards the end of 1794, in one of which Coleridge first declares himself her lover, a passion which he says he has 'for four years endeavoured to smother.' These letters will receive notice in their

[1] Afterwards a fellow-clerk with Lamb in the India House.
[2] *Letters*, etc., 1864, p. 170.
[3] Now in the great collection of Mr. Alfred Morrison at Fonthill, who has kindly permitted me to use them.
[4] *A Wish*, the two poems which follow it, and the *Complaint of Ninathóma*. See *Poetical Works*, 1893, pp. 19, 20.

proper place—here it is enough to show that in all probability Coleridge was fancy-free until the end of 1790. As Mrs. Evans was as a mother or an aunt to him, so were her daughters as his sisters or cousins. Unless we are to believe implicitly Coleridge's dating of *Genevieve*, it is clear that ' Poetry ' (or, at all events, verse) preceded ' Love ' in his development, for the contributions to Boyer's albums [1] begin with 1787 ; and the dates attached to these are the only ones which can be depended on. But it was not until the end of 1789 that the poetical faculty in Coleridge was quickened. The school exercises [2] were regarded by him strictly as such, and at this particular period poetry had become 'insipid,' and everything but metaphysics distasteful. [3]

From 'this preposterous pursuit' he was 'auspiciously withdrawn,' first by 'an accidental introduction to an amiable family' (Evanses) ; next, and 'chiefly,' by another accidental introduction—to the poetry of Bowles. 'I had just entered on my seventeenth year [October 1789] when the Sonnets of Mr. Bowles,[4] twenty in number, and just then published in a quarto pamphlet, were first made known and presented to me.' [5] The donor was his friend Middleton, who had left Christ's Hospital for Cambridge a year before. These mild sonnets stirred Coleridge.

---

[1] The books into which the headmaster of Christ's caused his boys to transcribe their best exercises, and which his grandson, Mr. James Boyer of Coopers' Hall, has kindly placed at my disposal.

[2] See *Dura Navis, Nil pejus est cælibe vitâ, Quæ nocent docent*, first printed in *Poetical Works* (1893) ; and *Julia*, first printed in Trollope's *History of Christ's Hospital*, 1834 (*P. W.* 1893, p. 4).

[3] *Biog. Lit.* 1817, i. 16.

[4] Probably the second edition, which contained twenty-one sonnets. The first was anonymous : *Fourteen Sonnets, Elegiac and Descriptive, written during a Tour*. Bath, MDCCLXXXIX. Quarto.

[5] *Biog. Lit.* i. 13.

My earliest acquaintances (he adds) will not have forgotten the undisciplined eagerness and impetuous zeal with which I laboured to make proselytes. . . . As my school finances did not permit me to purchase copies, I made within less than a year and a half more than forty transcriptions as the best presents I could offer to those who had in any way won my regard, and with almost equal delight did I receive the three or four following publications of the same author.

One cannot help regretting that the inspiration did not come more directly from Cowper or Burns, or from both ; but I confess my inability to join in the expression of amused wonder which has so often greeted Coleridge's acknowledgments of his obligation to Bowles. Had he first met with Cowper, or with Burns, doubtless Coleridge would have been less strongly impressed by Bowles—certainly less strongly impressed by his novelty or originality; perhaps (but only perhaps) less influenced by his work as a whole. As a matter of fact, however, it happened that the first breath of Nature, unsophisticated by the classical tradition, came to Coleridge from Bowles's sonnets ; and he recognised it at once. Nor was he alone in this experience. Four years later, the same sonnets captivated Wordsworth. He first met with them as he was starting on a walk, and kept his brother waiting on Westminster Bridge until, seated in one of its recesses, he had read through the little quarto. Of course, much that Coleridge and Wordsworth saw in Bowles's sonnets is hidden from us ; but surely, even to eyes looking across the century, they exhibit qualities, both intrinsic and adventitious, which sufficiently explain the influence they exercised.

How this influence affected Coleridge is set forth in the opening chapters of the *Biographia*, and is best illustrated by the youthful poems of 1790 and following

years, which can now be read in something which
approximates to chronological order.[1]   In one of the
earliest, the *Monody on Chatterton* (1790), he passed
beyond his master, but the new influence pervades
others of succeeding years.   The old leaven was not
purged out all at once, and throughout there is dis-
cernible more of the besetting weakness of the new, as
represented by the model, and less of the individuality
it helped to emancipate, than we could have wished or
expected.   Even at the end of 1796 Coleridge wrote
to Thelwall of Bowles as 'the god of his idolatry,'
and presented Mrs. Thelwall with a copy of his idol's
poems (Bath, 1796)—it is now in the Dyce collection
at South Kensington — thus inscribed : ' I entreat
your acceptance of this volume, which has given me
more pleasure, and done my heart more good than
all the other books I ever read, excepting my Bible '
(Dec. 18, 1796).   How closely Coleridge would sometimes follow his model in subject, sentiment, and
language, may be seen by comparing his sonnet *To
the River Otter*, written either in 1792 or 1793 (p. 7
*supra*), with Bowles's verses *To the River Itchin, near
Winton*.[2]

The winter of 1790-1 brought two severe trials to

---

[1] *The Poetical Works of S. T. Coleridge.*   Macmillan and Co.   1893.

[2]  Itchin, when I behold thy banks again,
    Thy crumbling margin, and thy silver breast,
    On which the self-same tints still seem to rest,
Why feels my heart the shiv'ring sense of pain ?
    Is it, that many a summer's day has past
Since, in life's morn, I carol'd on thy side ?
Is it, that oft, since then, my heart has sigh'd
    As Youth, and Hope's delusive gleams, flew fast ?
Is it, that those, who circled on thy shore,
Companions of my youth, now meet no more ?
    Whate'er the cause, upon thy banks I bend
Sorrowing, yet feel such solace at my heart,
    As at the meeting of some long-lost friend,
    From whom, in happier hours, we wept to part.
            (*Fourteen Sonnets*, 1789.   No. VIII.)

Coleridge in the deaths successively of his brother Luke
—who had been the kindest of elder brothers during
the time they were together in London—and his
sister Ann.   In the short space which intervened
between these bereavements he wrote the well-known
lines *On receiving an account that his only sister's
death was inevitable*—

> The tear which mourn'd a brother's fate scarce dry—
> Pain after pain, and woe succeeding woe—
> Is my heart destined for another blow ?
> O my sweet sister ! and must thou too die ?

And four years later, during a serious illness of Mary
Lamb, Coleridge thus wrote to her brother Charles :—

> I too a Sister had, an only Sister—
> She loved me dearly, and I doted on her !
> To her I pour'd forth all my puny sorrows,
> (As a sick Patient in his Nurse's arms)
> And of the heart those hidden maladies
> That even from Friendship's eye will shrink ashamed.
> O ! I have woke at midnight, and have wept,
> Because she was not !—Cheerily, dear Charles !
> Thou thy best friend shalt cherish many a year :
> Such warm presagings feel I of high Hope.[1]

The sadness of this winter was doubtless greatly
relieved by the knowledge that the next would be
spent at Cambridge.   The worst of the school-boy
hardships had already been left behind, but even the
life of a Grecian was subject to restraints unknown to
an undergraduate ; and no doubt Coleridge had long
been looking forward to freedom.   Yet when the day
came round for entering upon it, it was but natural
that the drawbacks of the change should have been
uppermost in his mind.   Of his special school-friends,
only Middleton, who was three years his senior in age,
would greet him at Cambridge, while he was leaving

---

[1] *To a Friend together with an unfinished Poem.*

behind not a few with whom his relations had been
on a footing of greater equality—Lamb, who, though
he had left the Cloisters two years before, was still
within hail; Robert Allen, the brothers Le Grice,
Favell, and others, doubtless, whose names have
not come down to us. For the moment at least the
boy felt as the child had done nine years before,—
that he was leaving *home*, and it was in this regretful
strain that he sang his *Dulce Domum* :—

> Farewell parental scenes ! a sad farewell !
> To you my grateful heart still fondly clings,
> Tho' fluttering round on Fancy's burnish'd wings
> Her tales of future Joy Hope loves to tell.
> Adieu, adieu ! ye much-loved cloisters pale !
> Ah ! would those happy days return again,
> When 'neath your arches, free from every stain,
> I heard of guilt and wonder'd at the tale !
> Dear haunts ! where oft my simple lays I sang,
> Listening meanwhile the echoings of my feet,
> Lingering I quit you, with as great a pang,
> As when erewhile, my weeping childhood, torn
> By early sorrow from my native seat,
> Mingled its tears with hers—my widow'd Parent lorn.

# CHAPTER II

## CAMBRIDGE, ETC.

### A.D. 1791–1794

On the 12th January 1791 the Committee of Almoners of Christ's Hospital appointed Coleridge to an Exhibition at Jesus College, Cambridge, on the books of which he was entered as a sizar on the 5th February. His 'discharge' from the school is dated September 7th, 1791, and he went into residence at Jesus in the following month. He became a pensioner on November 5, and matriculated on March 26, 1792. The Official 'List of [C.H.] University Exhibitioners' states that Coleridge 'was sent to Jesus College, Cambridge, as the prospect of his preferment to the Church would be very favourable if he were preferred to that College.' His Exhibition from the Hospital (besides the usual allowance of £40) was fixed at £40 per annum for the first four years, and £30 for each of the three remaining years of the then usual period of C.H. Exhibition tenure. Mr. Leslie Stephen states,[1] on official authority, that Coleridge obtained one of the Rustat scholarships belonging to Jesus which are confined to the sons of clergymen. 'He received something from this source in his first term, and

---

[1] *Dictionary of National Biography*—Art. 'S. T. Coleridge.'

about £25 for each of the years 1792-94. He
became also a Foundation scholar on 5th June 1794.'

There is no certainty that Coleridge's London
school-life was ever broken by holiday visits to his
old home. A letter to his mother of 1785 suggests
a bare possibility that he went to Ottery in 1784;
if we are to accept the family date of 1789 given
to *Life*, and that of 1790 to *Inside the Coach* and
*Devonshire Roads*, he must have spent some of the
holidays of these years at Ottery. But these family
dates seem little to be depended on. There is,
however, no reasonable doubt that Coleridge went
home in 1791, between school and college, or that
*Happiness* must have been written at Ottery in that
year. In some cancelled lines of that doleful poem
he drew an unflattering portrait of himself, the faith-
fulness of which is to some extent certified by the
testimony of the member of the family who transcribed
the verses : ' The Author was at this time remarkable
for a plump face '—

> Ah ! doubly blest, if love supply
>   Lustre to this now heavy eye,
> And with unwonted Spirit grace
>   That fat vacuity of face.
> Or if e'en Love, the mighty Love
>   Shall find this change his powers above ;
> Some lovely maid perchance thou'lt find
>   To read thy visage in thy mind.

Of his University career we know little. On
entering, he found Middleton at Pembroke College,
and to this old school 'patron and protector' he
probably owed the stimulus which made him an
industrious student for the first year or two. He
certainly began well, for in his first year (1792) he
gained the Browne Gold Medal for a Sapphic Ode

on the Slave Trade ;[1] and in the winter of the same
year he was selected by Porson as one of a 'short
leet' of four (out of seventeen or eighteen) to com-
pete for the Craven Scholarship.[2]   This was gained by
Samuel Butler, afterwards headmaster of Shrewsbury
and Bishop of Lichfield; but as Coleridge's failure
has been reported to have depressed his spirits and
injuriously affected his future, it may be mentioned
that this view receives no confirmation from his
letter to Mrs. Evans, written immediately after the
award.

MY DEAR MRS. EVANS— . . . The event of our examination
was such as surpassed my expectation, and perfectly accorded with
my wishes.   After a very severe trial of six days' continuance, the
Number of the Competitors was reduced from 17 to 4—and after a
further process of ordeal, we, the survivors, were declared equal each
to the other, and the Scholarship, according to the will of the Founder,
awarded to the youngest of us, who was found to be a Mr. Butler of
St. John's College.   I am just two months older than he is ; and
though I would doubtless have rather had it myself, I am not yet
at all sorry at his success, for he is sensible and unassuming, and,
besides, from his circumstances, such an accession to his annual
income must have been very acceptable to him.—So much for
myself.

I should be afraid to guarantee the strict accuracy
of this account of the award, but it shows clearly enough
that Coleridge did not take his loss of the scholarship
very much to heart.   The whole letter is a cheerful
and hopeful one, much occupied by mock-heroics on
his sufferings from toothache, and thus it ends :—

[1] Printed only in *Poetical Works*, 1893, p. 476.   He also entered for the
Latin Ode and the Epigrams.
[2] The other three were Butler, Keate (afterwards headmaster of Eton), and
Bethell (afterwards Bishop of Bangor).   One of the subjects set was a Greek
poem on 'Astronomy,' and though no copy of Coleridge's composition is extant,
an English translation of it was made by Southey, and included by him in the
1806 collection of his *Poems*.   The translation is reprinted in the Appendix to
*The Poetical and Dramatic Works of Samuel Taylor Coleridge*, ed. 1878
(i. 219).

My dear Mrs. Evans! excuse the wanderings of my castle-building Imagination! I have not a thought which I conceal from you. I *write* to others, but my Pen *talks* to you. Convey my softest affection to Betty [an old servant], and believe me, your grateful and affectionate Boy,        S. T. COLERIDGE.
        Feb. 5th [1793].

Unfortunately, Middleton, from whom a coveted and deserved fellowship had been withheld as a punishment for his 'republicanism,' left the University in 1792, and there seems to have been no one to take his place as a steadying influence. In a letter to the Evanses of February 14, 1792, Coleridge speaks of a wine-party he attended, at which 'three or four freshmen were most deplorably intoxicated.'[1] On the way home two of them fell into the gutter, and one who was being assisted 'generously stuttered out' a request that his friend might be saved as he (the speaker) 'could swim.' In another letter,[2] written a year later, he describes himself as 'general' of a party of six undergraduates who 'sallied forth to the apothecary's house with a fixed determination to thrash him for having performed so speedy a cure' on Newton, their mathematical tutor, who had been half-drowned in a duck-pond a week before. The same letter announces that he is taking lessons on the violin in self-defence against fiddling and fluting neighbours. It also contains this passage—'Have you read Mr.

---

[1] Writing to his wife from Gottingen in March 1799, Coleridge describes a wild supper-party of students he had been attending, at which nearly all but himself had drunk to excess: 'I thought of what I had been at Cambridge, and of what I was, of the wild bacchanalian sympathy with which I had formerly joined similar parties, and of my total inability now to do ought but meditate, and the feeling of the deep alteration in my moral being, gave the scene a melancholy interest to me' (*Illustrated London News*, April 29, 1893). I have an assured faith in the accuracy of the Cambridge reminiscence.

[2] Printed in full in the *Illustrated London News* for April 8, 1893. It was addressed to Mary Evans, and included a copy of *The Complaint of Ninathôma*.

Fox's letter to the Westminster Electors? It is quite the *political Go* at Cambridge, and has converted many souls to the Foxite Faith.' Coleridge himself had already been converted to a political faith far in advance of that held by the average Foxite. C. V. le Grice [1] describes Coleridge's rooms at this time as crowded by friends who came to hear their host declaim, and repeat 'whole passages verbatim' from the political pamphlets which then swarmed from the press. The rooms were also a centre for the sympathisers with William Frend, a Fellow of Jesus, who in May 1793 was tried in the Vice-Chancellor's Court for having expressed too freely liberal views in politics, and Unitarian opinions in religion. Coleridge, who was in everything but mathematics, the earnest disciple of Frend, made himself dangerously conspicuous at the trial.[2]

In October of that year Christopher Wordsworth entered at Trinity (of which he was afterwards Master), and speedily became acquainted with Coleridge.[3] In November they joined with some other undergraduates in forming a Literary Society. On the 5th the pair discussed a review in the current *Monthly* of the poems of Christopher's brother

---

[1] *Gentleman's Magazine*, Dec. 1834. He had come up, a year after Coleridge, with a C.H. Exhibition to Trinity.

[2] In the long vacation of this year Coleridge visited his family at Ottery. See the following note attached in *Poems*, 1852, to the verses called *Kisses* (beginning 'Cupid, if storying legends tell aright'): 'This *Effusion* and *The Rose* were originally addressed to a Miss F. Nesbitt, at Plymouth, whither the author accompanied his eldest brother, to whom he was paying a visit, when he was twenty-one years of age. Both poems are written in pencil on the blank pages of a copy of Langhorne's *Collins*. *Kisses* is entitled *Cupid turned Chymist;* is signed S. T. Coleridge, and dated Friday evening, [July] 1793. *The Rose* has this heading: "On presenting a Moss Rose to Miss F. Nesbitt." In both poems the name of Nesbitt appears instead of Sara, afterwards substituted.' The *Songs of the Pixies* belongs also to this summer. In the 'Pixies' Parlour,' near Ottery, Coleridge's initials, cut by his own hand in the rock, are still legible.

[3] *Social Life at the English Universities*, by Christopher Wordsworth, M.A., Fellow of Peter House, Cam., 1874. *Appendix.*

William, on which occasion Coleridge spoke of the
esteem in which William 'was holden by a Society
at Exeter.[1] . . . Coleridge talked Greek, Max. Tyrius,
he told us, and spouted out of Bowles.' On the 7th
he repeated his *Lines on an Autumnal Evening* and
had them criticised. On the 13th the Society met
for the first time at Wordsworth's rooms. 'Time
before supper was spent in hearing Coleridge repeat some original poetry (he having neglected to
write his essay, which is therefore to be produced
next week).'

But there is no record of that essay having ever
been read, and it is probable that before the Society's
next meeting Coleridge had left Cambridge. Of the
immediate causes of his flight nothing positive is
known. Gillman[2] attributes it to debts incurred for
the furnishing of his college rooms; Coleridge himself[3] to his debts generally, denying passionately a
report, believed by his family, that they had been
incurred disreputably; Cottle[4] ascribes to Coleridge
the statement that he ran away in a fit of disgust
arising from Mary Evans's rejection of his addresses.
It is not improbable that debts and disappointed love
combined to drive him out of his course. Debts, however contracted, were evidently weighing on him at
the time. The artless appeal *To Fortune—On buying a
Ticket in the Irish Lottery*[5] seems to point to a speculative attempt to retrieve his position. The lines are
described as having been 'composed during a walk to
and from the Queen's Head, Gray's Inn Lane, Hol-

---

[1] See an allusion to such a Society in *Biog. Lit.* i. 19.      [2] *Life*, p. 42.
[3] *Ib.* p. 64.              [4] *Early Recoll.* ii. 54 ; and *Rem.* p. 279.
[5] First collected in *Poetical Works* (1893) from the *Morning Chronicle* of
Nov. 7, 1793. This probably was the poem Stuart tells us Coleridge sold
about this time to the *Morning Chronicle* for a guinea (*Gent. Mag.* Aug. 1838,
p. 125).

born, and Hornsby and Co.'s, Cornhill,' and in spite of
the conventionality of the phraseology are quite as
characteristic of the suppliant at any given period of
his life as anything he ever wrote. 'Mine is no
common case,' was Coleridge's constant plea. It
always came from his heart as well as from his lips,
and to the end he never fully realised that the goddess
Fortune is deaf as well as blind :—

> Promptress of unnumber'd sighs,
> O snatch that circling bandage from thine eyes !
> O look, and smile !   No common prayer
> Solicits, Fortune ! thy propitious care !
> For, not a silken son of dress,
> I clink the gilded chains of *politesses*,
> Nor ask thy boon what time I scheme
> Unholy Pleasure's frail and feverish dream ;
> Nor yet my view life's *dazzle* blinds—
> Pomp !—Grandeur ! Power !—I give you to the winds !
>
> .  .  .  .  .  .
>
> But oh ! if ever song thine ear
> Might soothe, O haste with fost'ring hand to rear
> One Flower of Hope !   At Love's behest,
> Trembling, I plac'd it in my secret breast :
> And thrice I've viewed the vernal gleam,
> Since oft mine eye, with joy's electric beam,
> Illum'd it—and its sadder hue
> Oft moistened with the tear's ambrosial dew !
> Poor wither'd floweret ! on its head
> Has dark Despair his sickly mildew shed !
> But thou, O Fortune ! can'st relume
> Its deaden'd tints—and thou with hardier bloom
> May'st haply tinge its beauties pale,
> And yield the unsunn'd stranger to the western gale !

In one of his accounts of the adventure Coleridge
speaks of having spent only a couple of days in London,
in another he gives himself a week.[1] The latter is probably the correct version, for he may have come up to
await the lottery drawing, and, having drawn a blank,
he apparently could not face a return to Cambridge.
On the 2nd December 1793 he enlisted under the

---

[1] Gillman's *Life*, pp. 57 and 64 respectively.

name of Silas Tomkyn Comberbacke, in the 15th, or
King's Regiment of Light Dragoons.    Two days
later he was inspected, attested, and sworn at Reading,
the headquarters of the regiment.    His Majesty's
military needs must have been urgent at this time, for
Comberbacke was one of the few Englishmen of any
degree who could truthfully affirm that he had had all
his life 'a violent antipathy to soldiers and horses.'    Of
course, the dragoonship was a sorry farce.    He could
not stick on his horse ; he could not even groom it, or
clean the accoutrements.    But he could charm his com-
rades into taking these latter duties off his hands by
writing their love-letters, telling them stories, and
nursing them when they were sick.    In rather less than
two months Coleridge, feeling that he had had enough
of it, revealed his whereabouts in a letter to certain of
his old cronies who were still at Christ's, and they in
turn confided the intelligence to another—Tuckett, by
name—who had gone up to Cambridge.    Tuckett
seems to have forwarded the letter to Ottery, and also
to have communicated with the commanding officer,
duly informing the trooper of what he had done.    In
his reply to Tuckett, Coleridge makes some show of
indignation at what he calls the abuse of his confidence ; but his gratitude for the results is even more
apparent.    Tuckett seems to have sent on a letter
from Ottery, the seal of which Coleridge feared to
break—the earliest recorded instance we have of what
was a life-long habit :—

A letter from my brother George !  I feel a kind of pleasure
that it is not directed—it lies unopened—am I˙ not already sufficiently miserable ?  The anguish of those who love me, of him
beneath the shadow of whose protection I grew up—does it not
plant the pillow with thorns and make my dreams full of terrors ?
Yet I dare not burn the letter—it seems as if there were an horror

in the action. . . .   Alas! my poor mother!   What an intolerable
weight of guilt is suspended over my head by a hair on one
hand; and if I endure to live—the look ever downward—insult,
pity, and hell!   God or Chaos preserve me!   What but infinite
Wisdom or infinite Confusion can do it?[1]

Coleridge apparently soon summoned up courage
to open the letter, and it was probably after some confidential correspondence with George that a properly
humble and dutiful letter was concocted, and addressed,
on February 20, by Samuel to the head of the family,
his brother Captain James Coleridge.[2]   His discharge
was procured, but not until the 10th of April.   The
many romantic stories afloat as to the circumstances
of Coleridge's release have little, if any, foundation.
Miss Mitford's and Mr. Bowles's Captain Ogle, who
did not appear on the scene until the secret was out,
may have rendered some kindly assistance, but the
caged bird himself took the initiative, and the business
of uncaging him, no doubt a troublesome one, was
carried through by his brothers.   Little time was lost
by the prodigal son in returning to his Alma Mater—
for, according to Jesus College Register, it was on the
12th April that he was admonished by the Master in
the presence of the Fellows.   No further notice of the
escapade seems to have been taken by the College
authorities, nor any report made to those at Christ's
Hospital, so that Coleridge got off very cheaply.

Before the middle of June, and in company with J.
Hucks (who afterwards became a Fellow of Catherine
Hall), Coleridge went to Oxford on a visit, which was
prolonged to three weeks, to his old schoolfellow Allen,

[1] To G. L. Tuckett.   Written Feb. 6 and 7, 1794, from Henley-on-Thames
Workhouse Hospital, where he had been left behind in charge of a sick comrade.
The letter is printed in full in the *Illustrated London News* for April 15, 1893.
[2] See the letter (or part of it), in Brandl's *Life of Coleridge*, p. 65, where it
was first printed.

who had gone up two years before to University College with a C.H. Exhibition.   One of Allen's friends was Robert Southey of Balliol, who thus wrote to Grosvenor Bedford on June 12th :—

> Allen is with us daily, and his friend from Cambridge, Coleridge, whose poems you will oblige me by subscribing to, either at Hookham's or Edwards's.   He is of most uncommon merit,—of the strongest genius, the clearest judgment, the best heart.   My friend he already is, and must hereafter be yours.[1]

The poems mentioned by Southey must have been a proposed volume of *Imitations from the Modern Latin Poets*, which Coleridge was at this time advertising in the *Cambridge Intelligencer*,[2] interesting chiefly as the first in a long series of 'projected works' which came to nothing.   Probably little had been provided for the volume except the translation of Casimir's *Ad Lyram*,[3] printed in the *Watchman* two years later.   The first draft of *Lewti* had probably been written shortly before, for in it the lines are addressed to 'Mary'—doubtless Mary Evans— but they underwent much polishing before publication in 1798.   Even in its earliest form, however, the poem marks a great advance in lightness and individuality of touch.[4]

---

[1] *Life and Corr. of R. S.* i. 210.

[2] June 14 and July 26, 1794.   'Proposals for publishing by subscription *Imitations from the Modern Latin Poets, with a Critical and Biographical Essay on the Restoration of Literature.*   By S. T. Coleridge, of Jesus College, Cambridge.   'The work will consist of two volumes, large octavo, elegantly printed on superfine paper : Price to Subscribers, 14s. in boards ; to be paid on delivery.   [Here follows a lengthy "Design."]   In the course of the Work will be introduced a copious Selection from the Lyrics of Casimir, and a new Translation of the Basia of Secundus.   The Volumes will be ready for delivery shortly after next Christmas.   *Cambridge, June* 10, 1794.'

[3] *Poetical Works*, 1893, p. 28.

[4] It opened thus :—

> High o'er the silver rocks I roved
> To forget the form I loved ;
> In hopes fond fancy would be kind
> And steal my Mary from my mind.

It was during the visit to Oxford that Pantisocracy was hatched.   Southey gave his recollections of
the matter to Cottle in a letter dated March 5,
1836 :—

In the summer of 1794 S. T. Coleridge and Hucks came to
Oxford on their way into Wales for a pedestrian tour.   Then Allen
introduced them to me, and the scheme was talked of, but not by
any means determined on.   It was talked into shape by Burnett
and myself, when, upon the commencement of the long vacation,
we separated from them, they making for Gloucester, he and I proceeding on foot to Bath.   After some weeks, S. T. C., returning
from his tour, came to Bristol on his way and slept there.   Then it
was that we resolved upon going to America, and S. T. C. and I
walked into Somersetshire to see Burnett, and on that journey it
was that he first saw Poole.   He made his engagement with Miss
[Sarah] Fricker on our return from this journey at my mother's
house in Bath, not a little to my astonishment, because he had
talked of being deeply in love with a certain Mary Evans.   I had
previously been engaged to my poor Edith [Fricker]. . . . He
remained at Bristol till the close of the vacation [?]—several weeks.
During that time it was that we talked of America.   The funds
were to be what each could raise—S. T. C. by the *Specimens of the
Modern Latin Poets*, for which he had printed proposals, and obtained a respectable list of Cambridge subscribers before I knew
him ; I, by *Joan of Arc*, and what else I might publish.   I had no
. . . other expectation.   We hoped to find companions with
money.[1]

The material required for filling in Southey's
rapid sketch is happily abundant.   A minute itinerary
of the Welsh tour was published by Coleridge's com-

'Twas twilight, and the lunar beam
Sailed slowly o'er Tamaha's stream
As down its sides the water strayed.
Bright on a rock the moonbeam play'd,
It shone half-sheltered from the view,
By pendent boughs of tressy yew.

In another early MS. ' Sara ' held the place of ' Mary,' but in this the poet's
pen crossed out ' Sara ' and substituted the impersonal ' Lewti.'

[1] The letter is printed in Cottle's *Reminiscences*, pp. 402-407, but very inaccurately.   I quote from the original now in the Fonthill collection.   Cottle has
falsified the second sentence of the above extract, printing it thus : ' Allen introduced them to me, and the scheme of *Pantisocracy* was introduced *by them ;*
talked of, by no means determined on.'   (The italics are Cottle's).   There are
many other garblings, but this is the most important.

panion Hucks,[1] and Coleridge himself wrote a brief
account of part of it to a friend at Jesus,[2] while the
earlier developments of the visionary scheme which
then absorbed all the energies of both Southey and
Coleridge are vividly pictured in contemporary documents supplied by Mrs. Sandford in her admirable
account of *Thomas Poole and his Friends*.[3]   It was on
the 18th August that the visit to Poole mentioned by
Southey took place, and, fortunately for us, Poole had
an opportunity given him of recording his impressions
while they were yet fresh.   An acquaintance who had
heard rumours of Pantisocracy asked for information,
and to him Poole replied at length on the 22nd September :—

'Coldridge' [for so he spells the name], whom I consider the
Principal in the undertaking, and of whom I had heard much
[probably from George Burnett] before I saw him, is about five
and twenty [read, barely two and twenty], belongs to the University of Cambridge, [and] possesses splendid abilities. . . . He
speaks with much elegance and energy, and with uncommon facility,
but he, as it generally happens to men of his class, feels the

---

[1] *A Pedestrian Tour through North Wales, in a Series of Letters.*  By J.
Hucks, B.A.   London : printed for J. Debrett, 1795, 12mo, pp. 160.   It was on
this tour that Coleridge wrote the *Lines at the King's Arms, Ross*, and *On Bala
Hill.*   The last-mentioned poem is printed only in *Poetical Works*, ed. 1893.

[2] H. Martin, to whom *The Fall of Robespierre* was dedicated, and afterwards
incumbent of Cucklington, Somerset.   The letter was written at Carnarvon,
July 22, 1794, and was first printed in the *New Monthly Mag.* for August 1836 ;
and again in *Biog. Lit.* 1847, ii. 338, but somewhat inaccurately.

[3] *Thomas Poole and his Friends.*  By Mrs. Henry Sandford.  2 vols.  1888.
Vol. i. chap. vi.—Thomas Poole was then his father's partner in a large tannery
business carried on in the little market-town of Nether Stowey, which lies at the
foot of the Quantock Hills, about seven miles from Bridgwater.   In August
1794 he had almost completed his twenty-ninth year—a man of high and strong
character, eagerly interested in all that was going on in the national life, and himself a centre of progress in his neighbourhood.   Unlike the great majority of his
family connections, he was in full sympathy with the principles of the French
Revolution, until the Reign of Terror began.   So much is all that need be pre-
mised regarding this sterling Englishman, whose name is indissolubly connected
with that of Coleridge.   The poet's vivid sketch of Poole in the tenth chapter
of *Church and State* has been worthily filled in by Mrs. Sandford, whose book is
one of the best biographies in our literature.   It comprises the fullest account of
Coleridge's life from 1795 to 1804.

justice of Providence in the want of those inferiour abilities which are necessary to the rational discharge of the common duties of life. His aberrations from prudence, to use his own expression, have been great; but he now promises to be as sober and rational as his most sober friends could wish. In religion, he is a Unitarian, if not a Deist; in politicks a Democrat, to the utmost extent of the word.

Southey impressed Poole as lacking his companion's 'splendid abilities,' but as more violent in his principles. ' In Religion, shocking to say in a mere Boy as he is [Southey was just twenty], I fear he wavers between Deism and Atheism.' And then Poole goes on to give the most complete account[1] which has come down to us of the scheme which soon afterwards was named ' Pantisocracy,' and which I thus summarise :—

' Twelve gentlemen of good education and liberal principles are to embark with twelve ladies in April next,' fixing themselves in some 'delightful part of the new back settlements' of America. The labour of each man, for two or three hours a day, it was imagined, would suffice to support the colony. The produce was to be common property, there was to be a good library, and the ample leisure was to be devoted to study, discussion, and the education of the children on a settled system. The women were to be employed in taking care of the infant children and in other suitable occupations, not neglecting the cultivation of their minds. Among other matters not yet determined was 'whether the marriage contract shall be dissolved, if agreeable to one or both parties.' Every one was 'to enjoy his own religious and political opinions, provided they do not encroach on the rules previously made.' 'They calculate that every gentleman pro-

---

[1] A less detailed account was written about this time by Coleridge himself to Mr. C. Heath of Monmouth. See *Biog. Lit.* 1847, ii. 344-5.

viding £125 will be sufficient to carry the scheme into
execution.'

It is necessary here to revert to the Welsh tour
of the previous month.  In the letter written by
Coleridge to Martin, there is a remarkable passage
regarding Mary Evans.  The travellers were at
Wrexham on the 13th and 14th of July.

It had entirely escaped my memory (wrote Coleridge on the
22nd) that Wrexham was the residence of a Miss E. Evans, a
young lady with whom, in happier days, I had been on habits of
fraternal correspondence ; she lives with her grandmother.  As I
was standing at the window of the inn she passed by, and with her,
to my utter astonishment, her sister Mary Evans, *quam efflictim et
perdite amabam*, yea, even to anguish.  They both started, and gave
a short cry, almost a shriek.  I sickened, and well-nigh fainted, but
instantly retired.  Had I appeared to recognise her, my fortitude
would not have supported me.

> Vivit, sed mihi non vivit—nova forte marita.
> Ah ! dolor ! alterius nunc a cervice pependit.
> Vos malefida valete accensæ insomnia mentis
> Littora amata, valete ! vale, ah ! formosa Maria.

Hucks informed me that the two sisters walked by the window
four or five times, as if anxiously.  Doubtless, they think themselves deceived by some face strangely like me.  God bless her !
Her image is in the sanctuary of my bosom, and never can it be
torn from thence but with the strings that grapple my heart to life.
This circumstance made me quite ill.  I had been wandering
among the wildwood scenery and terrible graces of the Welsh
mountains to wear away, not to revive, the images of the past !  But
love is a local anguish: I am fifty miles distant, and am not half
so miserable.

This incident makes it clear that the even flow of
brother-and-sisterly affection between Coleridge and
Mary Evans had been disturbed, and imparts some
colour to the theory that disappointed love had had
more or less to do with the flight from Cambridge
eight months before.  It explains, though it hardly
justifies, the readiness with which Coleridge, to

Southey's natural surprise, engaged himself, a few
weeks afterwards, to Sarah Fricker. The engagement seems to have been a mere detail in the
preparations for carrying out the Pantisocracy.

Coleridge (wrote Southey to his midshipman brother Tom)
was with us nearly five weeks [*read* four] and made good use of his
time. We preached Pantisocracy and Aspheterism everywhere.
These, Tom, are two new words, the first signifying the equal
government of all, and the other the generalisation of individual
property ; words well understood in the city of Bristol. . . .
The thoughts of the day, and the visions of the night, all centre
in America. Time lags heavily along till March. . . . In
March we depart for America, Lovell, his wife [*née* Fricker],
brother and two of his sisters ; all the Frickers ; my mother, Miss
Peggy, and brothers ; Heath the apothecary, etc. ; G. Burnett, S. T.
Coleridge ; Robert Allen, and Robert Southey. . . . We shall be
on the bank of a navigable river, and appoint you admiral of the
cock-boat.[1]

One of the distractions of the Pantisocrats met
together in Bristol had been the joint composition of
a drama on the *Fall of Robespierre*. 'It originated,'
remembered Southey, 'in sportive conversation at
Lovell's, and we agreed each to produce an Act by
the next evening—S. T. C. the first, I the second,
and Lovell the third.' But it ended in Southey
writing both second and third. 'A dedication to
Mrs. Hannah More was concocted, and the notable
performance was offered for sale to a bookseller in
Bristol, who was too wise to buy it.' So, towards the
end of August, Coleridge carried off the MS. to
London, but in spite of encouragement from George
Dyer (who, as Lamb said, had an utter incapacity of
comprehending that there could be anything bad in
poetry), no publisher could be found. Cambridge
was more hospitable, and there it appeared in October,

[1] Sept. 20, 1794, *Life and Corr. of R. S.* i. 220, 221.

with Coleridge's sole name on the title-page and ' Dedication.' [1]

While in London, Coleridge saw much of an old schoolfellow, who had returned from a five-years' residence in America to act as agent for the sale of land there, and who strongly recommended the banks of the Susquehannah as suitable for the Pantisocrats' purpose—'from its excessive beauty, and its security from hostile Indians,' bisons, and mosquitos. ' Literary characters,' added this precursor of Generals Scadder and Choke, 'make money there.' These delightfully practical details were transmitted to Southey on the 6th September. A fortnight later Coleridge announces his arrival at his rooms at Jesus :—

> Since I quitted this room what and how important events have been evolved! America! Southey! Miss Fricker! . . . Pantisocracy! Oh! I shall have such a scheme of it! My head, my heart, all are alive. I have drawn up my arguments in battle-array; they shall have the *tactician* excellence of the mathematician, with the enthusiasm of the poet. The head shall be the mass; the heart, the fiery spirit that fills, informs, and agitates the whole. . . . C—— has been laughing at me. Up I arose, terrible in reasoning. He fled from me because ' he would not answer for his own sanity, sitting so near a madman of genius.' He told me that the strength of my imagination had intoxicated my reason, and that the acuteness of my reason had given a directing influence to my imagination. Four months ago the remark would not have been more elegant than just; now it is nothing.

There were few periods in Coleridge's life at which this remark would have been unjust, but it could hardly be expected that he should have detected its special aptitude just then. In the largest possible letters he goes on : 'SHAD GOES WITH US : HE IS MY BROTHER!!

[1] *The Fall of Robespierre.* An Historic Drama. By S. T. Coleridge, of Jesus College, Cambridge. Cambridge : Printed by Benjamin Flower, for W. H. Lunn [etc.], 1794. Price One Shilling. The Dedication was addressed to ' H. Martin, Esq., of Jesus College, Cambridge,' and served as preface.

—'Shad' being the man of all work of Southey's rich
aunt, Miss Tyler, who a month later turned Southey
out of her house on a wet night on hearing of his
projected marriage and of Pantisocracy, vowing never
to see his face again. If Coleridge gave any
attention to his duties and privileges as an undergraduate at this period, it must have been intermittent. On the 24th October, Pantisocracy over-
flowed into, if it did not suggest, a serio-comic
*Monologue to a Young Jackass in Jesus Piece,*[1]
which was afterwards toned down into unmitigated
sentimentality and sent to the *Morning Chronicle.*[2]

In November Coleridge lost a friend (a son of
Mr. Smerdon, the Vicar of Ottery), and mourned over
him in an elegy. It contains lines bewailing his own
condition—lines ever memorable, though rather as a
prophecy than on account of the passing mood which
prompted them.

> As oft at twilight gloom thy grave I pass,
> And sit me down upon its recent grass,
> With introverted eye I contemplate
> Similitude of soul, perhaps of—Fate !
> To me hath Heaven with bounteous hand assigned
> Energic Reason and a shaping mind,
> The daring ken of Truth, the Patriot's part,
> And Pity's sigh, that breathes the gentle heart—
> Sloth-jaundiced all ! and from my graspless hand
> Drop Friendship's precious pearls, like hour-glass sand.
> I weep, yet stoop not ! the faint anguish flows,
> A dreamy pang in Morning's feverish doze.[3]

But there was another and a principal cause of
distraction and agitation of which nothing has hitherto
been known. It is revealed in the two letters to Mary
Evans before mentioned. The sight of her in July

---

[1] Printed only in *Poetical Works,* 1893, 'APPENDIX C,' p. 477.

[2] The well-known lines *To a Young Ass, its mother being tethered near it,*
to be found, in their modified form, in all editions of Coleridge's *Poems.*

[3] *Lines on a Friend who died of a Frenzy Fever.*

had stirred his heart ; but out of sight was out of mind, and believing there was a vacuum he incontinently filled it—as he thought, honestly enough, no doubt — with love for Sarah Fricker.   Again, in respect of Sarah, out of sight was out of mind, and, further, he learned that there had been no vacuum to be filled.   The old love was still there, and from his despair of any fruition of it were wrung the well-known lines *On a discovery made too late*, the precise interpretation of which has hitherto been a puzzle.   When first published in 1796 the title was *To my own Heart :—*

> Thou bleedest, my poor Heart! and thy distress
> Reasoning I ponder with a scornful smile
> And probe thy sore wound sternly, though the while
> Swoln be mine eye and dim with heaviness.
> Why didst thou listen to Hope's whisper bland ?
> Or, listening, why forget the healing tale,
> When Jealousy with feverish fancies pale
> Jarred thy fine fibres with a maniac's hand ?
> Faint was that Hope, and rayless !—Yet 'twas fair
> And soothed with many a dream the hour of rest :
> Thou should'st have loved it most, when most opprest,
> And nursed it with an agony of care,
> Even as a mother her sweet infant heir
> That wan and sickly droops upon her breast !

The autograph copy of these lines is dated 'Oct. 21, 1794.'   The very despair which would seem to have prompted them appears to have provoked a final attempt to fan an answering spark should such remain ; or, in default, to learn his fate, beyond all doubt.   This attempt was made by a letter to Mary Evans which, though undated, was probably written some time in December.   It opens thus abruptly :—

Too long has my heart been the torture-house of suspense. After infinite struggles of Irresolution, I will at least dare to request of you, Mary ! that you will communicate to me whether or no you are engaged to Mr. —— [*sic in orig.*]   I conjure you not to con-

sider this request as presumptuous Indelicacy. Upon mine Honor
I have made it with no other design or expectation than that of
arming my fortitude by total hopelessness. Read this letter with
benevolence, and consign it to oblivion. For four years I have
*endeavoured* to smother a very ardent attachment—in what degree
I have succeeded, you must know better than I can. With quick
conceptions of moral Beauty, it was impossible for me not to
admire in you your sensibility regulated by Judgment, your Gaiety
proceeding from a cheerful Heart, acting on the stores of a strong
Understanding. At first, I voluntarily invited the recollection of
these qualities into my mind. I made them the perpetual object of
my reveries—yet I entertained no Sentiment beyond that of the
immediate Pleasure annexed to the thinking of You. At length it
became a habit. I awoke from the delusion and found that I had
unwittingly harboured a Passion which I felt neither the power or
the courage to subdue. . . . I thought of you incessantly : yet that
Spirit (if Spirit there be that condescends to record the lonely
Beatings of my Heart), that Spirit knows that I thought of you with
the purity of a Brother. Happy were I, had it been with no more
than a Brother's ardor. . . . I saw that you regarded me merely
with the kindness of a sister.——What expectations *could* I form ? I
formed no expectations. I was ever resolving to subdue the disquieting Passion : still some inexplicable suggestion palsied my
efforts, and I clung with desperate fondness to this Phantom of
Love, its mysterious Attractions, and hopeless Prospects. It was a
faint and rayless Hope ![1] Yet it soothed my solitude with many a
delightful Day-dream. It was a faint and rayless Hope ! yet I
nursed it in my bosom with an agony of Affection, even as a
Mother her sickly infant. . . . Indulge, Mary ! this my first, my
last request—and restore me to *Reality*, however gloomy. Sad and
full of heaviness will the intelligence be—my heart will die within
me. . . . I will not disturb your peace by even a *look* of Discontent,
still less will I offend your ear by the whine of selfish Sensibility.
In a few months I shall enter at the Temple,[2] and there seek
forgetful calmness where only it can be found — in incessant and
useful activity.

The letter closes with an assurance that if a rival
is to be made happy he will be congratulated and not
hated ; and ends as abruptly as it began, with the

---

[1] Compare with the lines *To my own Heart*.

[2] So far as I am aware the sole record of this project—if any such was ever
seriously entertained. About this time, proposals respecting the adoption of a
profession were made to Coleridge by his brothers, and the study of law may
have been one.

simple signature, 'S. T. Coleridge,'—followed by this postscript, ' I return to Cambridge to-morrow morning.' This seems to show that the letter was written before the end of the term (middle of December), in which case Mary's answer was far from being prompt, for Coleridge's response to it is dated ' 24th December, 1794.' It opens thus :—

> I have this moment received your letter, Mary Evans. Its firmness does honor to your understanding, its gentleness to your humanity. You condescend to accuse yourself most unjustly : you have been altogether blameless. In my wildest day-dream of Vanity, I never supposed that you entertained for me any other than a common friendship. To love you, habit has made unalterable. This passion, however, divested, as it now is, of all shadow of Hope, will lose its disquieting. Far distant from you, I shall journey through the vale of Men in calmness. He cannot long be wretched who dares to be actively virtuous. . . . May God infinitely love you !—S. T. COLERIDGE.

I think the Mary Evans affair, the termination of which brought about one of the most important crises in Coleridge's life, is only to be understood by assuming that, soon before his enlistment he had become convinced that while Mary continued to look upon him as merely a clever boy whose companionship was pleasant, she was giving her affections to ' Mr. ——'; and that thereupon, and without a word of declaration or explanation, he had suddenly broken off all relations with the family. It is clear that, at Wrexham, the Evans sisters had been anxious to meet Coleridge, hoping, doubtless, in their innocence, to receive some explanation of conduct which appeared to them mysterious ; while Coleridge's determination to avoid the encounter is easily comprehensible. His first letter of the December following must have come to Mary as at once an explanation and a surprise, and the delay in her reply was natural enough. The letter was one not easy to answer, and she must have learned from it that the writer could no longer be looked upon as a boy, and was worthy of a serious response. That her reply was dictated by the old sisterly affection mingled with pity and remorse, and that it was expressed in terms of simple womanliness may readily be gathered from the soothing effect it exercised on Coleridge's mind. Had he carried out his wise resolve to 'seek forgetful calmness in incessant and useful activity,' he would no doubt have been successful. The whole episode, so far as we know it, appears to have been highly creditable to Mary Evans, and in no respect discreditable to Coleridge.

About the middle of December, a few days before the close of term, Coleridge quitted Cambridge without taking his degree. Apparently, on the authority of Dr. Pearce himself, Dr. Carlyon[1] informs us that the Master of Coleridge's college ' made repeated efforts to reclaim' his errant pupil, but to no purpose. ' Upon one occasion, after a long discussion on the visionary and ruinous tendency of his conduct and schemes, Coleridge cut short the argument by bluntly assuring him, his friend and master, that he mistook the matter altogether—"he was neither Jacobin," he said, "nor Democrat, but a Pantisocrat."' Dr. Brandl[2] suggests that Coleridge did not take his degree because he could not have signed the Thirty-nine Articles, and adds (on what authority is not stated) that ' Dr. Pearce gave him the benefit of the whole winter term for his return, before removing, as he was bound to do, his name from the College boards. Finally, he obtained for him one reprieve more, up to the 14th June 1795.'

[1] *Early Years*, etc. i. 27.   [2] *Life of Coleridge*, p. 80.

In the official 'List of [C.H.] University Exhibitioners' it is stated that, on the 22nd April 1795, Coleridge's case was considered by the C.H. Committee,
which then seems to have learnt for the first time of
his absence from Cambridge from Nov. 1793 to April
1794; and also that he had left Cambridge a few days
before the expiration of the Michaelmas term in
1794.    In this way ended Coleridge's official relations
with Christ's Hospital and Jesus College.

He left Cambridge,—but not for Bristol.   He did
not even write, either to his *fiancée* or to Southey.  They,
and also Pantisocracy, seem to have been forgotten.
He went to London and remained there, solacing
his grief in the sympathetic society of Charles Lamb,
and confiding his opinions on things in general to the
public by way of 'Sonnets on Eminent Characters,'
which were printed in the *Morning Chronicle*.   It
was of this period that Lamb wrote two years later :
'You came to town, and I saw you at a time when
your heart was yet bleeding with recent wounds.   Like
yourself, I was sore galled with disappointed hope. . . .
I image to myself the little smoky room at the "Salutation and Cat," where we have sat together through
the winter nights, beguiling the cares of life with
Poesy.'[1]   The friends at Bristol gradually lost all
patience.   'Coleridge did not come back to Bristol,'
wrote Southey to Cottle,[2] 'till January 1795, *nor would
he, I believe, have come back at all*, if I had not gone to
London to look for him.   For having got there from
Cambridge at the beginning of winter, there he remained without writing to Miss F[ricker] or to me,

---

[1] Letter to Coleridge, June 10, 1796.  *Letters*, i. 14.  (Cf. letters of June 14
and December 2, 1796.)   The tavern (17 Newgate Street) survived as such till
1884, when it was burnt down.
[2] Cottle's *Reminiscences*, p. 405—text corrected by the original letter.

till we actually apprehended that his friends [family ?] had placed him somewhere in confinement.' After some difficulty, Southey found him at the 'Angel' Inn in Butcher Hall Street, and carried him off to Bristol. There was probably too much joy there over the recovery of the truant to permit of reproaches, for the relations with Sarah and with Pantisocracy, broken by Coleridge's long silence (the result, it is to be feared, of faded interest), were renewed. At all events they were patched up, and Coleridge recommenced ardent lover and Pantisocrat. 'The scheme,' Cottle assures us, was 'the favourite theme of his discourse.'

Finance, naturally, was the difficulty. Coleridge, Southey, and Burnett lodged together at 48 College Street. Burnett's father was a well-to-do Somersetshire farmer, and sympathetic ; Southey had nothing, and such of his relatives as had something were antagonistic ; Coleridge had nothing, and ignored his relatives altogether. Lovell, who had married Mary Fricker, could probably have provided his share of the common capital, but without Coleridge and Southey no move could be made. About a month after Coleridge's recapture, Southey wrote to Bedford (February 8, 1795)[1]: 'Coleridge is writing at the same table ; our names are written in the book of destiny, on the same page'; and he went on to expound a plan for publishing a magazine, to be edited by Coleridge and himself. Both hoped to get money by journalism, but

[1] *Life and Corr. of R. S.* i. 231. On January 29, 1810, Southey wrote to Miss Barker (*Letters of R. S.* ii. 188) of his intercourse with Coleridge in 1795 : 'Disliking his inordinate love of talking, I was naturally led to avoid the same fault ; when we were alone, and he talked his best (which was always at those times), I was pleased to listen ; and when we were in company, and I heard the same things repeated—repeated to every fresh company, seven times in the week if we were in seven parties—still I was silent. . . . His habits have continued, and so have mine.' This habit of unlimited repetition was noted by Coleridge's clerk at Malta. (Dilke's *Papers of a Critic*, i. 32.)

their opportunities were few; and they tried lecturing—Coleridge on politics and religion, Southey on history. Their relations seem to have been 'Aspheteric,' for two years later Southey declared that his earnings during the earlier half of 1795 were as four to one of Coleridge's, and that, besides supporting himself, he almost supported Coleridge. Of all the lecturing, nothing remains to us but what is contained in three little pamphlets.[1]

Lovell had lost no time in introducing Coleridge to Cottle, then a young printer, bookseller, and poetaster. He was very friendly to the Pantisocrats, and when they could not quite make up a seven weeks' lodging bill, he lent them a five-pound note, delighted to be thus assured that the foolish emigration scheme was not progressing materially. Soon after this he offered Coleridge thirty guineas[2] for a volume of poems, the money to be advanced as required. Coleridge had a good many short poems ready, but his *magnum opus*

[1] *A Moral and Political Lecture*, delivered at Bristol, by S. T. Coleridge, of Jesus College, Cambridge. Bristol : printed by George Routh, in Corn Street. Price Sixpence. [1795.] This was probably published soon after the oral delivery in February. In November it was reprinted with some alterations as the first of two *Conciones ad Populum ; or, Addresses to the People.* By S. T. Coleridge. 1795. I. Introductory Address. II. On the present War. The Preface is dated 'Clevedon, Nov. 16, 1795.' At the same time was published *The Plot discovered ; or, An Address to the People against Ministerial Treason.* By S. T. Coleridge. Bristol, 1795. On the wrapper was the legend : A Protest against certain Bills. Bristol : printed for the Author, Nov. 28, 1795.' The 'Bills' were the Pitt and Grenville Acts for gagging Press and Platform. The *Conciones* and *The Plot discovered* are reprinted in *Essays on his own Times.* The first-named pamphlet is excessively rare. The other two have survived in numbers, and are constantly advertised as 'privately printed.' The title pages have no publisher's name, but they were advertised for sale at ninepence each, and sent to the magazines for review.

[2] A statement that he only received half the sum, having been forgetfully made by Coleridge in later life, and adopted by some biographers, it seems only fair to Cottle to say that I have seen Coleridge's stamped receipt for the whole. It runs as follows :—' Received, the 28th March 1796, the sum of Thirty guineas, for the copyright of my Poems, beginning with the " Monody on the Death of Chatterton," and ending with " Religious Musings." (Signed) S. T. COLERIDGE.'

of those days, *Religious Musings*, was incomplete,[1] and,
indeed, was not completed until the following year,
after all the rest of the volume had been printed.
Probably one of the first of the early poems which he
revised was the *Monody on the Death of Chatterton*,
adding to the Christ's Hospital version,[2] which had
been printed in Lancelot Sharpe's edition of 'Rowley's
Poems' (1794), the lines respecting Pantisocracy, which
scheme, however, had become but a bitter memory
before the volume was published.   We are principally
dependent on Cottle for information regarding this
period, and he may be believed when he pictures
Coleridge as spending much time in 'conversation.'
It was probably, as in after-days, chiefly monologue,
and besides Pantisocracy ('an everlasting theme'), his
'stock subjects were Bishop Berkeley, David Hartley,
and Mr. Bowles, whose sonnets he delighted in reciting.'   Cottle forgets politics, but the lecture-
pamphlets are there to testify to the vigour of
Coleridge's campaign against the tyranny of Pitt.

The course of true love seems to have run smooth,
but not so that of friendship.   Letters written by
Southey and Coleridge show that up to the middle of
September no breach had taken place, but on July 19,
1797, Southey states[3] that he had lost confidence in his
friend 'as early as the summer of 1795.'   The joint
lodging had to be given up, for financial reasons, says
Southey, who returned to his mother at Bath.   'Our
arrears were paid with twenty guineas which Cottle

---

[1] It was doubtless the 'unfinished poem' sent to Lamb (*Poetical Works*,
1893, p. 37).

> Thus far my scanty brain hath built the rhyme
> Elaborate and swelling : yet the heart
> Not owns it.

[2] Given in *Poetical Works*, 1893, p. 8.

[3] *Letters of R. S.* i. 41.

advanced [to Southey]. During all this —— [Cole-
ridge] was to all appearance as he had ever been towards
me; but I discovered that he had been employing
every possible calumny against me, and representing
me as a villain.'[1]  The only probable explanation of
the conduct attributed to Coleridge is that he must
have seen that Southey's enthusiasm for Pantisocracy
had been waning.  When summer came it had so far
waned that, although he could not agree to prepare
for the Church, as he was urged to do by his uncle
Hill, he somewhat suddenly determined to study law.
In Coleridge's eyes this must have been black treason,
and it is much to be regretted that he did not at
once accuse Southey to his face.  It was only in
November, that Southey, when about to sail for
Lisbon, formally announced to Coleridge his abandonment of Pantisocracy.  Coleridge then broke out in
extravagantly-worded upbraidings, and the quarrel
was not made up until Southey's return in the summer
of the following year.[2]

When he betook himself to his solitary lodging at
25 College Street, Coleridge must have earned some
ready money by his pen, for the thirty guineas received for the copyright of his poems could not nearly
have sufficed to support him during the many months
which preceded publication, or the settlement of
accounts with Cottle which took place on the 28th
March 1796.  But Cottle must be held responsible
for Coleridge's determination not to postpone his
marriage.  He offered to buy an unlimited number of
verses from the poet at the fixed rate of a guinea and
a half per hundred lines (which works out at nearly

---

[1] *Letters of R. S.* i. 41.  See also letter in Cottle's *Rem.* p. 406.
[2] Cottle's *Rem.* pp. 104-107.

fourpence apiece), for when asked by a friend 'how he
was to keep the pot boiling when married,' Coleridge
'very promptly answered that Mr. Cottle had made
him such an offer that he felt no solicitude on that
subject'!¹

We are fortunate in possessing two graphic de-
scriptions of Coleridge as he appeared in this autumn
of 1795.  The acquaintance with Thomas Poole, made
a year before, appears to have been renewed on
Coleridge's return to Bristol, and to have ripened into
intimacy.  In September he paid a visit to Stowey,
during which he was thus sketched in the diary of a
keen but unsympathetic cousin of his host, Miss
Charlotte Poole of Marshmills :—

> Tom Poole has a friend with him of the name of Coldridge : a
> young man of brilliant understanding, great eloquence, desperate
> fortune, democratick principles, and entirely led away by the
> feelings of the moment.²

There is a fact undeniable in every stroke of the
etcher's needle, and a certain incomplete truth in the
general impression produced by the whole portrait.
It will be interesting as well as instructive to compare
and contrast it with another, drawn just a week before,
by an artist at least equally keen-sighted, but whose
vision was directed by sympathy.  It is contained in a
copy of verses addressed to Coleridge by Poole.

'However conventional the phrasing,' says Mrs.
Sandford, '*they describe Coleridge*—and Coleridge as

¹ *Rem.* p. 39.   To Poole, Coleridge wrote on the third day after his
marriage :—'Cottle has entered into an engagement to give me a guinea
and a half for every hundred lines of poetry I write, which will be perfectly
sufficient for my maintenance, I only amusing myself in the mornings—and all my
prose works, he is eager to purchase.'   In the same letter Coleridge says he is
going to return to Cambridge, but free from 'University control,' there to finish
his 'great work on *Imitations* in two volumes.'   (Unpublished portion of a letter
partially printed in the Biographical Supplement to *Biog. Lit.* ed. 1847, ii. 347.)
² *T. Poole and his Friends*, i. 124.

he was in the first early freshness of the dawn of his
marvellous powers " [1] :—

> Hail to thee, Coldridge, youth of various powers !
>　　I love to hear thy soul pour forth the line,
> To hear it sing of love and liberty
>　　As if fresh-breathing from the hand divine.
>
> As if on earth it never yet had dwelt,
>　　As if from heaven it now had wing'd its way ;
> And brought us tidings how, in argent fields,
>　　In love and liberty blest spirits stray.
>
> I love to mark that soul-pervaded clay,
>　　To see the passions in thine eye-balls roll—
> Their quick succession on thy weighty brow—
>　　Thy trembling lips express their very soul.
>
> I love to view the abstracted gaze which speaks
>　　Thy soul to heavenward towering—then I say,
> He's gone—for us to cull celestial sweets
>　　Amid the flowerets of the milky way.
>
> And now at home, within its mortal cage,
>　　I see thy spirit pent—ah me ! and mourn
> The sorrow sad, that weighs it down to earth,
>　　As if the Cherub Hope would ne'er return.
>
> And then I mark the starting tear that steals
>　　Adown thy cheek, when of a friend [2] thou speak'st,
> Who erst, as thou dost say, was wondrous kind,
>　　But now, unkind, forgets—I feel and weep.
>
> I hear thee speak indignant of the world,
>　　Th' unfeeling world crowded with folly's train ;
> I hear thy fervent eloquence dispel
>　　The murky mists of error's mazy reign.
>
> Anon thy Sarah's image cheers thy soul,
>　　When sickening at the world, thy spirits faint ;
> Soft balm it brings—thou hail'st the lovely maid,
>　　Paint'st her dear form as Love alone can paint.
>
>　　*　　　　*　　　　*　　　　*　　　　*

---

[1] *T. Poole and his Friends*, i. 124-126. It seems strange that the Pooles
should still have mistaken Coleridge's name. There is a Devonshire village
named 'Coleridge,' which, says the Rev. Isaac Taylor, in *Words and Places*,
means *Cold*-ridge (cf. *Mount Algidus*). In 1811, a 'John Coldridge' compiled a
'Survey of the Rectorial Tythes of Pinhoe.' Poole first spells his friend's name
correctly in a letter of the following month.

[2] Southey, doubtless.

No reader of Poole's opening stanzas can fail to be reminded of Lamb's description, written in 1816, of Coleridge's recitation of *Kubla Khan*—'which said vision he repeats so enchantingly that it irradiates and brings heaven and elysian bowers into my parlour when he sings or says it . . . his face when he repeats his verses, hath its ancient glory; an archangel a little damaged.' Lamb was writing as he watched Coleridge retiring from the battle: Poole as he saw him entering it, radiant as the Michael of Perugino.

# CHAPTER III

## MARRIAGE—*THE WATCHMAN*

### A.D. 1795–1796

THE visit to Stowey took place on the eve of Coleridge's marriage. In August a cottage at Clevedon had been taken—that

> cot o'ergrown
> With white-flowered Jasmin, and the broad-leaved Myrtle [1]—

which is still shown to the pilgrim and the tourist; and on the 4th October, Coleridge and Sarah Fricker were married at the great church of St. Mary Redcliffe, and the honeymoon began. The cottage wanted papering, and a good many indispensable housekeeping articles [2] had been forgotten, but Cottle promptly supplied all deficiencies. Burnett and one of Sarah's sisters for a time shared the limited accommodation of the jasmin-bound dwelling; and we learn by some jottings in a note-book that the household work was shared by all. The two men got up at six, put on the kettle and cleaned the shoes; at eight Sarah laid the breakfast table, and so on. But Clevedon being found too far

---

[1] *The Eolian Harp;* but the poem did not receive its title until 1817. When first published in *Poems*, 1796, it was called 'Effusion XXXV. Composed August 20th, 1795, at Clevedon, Somersetshire.'

[2] The amusing list is given in *Rem.* p. 40.

from Bristol Library, was soon abandoned for rooms
on Redcliffe Hill. No doubt it had been an idle
honeymoon, and Coleridge's conscience smote him.
'Ah! quiet dell!' was one of his 'Reflections on
leaving' this 'place of retirement'—

> dear cot, and mount sublime!
> I was constrained to quit you. Was it right,
> While my unnumbered brethren toiled and bled,
> That I should dream away the entrusted hours
> On rose-leaf beds, pampering the coward heart
> With feelings all too delicate for use?

The *Poems on various subjects* still lingered at press,
and Cottle's printers often waited in vain for ' copy.'

*Religious Musings* was still on the anvil, but it was
left there, for the prosecution of a great project in
which he had interested a number of friends, probably
as inexperienced, if not quite as enthusiastic and un-
businesslike, as himself. One evening in December
the party met 'at the Rummer tavern,' in Bristol, and
it was settled that Coleridge should bring out a
periodical, something between a newspaper and a
magazine, to be called *The Watchman*.[1] To avoid
the stamp-tax it was to be issued, not weekly, but
on every eighth day; and No. I. was announced to
appear on 'Friday the 5th day of February, price
four-pence.' Early in January, Coleridge started on a
tour of the north country to procure subscribers—
'preaching,' as he says,[2] 'by the way in most of
the great towns, as an hireless volunteer, in a blue
coat and white waistcoat, that not a rag of the woman

---

[1] A document which Cottle calls the prospectus of *The Watchman* was
printed by him in his *Early Recollections* and *Reminiscences* (p. 75). It may
possibly be a transcript of some later hand-bill, but it is not the original prospectus. A copy of this, unique so far as I am aware, recently came into
the possession of Mr. H. Buxton Forman, who kindly allows me to print it. See
APPENDIX.

[2] *Biog. Lit.* chap. x.

of Babylon might be seen on me. For I was at that time and long after, though a Trinitarian (i.e. *ad normam Platonis*) in philosophy, yet a zealous Unitarian in religion.' Through eight pages of the *Biographia* Coleridge gives a most vivid and humorous account of his tour, from which, he says, he returned with a subscription list of nearly a thousand names.[1]

Not on the 5th February, but on March 1st, No. I. appeared, but it disappointed the subscribers by its dulness. No. II. offended many by reason of an essay it contained on ' National Fasts,' with the motto —'Wherefore my Bowels shall sound like an Harp'; succeeding numbers gave umbrage to Jacobin, Democrat, and Godwinite patrons, without attracting opposite factions—and on the last page of ' No. X.' (May 13, 1796) an ' address to the reader' informed him that ' this is the last number of the *Watchman*. Henceforward I shall cease to cry the state of the political Atmosphere. . . . The reason is short and satisfactory— the Work does not pay its expenses.' Six weeks before, the ever-helpful Thomas Poole had foreseen the inevitable. He set to work to gather a little money for Coleridge, and on the last ' magazine-day' of the *Watchman*, its baffled proprietor was cheered by the receipt of a well-filled purse, together with a kindly and delicately-worded letter.[2] This produced

---

[1] See also an account of the *Watchman*, with some letters written by Coleridge on the tour, in Cottle's *Rem.* pp. 74 *et seq.*

[2] Which see, with Coleridge's response, in *Thomas Poole and his Friends*, i. 142-145. Poole's scheme was a testimonial in the form of an annuity. Each subscriber was to give five pounds a year for six years. Some seven or eight of Coleridge's friends subscribed, so that the purse must have contained £35 or £40. It will be seen that the scheme was again acted on in the following year, but not afterwards, as, says Mrs. Sandford, ' it may have been thought that the Wedgwoods' annuity [begun in 1798] removed all further necessity for going on with it.' There is an allusion to Poole's scheme in the Biog. Supp. to *Biog. Lit.* ed. 1847 (ii. 366), but it is inaccurate.

a grateful reply, which the ex-dragoon ended by asking for 'a horse of tolerable meekness' on which to ride over to Stowey. The request was granted, and he spent a peaceful fortnight with Poole.

Before this, probably in the first days of April, the *Poems*[1] had been published. The volume attracted the notice of the principal reviews and magazines— its reception being generally favourable, and in one or two instances enthusiastic. Some reviewers detected 'turgidity'—the *Monthly Magazine* thought that *Religious Musings* reached 'the top scale of sublimity.' Coleridge agreed with both sets of critics, and so did Lamb.

The praise was gratifying, but the pudding had long ago been eaten; the *Watchman's* audience was dwindling; and when the purse collected by Poole arrived in mid-May the cupboard was empty. The purse had probably been considerably lightened by the end of June when Coleridge received, through the famous Dr. Beddoes, a proposal to go up to London to become assistant editor of the *Morning Chronicle*, then the leading daily paper. This he at once accepted, and on the 5th July he was hourly expecting to receive particulars from James Perry, the proprietor and editor-in-chief. 'My heart is very heavy' (he wrote to Estlin[2]), 'for I love Bristol, and I

---

[1] POEMS on various subjects, by S. T. Coleridge, late of Jesus College, Cambridge.

> Felix curarum, cui non Heliconia cordi
> Serta, nec imbelles Parnassi e vertice laurus !
> Sed viget ingenium, et magnos accinctus in usus
> Fert animus quascunque vices.—Nos tristia vitæ
> Solamur cantu.—Stat. *Silv.* Lib. iv. 4.

LONDON : Printed for G. G. and J. Robinsons, and J. Cottle, Bookseller, Bristol, 1796. Octavo pp. xvi. ; 188 (plus one page of 'Errata'). See Preface, Contents, etc., in *Poetical Works*, 1893, p. 537. The volume included four sonnets by Lamb, signed 'C. L.'

[2] *Unpublished Letters of S. T. C. to the Rev. J. P. Estlin*, printed for the Philobiblon Society, p. 17.

do not love London.    Besides, local and temporary
politics are my aversion. . . .  But there are two giants
leagued together, whose most imperious commands I
must obey, however reluctant,—their names are BREAD
and CHEESE.'    An undated letter from S. Purkis to T.
Poole[1] shows that Coleridge intended to go up to
London to see Perry, but at this point our information
fails, and we only know that the negotiations ended
fruitlessly.    Next came an arrangement by which
Coleridge was to undertake the education of the sons
of Mrs. Evans of Darley Abbey, near Derby—a lady,
it may be as well to mention, entirely unconnected with
the family of his old sweetheart, Mary Evans.    This
having been settled during a visit to Darley Abbey,
Coleridge left his wife there, and, about the end of
July, paid a visit of reconciliation to his family at
Ottery.    Of this visit he wrote to Estlin[2]: 'I was
received by my mother with transport, and by my
brother George with joy and tenderness, and by my
other brothers with affectionate civility.'    I describe
this visit as one of reconciliation, because, although I
have seen no documentary evidence of any preceding
rupture, there is good reason for believing that Coleridge's intercourse with his family had been suspended
since his departure from Cambridge in the winter of
1794.    Proposals made by his brothers, to aid him on
the adoption of some profession, had been rejected,
and they cannot have failed to disapprove of most of
his doings in the interval—his devotion to Pantisocracy, his revolutionary lecturing, and his imprudent
marriage.

On his return home from Ottery on the 7th August,

---

[1] Printed in *T. Poole and his Friends*, i. 151, 152.
[2] *Estlin Letters*, p. 11.    The letter is there misplaced.

a fresh disappointment awaited him in the shape of a
letter from Mrs. Evans, informing him that her trustees
would not consent to the arrangements which had
been made, but begging him to come to her at once.
This request he complied with.   At the end of a ten
days' visit there was an affectionate parting, and Mrs.
Evans, he wrote, 'insisted on my acceptance of £95,
and she had given Mrs. Coleridge all her baby-clothes,
which are, I suppose, very valuable.'[1]   Before leaving
Derby, Coleridge was further consoled by a proposition
made by Dr. Crompton, that he should set up a school
there, under the active patronage of Mrs. Evans's
influential family connections.   An unfinished house
was at once engaged 'to be completed by the 8th
October, for £12 a year,' and the landlord won
Coleridge's heart by promising 'to Rumfordize the
chimneys.'[2]   This scheme also came to nothing.   On
September 24, Coleridge writes to Poole[3] that his
'heart is heavy respecting Derby'—which I interpret
as meaning that he feared to settle so far away from
Bristol and from Poole.   A house at Adscombe (near
Stowey), with some land attached, was his desire,
and apparently with Poole's approval Derby was
given up,'[4] and a letter written to Dr. Crompton to
which Coleridge received 'a very kind reply.'[5]

On his way home from Derby, Coleridge had
spent a week at Moseley, near Birmingham,[6] and there

---

[1] *Estlin Letters*, pp. 12, 13.

[2] *Biog. Lit.* 1847, ii. 372.   See the Sonnet to Count Rumford in *Poetical
Works*, 1893, p. 64.   See also letter of S. T. C. to Poole, Dec. 1796, *T. Poole
and his Friends*, i. 196.

[3] *T. Poole and his Friends*, i. 158.

[4] *Ib.* i. 188.

[5] *Biog. Lit.* 1847, ii. 377.   See Lamb's letters to Coleridge of October 17
and 24, and November 8, 1796 (Ainger's ed. i. 39 *et seq.*)

[6] 'I preached yesterday morning from Hebrews iv. 1, 2.   It was my *chef
d'œuvre*.   I think of writing it down and publishing it with two other sermons.
. . . I should like you to hear me preach them.   I lament that my political

renewed the acquaintance with the Lloyds which had
been formed during the *Watchman* tour in January.
Charles Lloyd had been fascinated by Coleridge,
and having a turn for verse-making and meditation,
rather than for the family business of banking, was
extremely desirous of becoming a philosopher and
a poet under the guidance and under the roof of
the philosopher and poet who was but two years
his senior. Nothing was then settled, but towards
the end of September, Lloyd's parents gave their
consent, and invited [1] Coleridge to pay them a visit.
Mrs. Coleridge having miscalculated times and seasons
allowed him to go, and while at the Lloyds' house
he was surprised by an announcement that on the
previous day, the 19th September, he had become
a father. He hastened home, taking Charles Lloyd
with him. The poet's and the father's tumultuous
feelings in presence of this crisis required three
sonnets [2] for their expression, but they were summed
up in these lovely lines with which the third closes :—

> So for the mother's sake the child was dear,
> And dearer was the mother for the child.

The father having at this period a great dislike for
all sacramental rites, [3] the child was not baptized, but
he was named 'David Hartley,' in honour of the

notoriety prevented my relieving you occasionally at Bristol.'   S. T. C. to Estlin,
'Moseley, Birmingham, August 22, 1796' (*Estlin Letters*, p. 15).   To Poole
he wrote (same date) :—' In preaching on Faith yesterday, I said that Faith was
infinitely better than Good Works, as the cause is greater than the effect,—as a
fruitful tree is better than its fruits, and as a friendly heart is of far higher value
than the kindnesses which it naturally and *necessarily* prompts.   It is for that
*friendly heart* that I now have thanked you, and which I so eagerly accept of ;
for with regard to settlement, I am likely to be better off now than before, as I
shall proceed to tell you.' (*Biog. Lit.* 1847, ii. 370, corrected by original.)

[1] S. T. C. to Poole, September 24 ; printed in *Biog. Lit.* 1847, ii. 374.
[2] *Poetical Works*, 1893, p. 66.
[3] Letter to Estlin (*Estlin Letters*, p. 35).

'wisest of mortal kind,'[1] and solemnly dedicated to
the service of the truths 'so ably supported by that
great master of Christian Philosophy.'[2]   So he informed Poole, going on to write about his other
son, born to him, as it were, on the same day as
David Hartley.

> Charles Lloyd wins upon me hourly.   His heart is uncommonly
> pure, his affections delicate, and his benevolence enlivened, but not
> sicklied, by sensibility.   He is assuredly a man of great genius. . . .
> His joy and gratitude to Heaven for the circumstance of his domesti-
> cation with me, I can scarcely describe to you; and I believe his
> fixed plans are of being always with me. . . .   My dearest Poole,
> can you conveniently receive us in the course of a week?   We can
> both sleep in one bed, as we do now; and I have much, very much,
> to say to you, and to consult you about; for my heart is heavy
> respecting Derby; and my feelings are so dim and huddled, that
> though I can, I am sure, communicate them to you by my looks
> and broken sentences, I scarcely know how to convey them in a
> letter.   C. Lloyd also wishes much to know you personally.[3]

Poole, of course, replied, 'Come at once'; and truly
Coleridge was never more in need of the wise
sympathy and advice which always awaited him at
Stowey.   He had no settled prospects.   Lloyd's
contribution to the household expenses was limited
to £80 a year, and this was supplemented only by
the proceeds of a little reviewing, etc., which Coleridge hoped might yield £40 in a year.[4]   The
deficiency could not always be filled up by sympathetic offerings, nor could he have contemplated
with complacency the continued acceptance of such
aid.   His consuming desire was to live in the country,
near Poole, and to support himself by a combination
of literature and husbandry.

---

[1] *Religious Musings*, ll. 368, 369.
[2] Letter to Poole, Sept. 24, 1796 (*T. Poole and his Friends*, i. 157).
[3] *Biog. Lit.* 1847, ii. 375—corrected and supplemented from the original.
[4] *T. Poole and his Friends*, i. 189.

A vivid and comprehensive picture of Coleridge,
and of his views and tastes at this period, survives
in a series of unprinted letters addressed by him
to Thelwall, which once had a place in the late
Mr. F. W. Cosens's MS. collections. When Coleridge wrote the passage which follows (Nov. 19, 1796)
the two men had not yet met.

> Your portrait of yourself interests me.  As to me, my face, unless
> when animated by immediate eloquence, expresses great sloth, and
> great, indeed almost idiotic, good nature.  'Tis a mere carcase of a
> face : fat, flabby, and expressive chiefly of inexpression.   Yet I am
> told that my eyes, eyebrows, and forehead are physiognomically good;
> but of this the Deponent knoweth not.  As to my shape, 'tis a good
> shape enough, if measured—but my gait is awkward, and the walk of
> the whole man indicates *indolence capable of energies.* . . . I cannot
> breathe through my nose, so my mouth with sensual thick lips is
> almost always open. . . . I am, and ever have been, a great reader, and
> have read almost everything—a library cormorant.   I am *deep* in all
> out-of-the-way books, whether of the monkish times or of the puri-
> tanical æra.   I have read and digested most of the historic writers,
> but I do not *like* history.  Metaphysics and poetry and 'facts of
> mind' (*i.e.* accounts of all strange phantasms that ever possessed
> your philosophy-dreamers, from Theuth the Egyptian to Taylor the
> English pagan) are my darling studies.   In short, I seldom read
> except to amuse myself, and I am almost always reading.   Of useful
> knowledge—I am a so-so chemist, and I love chemistry—all else is
> *blank*—but I *will be* (please God) an horticulturist and a farmer.   I
> compose very little, and I absolutely hate composition.   Such is my
> dislike that even a sense of duty is sometimes too weak to over-
> power it. . . . In conversation I am impassioned, and oppose what
> I deem error with an eagerness which is often mistaken for personal
> asperity, but I am ever so swallowed up in the *thing* that I perfectly
> forget my opponent.   Such am I.

A month later he writes to the same unseen friend :
'As to my own poetry, I do confess that it frequently,
both in thought and language, deviates from "nature
and simplicity." But that Bowles, the most tender,
and with the exception of Burns, the only always
*natural* poet in our language, that he should not
escape the charge of Della - Cruscanism, this cuts

the skin and surface of my heart.' His own poetry, he goes on to say—

seldom exhibits unmixed and simple tenderness or passion. My philosophical opinions are blended with or deduced from my feelings, and this, I think, peculiarises my style of writing, and like everything else it is sometimes a beauty and sometimes a fault. But do not let us introduce an Act of Uniformity against Poets. I have room enough in *my* brain to admire, aye, and almost equally, the *head* and fancy of Akenside and the *heart* and fancy of Bowles, the solemn lordliness of Milton, and the divine chit-chat of Cowper : and whatever a man's excellence is, that will be likewise his fault.

In the same letter he speaks of Bowles as 'the bard of my idolatry,' and sends a commission to Thelwall to buy for him the works of Iamblichus, Proclus, Porphyry,[1] the Emperor Julian, Sidonius Apollinaris, and Plotinus—a little Neo-Platonic library.

In the summer of this year (1796) Southey had returned from Portugal. The quarrel revived, but about the time of Hartley's birth Southey made overtures which were accepted with seeming cordiality.[2] But it was only seeming, for at the end of the year Coleridge wrote to Thelwall : 'We are now reconciled ; but the cause of the difference was solemn, and "the blasted oak puts not forth its buds anew"; we are *acquaintances*, and feel *kindliness* towards each other, but I do *not esteem* or *love* Southey as I must esteem and love whom I dare call by the holy name of Friend! . . . And *vice versa*, Southey of me.'[3]

As the days shortened, Coleridge grew more and more impatient with the delays and disappointments which dogged his efforts to find a house near Poole. He was sick at heart, and the depression brought on neuralgia, and the neuralgia brought on laudanum—

[1] See also Lamb's letter to Coleridge, July 1st, 1796. *Letters*, i. 28.
[2] *Biog. Lit.* 1847, ii. 376.
[3] Unprinted letter once in Mr. F. W. Cosens's collection.

a disease of which he was never completely cured.
The attack of the temporary evil, which began on the
2nd November, was renewed on the 3rd, when Coleridge took

between 60 and 70 drops of laudanum, and *sopped* the Cerberus just
as his mouth began to open. . . . My medical attendant decides it
to be altogether nervous, and that it originates either in severe
application or excessive anxiety.  My beloved Poole, in excessive
anxiety, I believe, it might originate.  I have a blister under my
right ear, and I take 25 drops of laudanum every five hours, the
ease and *spirits* [italics in original] gained by which have enabled
me to write you this flighty but not exaggerating account.[1]

'Two days later,' says Mrs. Sandford, 'he wrote that
he was better, though "totally inappetent of food, and
languid even to an inward perishing."'

The baby son flourished, but not so Lloyd; and
the epileptic fits to which he was subject, caused the
household much anxiety.  Its master had yet found no
money-making employment, so that a gift of fifteen
guineas, which came through Estlin, must have been
welcome.  On the 15th November Coleridge wrote
to Poole : 'My anxieties eat me up. . . . I want
consolation—my Friend! my Brother! write and con-
sole me.'[2]   Poole's consolation was of a modified
character.  He told his friend of a wayside cottage
obtainable at Stowey, but had little but evil to say of
its accommodations.  These seemed to be unequal
even to the poor poet's modest requirements.  But
by the end of the month Coleridge confesses to Poole
that he is 'childishly impatient,' and, as nothing better
offers, will put up with the cottage.  One day he
writes, 'I will instruct the maid in cooking'; the next
that he will 'keep no servant'—will himself be every-

[1] S. T. C. to Poole, Nov. 5, 1796 (*T. Poole and his Friends*, i. 177, and
*Biog. Lit.* 1847, ii. 380).
[2] *T. Poole and his Friends*, i. 179.

thing, even 'occasional nurse.' This last heroic resolve was communicated to Poole in a letter of the
11th December. It was crossed by one in which
Poole not only reiterated the disadvantages of the
cottage, but dissuaded the poet strongly from burying
himself in a village so remote, as was Stowey, from
libraries and from the society of a stimulating and
helpful group of friends. This letter caused Coleridge 'unexpected and acute pain.' His frenzied reply
must be read at its full length of ten printed pages in
Mrs. Sandford's book (i. 184-193). No summary could
do it the least justice. It is a whirl of appeals, adjura-
tions, reproaches, cries *de profundis*, plans and plans
of life framed and torn up, and resumed to be again
abandoned, in bewildering profusion : a vivid and
sincere (because unconscious) revelation, not merely
of the passing mood, but of the very deeps of character and nature, which is probably unique in autobiography. As truly as of any Lucy Gray—

> 'Tis of a little child
> Upon a lonesome wild,
> Not far from home, but she hath lost her way :
> And now moans low in bitter grief and fear,
> And now screams loud, and hopes to make her mother hear.
>
> *Dejection : an Ode.*

# CHAPTER IV

## NETHER STOWEY—*LYRICAL BALLADS*

### A.D. 1797–1798

THIS letter was begun immediately on the receipt of Poole's, and concluded on the following day, but it concluded as it began, with the expression of a determination to settle at once in the cottage, if only Poole will assure him that he has kept back no reason to the contrary—for he fears that Poole's family connections are at the bottom of the dissuasion. He must have received the reassurance he wanted, for he took up his abode in the cottage on the last day of the year.[1] A poor cottage now, then a poorer; but then it had a garden of an acre and a half, and that garden touched Poole's at the rear. Just at that time no place in the world could have been more attractive. 'Literature,' he told Poole, 'though I shall never abandon it, will always be a secondary object with me. My poetic vanity and my political furor have been exhaled, and

---

[1] On June 9, 1893, a tablet inscribed, 'Here Samuel Taylor Coleridge made his home—1797-1800,' was affixed to the cottage. An effort is now being made to obtain funds for the purchase of the cottage, that it may be preserved as a memorial of Coleridge, as Dove Cottage has been secured as a memorial of Wordsworth. For the moment it has been saved from impending mutilation by a lease, with option of purchase, and will be used as a Village Lending Library. The treasurer, both for the temporary scheme, and for the purchase money, is H. St. B. Goldsmith, Esq., Manager of Stuckey's Banking Company, Bridgwater. (See *Athenæum* for June 17, 1893—Art. 'Coleridge and Nether Stowey.')

I would rather be an expert self-maintaining gardener than a Milton, if I could not unite both.' To Thelwall he wrote, in an unpublished letter, Dec. 17, 1796 :—

My farm will be a garden of one acre and an half, in which I mean to raise vegetables and corn enough for myself and wife, and feed a couple of snouted and grunting cousins from the refuse. My evenings I shall devote to literature, and by reviews in the Magazine [*Monthly*] and other shilling - scavenger employments, shall probably gain £40 a year—which Economy and Self-denial, gold-beaters, shall hammer till it covers my annual expenses. . . . I am not fit for *public* life ; yet the Light shall stream to a far distance from the taper in my cottage window.

Coleridge's last employment before finally quitting Bristol with his wife and child on the 30th December was 'to get some review-books off his hands.'[1] A week before, he had executed an order from his friend Benjamin Flower for an ode to be published on the last day of the year in the *Cambridge Intelligencer*— the paper he had recommended to the disappointed subscribers to the *Watchman*. The ode duly appeared, and at the same time Coleridge published it in an expanded form in a thin quarto pamphlet with the title, *Ode on the Departing Year*,[2] and a dedication to Thomas Poole. The superfluous page at the end he filled with the lines *Addressed to a Young Man of Fortune who abandoned himself to an indolent and causeless melancholy*—probably intended for Charles Lloyd's benefit.

When Lamb heard of the 'farm,' he asked sceptically, 'And what does your worship know about farming ? ' and recommended the cultivation of the muse as something more in his friend's way, reminding him of

---

[1] *Estlin Letters*, p. 25.
[2] ODE ON THE DEPARTING YEAR, by S. T. Coleridge. [Motto from *Æschylus*.] Bristol : Printed by N. Biggs, and sold by J. Parsons, Paternoster Row, London, 1796. Quarto, 16 pp.

a project for an epic on the Origin of Evil. But the first thing to be done at Stowey was to continue preparations begun three months before for a second edition of the *Poems*, the first having been sold out. Passages contributed to Southey's *Joan of Arc* were to be reclaimed, and recast into an independent poem, *The Visions of the Maid of Arc*, with which the new edition was to lead off. 'I much wish' (wrote Coleridge to Cottle early in January 1797) 'to send my *Visions of the Maid of Arc* and my corrections to Wordsworth, who lives not above 20 [really about 40] miles from me, and to Lamb, whose taste and *judgment* I see reason to think more correct and philosophical than my own, which yet I place pretty high.'[1]

The arrangements for a 'second edition' of the *Poems* had been made in October 1796. Cottle proposed to give Coleridge twenty guineas for an edition of five hundred, reminding us (as he probably reminded Coleridge) that this was an act of pure charity, the copyright being his. If the poet chose to omit and alter and add, it was his affair. In his reply, Coleridge hinted very strongly that he thought the proposal unjust, but that 'bartering' with Cottle was 'abso-

[1] The letter is mutilated and inaccurately printed by Cottle. This portion occurs at p. 130 of the *Reminiscences*—another at p. 100. Wordsworth and his sister were then living at Racedown, in Dorsetshire (the post-town being Crewkerne), a house lent to them by a member of the Bristol family of Pinney. The precise date of the first meeting of Coleridge and Wordsworth (a point which has been discussed) has not been ascertained, but a careful examination of all the evidence available, published and unpublished, has all but convinced me that it may have probably taken place as early as September 1795. The men do not appear to have met a second time until the autumn of 1796, after which intercourse seems to have become more or less frequent. Nothing, however, like intimacy was formed until Coleridge's visit to Racedown in June 1797, when Dorothy saw him for the first time.

Cottle has added to the difficulty by garbling seriously the letter of Coleridge printed in the *Early Recollections*, i. 159 (*Reminiscences*, pp. 81-82). In Coleridge's list of persons to whom presentation copies of the *Poems* (1796) were to be sent, Cottle has *inserted* the names of Wordsworth, Lamb, and Dr. Parr; and *omitted* a suggestion that a copy should be sent by him to Mrs. Barbauld, or to her brother Dr. Aikin.

lutely intolerable.' He was clearing out the rubbish,
and especially the political verses—the absence of
which would 'widen the sphere of his readers'—and
supplying their place with new poems of better and
more attractive quality. If he left Cottle to reprint
the old volume, and himself published the new, he
would make more money, and save the copyright in
them. He ends, however, by accepting Cottle's proposal, being 'solicitous only for the omission of the
sonnet to Lord Stanhope, and the ludicrous poem'
(*Written after a Walk before Supper*).[1] The printing
dragged on till March 1797, and when the volume
was almost completed, Coleridge wrote thus to Cottle,
in a letter which has not been fully published:
'Charles Lloyd has given me his poems, which I give
to you on condition that you print them *in this volume*
—after Charles Lamb's poems.' He goes on to
explain that although the bulk of the volume will thus
be increased, so also will be its saleability, seeing that,
he doubts not, 'Lloyd's connections will take off a
great many, more than a hundred.'

It was about this time that Coleridge received a
request from Sheridan that he would write a play for
Drury Lane, and with a feeling in which confidence
and misgivings were pretty equally mingled, the
attempt was begun. The composition occupied a good
deal of his time until the middle of October, when the
finished manuscript of *Osorio* was despatched to the
theatre. But these months were varied by many
other interests and occupations, and by one fateful
event—the settlement of the Wordsworths at Alfoxden. On most Sundays—whether in blue coat and

---

[1] See Cottle's *Rem.* p. 115. In the *E. Recoll.* (1837) Cottle suppressed
most of Coleridge's letter; but in the *Reminiscences* professes to give it complete.
I have not seen the original.

white waistcoat, or in some more conventional costume,
is unknown—Coleridge preached in the Unitarian
chapels of Bridgwater or Taunton, often travelling
on foot, and never receiving hire : on week-days he
learned a hundred practical things by precept and
example in the kindly companionship of Thomas
Poole, whose well-assorted library was as much at
Coleridge's service as if it had been his own : Charles
Lloyd occupied some hours of each morning when the
neophyte's health permitted.  Stowey had not brought
wealth or even competency, but it had revived hope,
and Coleridge generally found that a sufficing diet.  He
had not, perhaps, like another great poet, waited very
patiently, but nevertheless his cry had been heard, he
felt that his feet had been set upon a rock, and his
goings established, and he was soon to learn that a
new song had been put into his mouth.

Coleridge was certainly not idle, but money was
not coming in, and about the beginning of June,
Poole saw that a fresh subscription was needful.
Confiding his views to Lloyd and Estlin, he begged
the latter to be treasurer,[1] and to apply to none 'but
to those who love him, for it requires affection and
purity of heart to offer, with due associations, assistance of this nature to such a man.'  Coleridge had
'preached an excellent sermon at Bridgwater' on the
previous day 'on the necessity of religious zeal in
these times,' and from Bridgwater he seems to have
proceeded to Racedown on a visit to Wordsworth.

---

[1] 'I stated to Mr. Garnett that, according to our agreement, it was necessary we should again come forward, and desired him to call on you, and make
the necessary arrangements.' (Poole to Estlin, June 5, 1797, in *T. Poole and
his Friends*, i. 230.)  Poole wrote to Lloyd on the same day, a letter of similar
purport, which is printed at the same reference.  Lloyd had not been one of the
original subscribers, but, now that he had ceased to live at Stowey, Poole
assumes he will join them.  'You will, I know, become one of us.'

Thence, probably on the 9th, and again on the 10th, he wrote to Estlin asking him to give to Mrs. Fricker and to Mrs. Coleridge five guineas each, out of the subscription money, expressing ' a hope and a trust that this will be the last year ' in which he can conscientiously accept of those contributions, which, ' in my present lot, and conscious of my present occupations, I feel no pain in doing.'   To Cottle he wrote [1] with some corrections for the *Ode on the Departing Year* (then at press for the *Poems*, 1797) and announcing his return to Stowey on a ' Friday,' which may be calculated as probably the 16th June.   Wordsworth, he announces, admires his tragedy, ' which gives me great hopes '; and then he goes on to estimate Wordsworth's own tragedy in terms which, when we remember he is speaking of *The Borderers*, compel a smile. ' His drama is absolutely wonderful. . . . There are in the piece those *profound* truths of the human heart, which I find three or four times in the *Robbers* of Schiller, and often in Shakespere, but in Wordsworth there are no *inequalities*.'   He feels himself a ' little man ' by Wordsworth's side ; and adds (a passage suppressed by Cottle), ' T. Poole's opinion of Wordsworth is that he is the greatest man he ever knew.   I coincide.'   This seems to point to a previous visit or visits to Stowey paid by Wordsworth, or of meetings with Poole at Bristol, of which direct record is lacking.   Curiously enough the letter makes no mention of Miss Wordsworth, who then saw Coleridge for the first time.   Yet in 1845—across the mists of nearly half-a-century—she as well as her brother retained the ' liveliest possible image ' of Coleridge on his arrival at

[1] Cottle prints this important letter (*Rem.* p. 142) in a form both garbled and incomplete, and with the date ' June 1796.'   The original was lent me by the late Mr. F. W. Cosens.

Racedown, how 'he did not keep to the high road, but leapt over a gate and bounded down the pathless field, by which he cut off an angle.'[1]   And at the time she thus recorded her first impressions of the visitor :—

He is a wonderful man.   His conversation teems with soul, mind, and spirit.   Then he is so benevolent, so good-tempered and cheerful, and, like William, interests himself so much about every little trifle.   At first I thought him very plain, that is for about three minutes : he is pale, thin, has a wide mouth, thick lips, and not very good teeth, longish, loose-growing, half-curling, rough black hair.   But, if you hear him speak for five minutes, you think no more of them.   His eye is large and full, and not very dark, but grey—such an eye as would receive from a heavy soul the dullest expression ; but it speaks every emotion of his animated mind ; it has more of 'the poet's eye in a fine frenzy rolling' than I ever witnessed.   He has fine dark eyebrows, and an overhanging forehead.[2]

If Coleridge carried out his first intention of returning to Stowey on the 16th June, he must soon have gone back, for he appears to have arrived again at Stowey from Racedown on the 28th, and again on the 2nd July, on the last occasion bringing with him[3] the two Wordsworths on that famous visit to the Quantock country, which was destined to be prolonged for a whole year.   The visitors spent a fortnight with Coleridge, and it was then that he drew his famous portrait of Wordsworth's 'exquisite sister.'[4]

It was about this time that the second edition of Coleridge's *Poems* appeared.[5]   Much of the ultra-

---

[1] Knight's *Life*, i. 111.

[2] *Memoirs of Wordsworth*, i. 99.

[3] Information from unpublished letters, kindly given me by Mr. Ernest H. Coleridge.

[4] Letter to Cottle, *Rem.* p. 144.

[5] POEMS by S. T. Coleridge, Second Edition.   To which are added POEMS by Charles Lamb, and Charles Lloyd.

Duplex nobis vinculum, et amicitiæ et similium junctarumque Camœnarum ; quod utinam neque mors solvat, neque temporis longinquitas !   *Groscoll. Epist. ad Car. Utenhov. et Ptol. Lux. Tast.*

Printed by N. Biggs, for J. Cottle, Bristol, and Messrs. Robinsons, London. 1797.   Octavo, pp. xx. ; 278.

Lloyd's verses occupied pp. 153-213 : and Lamb's, pp. 217-240.

juvenile and most of the political verse had been discarded in favour of new, or at least hitherto uncollected, matter, and he intended (as he expressed it to Cottle) to admit nothing to the new volume 'but my choicest fish, picked, gutted, and clean'd.' The most notable additions were the dedicatory poem to his brother George; a much revised version of the *Ode to the Departing Year;* the second and third sonnets on the birth of Hartley; and the companion poem to *The Eolian Harp*, entitled *Reflections on having left a place of retirement* (Clevedon). The *Religious Musings* was included, but in a much altered form.[1] *The Visions of the Maid of Arc*, intended, as we have seen, for the first place in the new edition, was never completed, having been abandoned in deference to the adverse criticisms of Lamb—possibly also to those of Wordsworth. The fragments first saw the light in 1817, when they were printed in *Sibylline Leaves*, under the title of *The Destiny of Nations*. Cottle pretends to remember that the 'Dedication' was prompted by himself, but the reasons he assigns for his alleged suggestion are so absurd that it is probable that his memory was altogether at fault. Opening with a description of his brothers' happy fate in being settled prosperously amid the surroundings of their youth, Coleridge proceeds to contrast it with his own :—

---

[1] The 'Preface to the Second Edition' thus opens :—

'I return my acknowledgments to the different Reviewers for the assistance, which they have afforded me, in detecting my poetic deficiencies. I have endeavoured to avail myself of their remarks : one-third of the former Volume I have omitted, and the imperfections of the republished part must be considered as errors of taste, not faults of carelessness. My poems have been rightly charged with a profusion of double-epithets, and a general turgidness, I have pruned the double-epithets with no sparing hand ; and used my best efforts to tame the swell and glitter both of thought and diction. This latter fault however had insinuated itself into my *Religious Musings* with such intricacy of union, that sometimes I have omitted to disentangle the weed from the fear of snapping the flower.'

To me the Eternal Wisdom hath dispensed
A different fortune and more different mind—
Me from the spot where first I sprang to light
Too soon transplanted, ere my soul had fixed
Its first domestic loves ; and hence through life
Chasing chance-started friendships.   A brief while
Some have preserved me from life's pelting ills.

## Others, he goes on, have proved ' most false.'

                                But, all praise to Him
Who gives us all things, more have yielded me
Permanent shelter ; and beside one friend,
Beneath the impervious covert of one oak,
I've raised a lowly shed, and know the names
Of Husband and of Father ; not unhearing
Of that divine and nightly-whispering voice,
Which from my childhood to maturer years
Spake to me of predestinated wreaths,
Bright with no fading colours !

                                Yet at times
My soul is sad, that I have roamed through life
Still most a stranger, most with naked heart
At mine own home and birth-place : chiefly then,
When I remember thee, my earliest friend !
Thee, who didst watch my boyhood and my youth ;
Didst trace my wanderings with a father's eye ;
And boding evil yet still hoping good,
Rebuked each fault, and over all my woes
Sorrowed in silence !   He who counts alone
The beatings of the solitary heart,
That Being knows, how I have loved thee ever,
Loved as a brother, as a son revered thee !
Oh ! 'tis to me an ever new delight,
To talk of thee and thine : or when the blast
Of the shrill winter, rattling our rude sash,
Endears the cleanly hearth and social bowl ;
Or when as now, on some delicious eve,
We in our sweet sequestered orchard plot
Sit on the tree crooked earth-ward ; whose old boughs,
That hang above us in an arborous roof,
Stirred by the faint gale of departing May,
Send their loose blossoms slanting o'er our heads !

Nor dost not *thou* sometimes recall those hours,
When with the joy of hope thou gavest thine ear
To my wild firstling-lays.   Since then my song

> Hath sounded deeper notes, such as beseem
> Or that sad wisdom folly leaves behind,
> Or such as, tuned to these tumultuous times,
> Cope with the tempest's swell !

I regret that considerations of space do not permit me to quote the whole of this beautiful and touching poem. I think it was conceived in a spirit of perfect sincerity; it is full of character and autobiography; in construction it is more firmly knit, and (spite of an intolerable passage about the ' Manchineel') in expression more natural, more individual, than anything which preceded it. The style moves in easy accord with the thought, gravity and pensive gaiety alternating and mingling with unfailing sweetness and grace. But withal, the deficiency of the poem, from one point of view, is more notable than its achievement: it gives no hint—nothing in the volume to which it is a prelude gives the least hint—that Coleridge's hand was already on the latch of the magic casements which were to open on the perilous seas sailed by the *Ancient Mariner*, and the fairy-lands of *Christabel* and *Kubla Khan*. He must have himself been unaware, for he was then contentedly and almost hopefully giving his days and nights to the tragedy called *Osorio*.

The Wordsworths were still at the Stowey cottage when Charles Lamb[1] came to spend his week's holiday—the visit which the host commemorated in *This Lime-tree Bower my Prison*.

---

[1] A marginal note which Coleridge in 1834 wrote on the explanatory introduction to the poem has led to the assumption that Mary Lamb accompanied her brother to Stowey in 1797. There can be little doubt that Coleridge's memory —after thirty-seven years—had failed him. In none of Lamb's letters to him, written either before or after the visit, is there any indication that he was to be, or had been, accompanied by his sister. Mary Lamb was at that period in a very precarious state of health, and living apart from her father and brother.

In this poem Coleridge addresses his three guests as—

Friends whom I never more may meet again.

Lamb, of course, was a bird of passage, and so, to all appearance on that evening, were the Wordsworths, for Alfoxden had not yet been seen, or if seen had not yet been secured.   But the delay was short.   On the 14th August, Dorothy Wordsworth wrote thus from Alfoxden : 'We spent a fortnight at Coleridge's ; in the course of that time we heard that this house was to let, applied for it, and took it.   Our principal inducement was Coleridge's society.   It was a month yesterday since we came to Alfoxden.'[1]   The Coleridges' guests had scarcely quitted them—Lamb for London, and the Wordsworths for Alfoxden—when, on the 17th July, a new claimant for hospitality, in the person of John Thelwall,[2] arrived at the cottage. It was nine o'clock in the evening, and he found only Sara, who had left her husband at Alfoxden for a day or two that she might 'superintend the wash-tub.' In the morning, between five and six, Sara and her guest 'walked over to Alfoxden—a distance of about three miles—to breakfast.'[3]   'Faith, we are a most

[1] The agreement, dated 14th July 1797, is printed in full in *T. Poole and his Friends*, i. 225.   It provided for a year's tenancy of the furnished house, etc., from Midsummer to Midsummer at the rent of £23, including all rates and taxes. Wordsworth may retain the house, etc., for an indefinite period beyond Midsummer 1798, at the same rent.

[2] Known as 'Citizen Thelwall' in those days, and hardly known at all in these.   Coleridge and he had been carrying on for about a year the correspondence from which I have already quoted, but they had now met for the first time. By this time Thelwall had abandoned his somewhat silly, but always honestly conducted career of political martyrdom, and desired to settle as meditative and poetical farmer in some remote part of the country.   In quest of a suitable retreat he had travelled, mostly on foot, from London, and had now arrived at Stowey in acceptance of an invitation from the ever-hospitable Coleridge.

[3] The details respecting Thelwall are partly taken from a letter to his wife printed in *T. Poole and his Friends* (i. 232) ; and partly from Thelwall's MS. Diary, now in my own possession.—Sarah had now become 'Sara.'

philosophical party' (Thelwall writes to his wife), 'the
enthusiastic group consisting of Coleridge and his
Sara, Wordsworth and his sister, and myself, without
any servant, male or female.   An old woman, who
lives in an adjoining cottage, does what is requisite
for our simple wants.'   The party remained there for
three days.   It was at this time, and in one of
Alfoxden's romantic glens, that (as Wordsworth remembered long afterwards) Coleridge exclaimed,
'This is a place to reconcile one to all the jarrings
and conflicts of the wide world!' and that Thelwall
replied, 'Nay, to make one forget them altogether!'[1]
A few days at Stowey succeeded.   The Wordsworths
accompanied their guests part of the way, and they
talked of many things—the 'moral character of Demo-
crats, of Aristocrats,' and of 'pursuits proper for literary
men—unfit for management of pecuniary affairs—
Rousseau, Bacon, Arthur Young!'[2]   This visit of
Thelwall shocked the neighbourhood, which considered Poole responsible, and he was called upon to
answer for Wordsworth to the owner of Alfoxden.
This Poole did manfully,[3] but a Government spy was
sent down to watch the poets and their patron.   Most
of Cottle's[4] stories of the suspicions excited in the
neighbourhood by the poets' goings on, and much
of Coleridge's[5] own account of the spy's proceedings,
wear a dubious complexion ; but there is no room for
doubt that it was Thelwall's visit which brought about
the cessation of Wordsworth's tenancy of Alfoxden.

[1] *Memoirs of Wordsworth*, i. 105.
[2] MS. Diary of Thelwall, July 21, 1797.
[3] *T. Poole and his Friends*, i. 240.
[4] *Reminiscences*, p. 181.
[5] *Biog. Lit.* 1847, i. 196-200.   That a spy was actually sent down to watch
the poets seems certain (Southey's *Life and Corr.* ii. 243), but in later life
Wordsworth declared that he never heard of the circumstance until the publication of the *Biog. Lit.*

In late life he stated, in reply to assertions that he
had been refused a renewal, that he had never asked
for one—but his memory had failed, and the truth was
that he either received notice to quit, or did not think
it worth while to attempt to assert the right to remain
which the agreement accorded him.   Coleridge's
friendship with Thelwall, begun by correspondence,
was cemented by personal intercourse, and continued
for some years ; but later on, when the ex-Citizen had
a short season of prosperity, he showed himself
the poor creature he was by alternately patronising
and sneering at Coleridge.   After leaving Stowey,
he asked Coleridge to interest Poole in securing him
a farm in their neighbourhood, but the passing visit
had caused Poole trouble enough, and Thelwall had
to move into Wales.   He ultimately procured a farm
at Llyswen, in Brecon, where he was visited by the
Wordsworths and Coleridge in 1798.[1]

Soon after Citizen Thelwall's departure, came a
Mr. Richard Reynell, who wrote to his brother a
pleasing picture of the cottage and its inmates :—' On
my arrival at Stowey and at Mr. Coleridge's house, I
found he was from home, having set out for Bristol to
see Mrs. Barbauld a few days before.   I think he had
never seen her, and that he now had *walked* all the
way to gratify his curiosity.   He returned on Saturday
evening after a walk of 40 miles in one day, apparently
not much fatigued.'   Mr. Reynell describes Mrs.
Coleridge as uniformly ' sensible, affable, and good-
natured—thrifty and industrious, and always neat and
prettily dressed.   I here see domestic life in all its
beauty and simplicity. . . . Love seems more pure
than it in general is to be found, because of the

---

[1] Fenwick-note to Wordsworth's *Anecdote for Fathers*.

preference that has been given in the choice of a
life-friend to mental and moral rather than to personal
and material charms—not that you are to infer that
Coleridge and his wife have no personal recommendation.   Mrs. Coleridge is indeed a pretty woman.
. . . It is a treat, a luxury, to see Coleridge hanging
over his infant and talking to it, and fancying what he
will be in future days.'  The house is described as
'very small and very simple.  Three rooms below,
and three above—all small.'  'Here you can be
happy,' he adds, 'without superfluities.'[1]

The intercourse between Coleridge and the
Wordsworths was almost daily.  Coleridge says
somewhere, that they were 'three people but one
soul.'  The character of the intimacy is fully shown
in his exquisite lines entitled *The Nightingale: a
Conversation Poem* (April, 1798), and in the printed
fragments of Miss Wordsworth's journal.[2]  The
entries cover the first four months of 1798, but
doubtless illustrate equally the whole year during
which the two families were neighbours.  'Feb. 11th.
Walked with Coleridge near to Stowey.   12th.
Walked alone to Stowey.  Returned in the evening
with Coleridge.   13th. Walked with Coleridge
through a wood.'  On the 17th they walked together.
On the 19th Dorothy walked to Stowey.  On the
21st 'Coleridge came in the morning. . . . William
went through the wood with him towards Stowey:
a very stormy night.  22nd. Coleridge came in the
morning to dinner. . . . 23rd. William walked with
Coleridge in the morning.  26th. Coleridge came in
the morning . . . walked with Coleridge nearly to

[1] 'Stowey, August, 1797.'  Printed in *Illustrated London News* for April
22, 1893.  The whole of Reynell's long letter is full of interest.
[2] Knight's *Life of Wordsworth*, vol. i. chap. ix.

Stowey after dinner'—and so on.    They saw as much
of one another as if the width of a street, and not a
pair of coombs, had separated their several abodes.
It was a rich and fruitful time for all three—seed-
time at once and harvest ; and its happy influences
spread far beyond their own individual selves.    The
gulf-stream which rose in the Quantocks warmed and
is still warming distant shores.    Although Dorothy
Wordsworth produced nothing directly, her influence
on both men was of the highest importance.    Coleridge answered to many a touch which the slower
Wordsworth could not feel ; but Dorothy's quick
sympathy, keen observation, and rapid suggestion—
qualities she possessed in greater measure than her
brother—were invaluable to both.    The best work of
both poets was done, alike by the Quantocks and by
the Lakes, under the direct influence of her companionship.    Nor was the influence, in action and
reaction, of the men on one another less potent.
Coleridge's was by far the most active, as well as the
finer and more penetrating, and the immense re-
ceptiveness of Wordsworth must have acted as a
strong incentive to its exercise.    And this is true, I
believe, notwithstanding that there are more distinct
traces of Wordsworth's influence on Coleridge's poetry
than of the converse.    It was a consequence of
Coleridge's quicker sense, that he took up readily the
tone and accent as well as the substance of another's
thoughts, whereas, in Wordsworth's case, everything
that entered his mind from without underwent a slow
process of assimilation, and when it re-appeared, substance and expression were equally his own.

There are several indications, however, that this
summer of 1797 was not to Coleridge one of unmingled

happiness. Poole's letter to Charles Lloyd, written on 5th June, already quoted, seems to show that Lloyd was then no longer 'domesticated' with Coleridge. The particular date at which domestication ceased, and with it the payment of the £80 a year, is unknown; but although Lloyd came and went[1] until the final rupture in the spring of 1798, he probably ceased to contribute regularly to Coleridge's household expenses after the summer of 1797. The deprivation must have been severely felt, and this it may have been which caused the fit of 'depression too dreadful to be described,' of which he wrote in an undated letter to Cottle[2]: 'A sort of calm hopelessness diffuses itself over my heart. Indeed every mode of life which has promised me bread and cheese, has been, one after another, torn away from me; but God remains. I have no immediate pecuniary distress, having received ten pounds from Lloyd. I employ myself now on a book of morals in answer to Godwin, and on my tragedy.' We have already seen that, in June, Coleridge was accepting pecuniary aid from Poole and other friends. Poole at that time describes him as 'industrious, considering the exertion of his mind necessary when he works,' adding that three acts of the tragedy are completed.[3]

About the 6th of September, having completed *Osorio* to the middle of the fifth act, he took it over to Shaftesbury to exhibit it to the 'god of his idolatry,' Bowles.[4] Idol and worshipper then met for the first time, and if we may believe Cottle,[5] some disillusion

---

[1] Cottle (*Rem.* p. 150) says he met Charles Lloyd at Coleridge's house in August 1797.

[2] *Rem.* p. 102. The reference to 'my tragedy' shows that the letter must have been written before the middle of October. The 'answer to Godwin' never appeared.

[3] *T. Poole and his Friends*, i. 231.

[4] Cottle's *Rem.* p. 133.       [5] *Ib.* p. 21.

must have resulted—on Coleridge's part, at all events.[1]
A month later *Osorio* was completed and sent off to
Drury Lane, without much hope that it would be
accepted.   Although Coleridge's memory so far failed
him that, during all his later life, he made it his pet
grievance that Sheridan returned him neither MS. nor
reply, he really received the reply by the beginning of
December.   It was to the effect that *Osorio* was
rejected on account of the obscurity of Acts III., IV.,
and V.[2]   Wordsworth stated [3] that in November 1797
*Osorio* was offered with his own tragedy to Covent
Garden, but his statement was made doubtfully, and
there is no corroborative evidence.   Both tragedies
were about this time proposed to Cottle for publication,
and he offered thirty guineas for each, but the offer
was declined—'from the hope' (says Cottle) 'of introducing one or both on the stage.' [4]

The air, as usual, was full of projects.   An epic, to
which at least twenty years should be devoted, was
not, strictly speaking, one of them, but the necessary
preparations were suggested—ten years for collecting
material, five for composition, five for correction—'So

[1] During his residence at Calne in 1814-1816, Coleridge saw much of
Bowles, whose parsonage at Bremhill was not far off.   Coleridge showed Bowles
the first chapter of his *Biographia*, and wondered what Bowles thought of it—
'if, indeed, he collated the passages concerning himself, with his own speeches,
etc., concerning *me*.   Alas !   I injured myself irreparably with him by devoting
a fortnight [probably in 1815] to the correction of his poems.   He took the
corrections, but never forgave the corrector.   *Nihil fecisse benigne est : Immo
etiam tædet, tædet obestque magis*' (Letter to Brabant, December 5, 1816, in
*West. Rev.* July 1870, p. 21).   The Latin words are from Catullus (Carmen
LXXIII.   *In Ingratum*).   The passage to which they belong is quoted, with
reference to Hazlitt, in the last chapter of the *Biog. Lit.* (ed. 1847, ii. 302).

[2] 'I received a letter from Linley [Sheridan's brother-in-law and secretary],
the long and short of which is that Sheridan rejects the Tragedy—his *sole*
objection is, the obscurity of the three last acts.'   (*From an unprinted letter
written by Coleridge at 'Cottle's shop,' undated, but received by Poole on 'Dec. 2,
1797.'*)

[3] Fenwick-note to *The Borderers*.

[4] *Rem.* pp. 166, 167.

would I write, haply not unhearing of that divine and nightly whispering voice, which speaks to mighty minds, of predestinated garlands, starry and unwithering.'[1] A great poem on Man and Nature and Society, to be symbolised by a brook in its course from upland source to sea,[2] was planned in conversation with Wordsworth, and a translation of Wieland's *Oberon* seems to have been actually undertaken. This was in November 1797. On the 13th of that month,[3] at half-past four in the afternoon, Coleridge and the two Wordsworths set off to walk to Watchet *en route* to Linton and the Valley of Stones—a little tour the expense of which they meant to defray (*solvitur ambulando*) by a joint composition of the two poets, to be sold for £5 to the editor of the *Monthly Magazine*.[4] Before the first eight miles had been covered the attempt at joint composition broke down, and Coleridge took the business into his own hands.[5]

---

[1] To Cottle. *Rem.* p. 103. *Cf.* the lines in the 'Dedication' to George Coleridge—quoted at p. 70 *supra*.

[2] See Coleridge's account of the projected poem on 'The Brook' in *Biog. Lit.* chap. x. 'My walks were almost daily on the top of Quantock, and among its sloping coombs. With my pencil and memorandum-book in my hand, I was *making studies*, as the artists call them, and often moulding my thoughts into verse with the objects and imagery immediately before my senses. Many circumstances, evil and good, intervened to prevent the completion of the poem which was to have been entitled "THE BROOK."' In the course of the 'Fenwick-note' to the Duddon sonnets, Wordsworth makes an interesting comparison between what he had accomplished in that series, and what Coleridge had planned for his poem on *The Brook*.

[3] Dorothy Wordsworth's letter, Nov. 20, 1797, in *Memoirs* of Wordsworth (1851, i. 106), and the 'Fenwick-note' which follows the letter. There the date of the *Ancient Mariner* tour is given as 'the autumn of 1797.' The date given to Miss Fenwick by Wordsworth seems to have been 'the spring of 1798,' but the error was silently corrected in the *Memoirs*. It has unfortunately been allowed to stand without a corrective note in all editions of Wordsworth's poems, and in later biographies.

[4] Commonly given as 'The *New* Monthly Magazine'—a periodical which did not begin until 1814.

[5] A few lines which Wordsworth had composed were adopted by Coleridge. The 'Fenwick-note,' in which Wordsworth gave an account of the genesis of the poem, with many other particulars regarding it, too voluminous for reproduction here (even were it the place), will be found in the 'Notes' to Coleridge's *Poetical Works*, 1893, pp. 593-599.

The magnificent result was *The Ancient Mariner*.
But it was not sent to the *Monthly Magazine*, and the
travellers' expenses must have come from some other
fund. It 'grew and grew' (says Wordsworth) until
March came round. On the 23rd of that month (1798)
Dorothy records: 'Coleridge dined with us; he
brought his ballad finished. We walked with him to
the miner's house. A beautiful evening, very starry,
the horned moon.' No doubt the poet read the
ballad to his friends—his one perfect and complete
achievement—'inimitable,' as with just pride he
affirmed.

Of *Christabel*, which Coleridge tells us was begun
at Stowey in 1797, there is no contemporary record
or manuscript. But the originals of the 'thin gray
cloud' which made the moon 'both small and dull';
of 'the one red leaf the last of its clan'; of ''Tis a
month before the month of May, And the Spring
comes slowly up this way,' and of other lines are
to be found in Dorothy Wordsworth's Journal from
January 21 to March 25, 1798, and show, not only
how much Coleridge was aided by her keen observation of nature, but fix unmistakably the date of composition of Part I. The enchantment was all his own,
but, as in the case of the *Ancient Mariner* and *Kubla
Khan*, the elements were gathered from every quarter.

Sometime in 1797, possibly earlier, Coleridge had
been introduced by Poole to Thomas and Josiah
Wedgwood, sons of the great potter. Their brother
John resided at Cote House, Westbury, near Bristol;
Thomas was a patient of Dr. Beddoes, and the com-
bined circumstances caused the brothers, Thomas and
Josiah, to be frequent visitors to the neighbourhood.
Coleridge probably often met them at Bristol and at

Poole's, and as both were cultivated men they could not fail to be greatly interested in the poet. In December 1797, and during the absence of the Words-worths in London, Coleridge received an invitation to preach at the Unitarian chapel at Shrewsbury, as a candidate for the pastoral charge about to become vacant by the retirement of the Rev. Mr. Rowe. In spite of old prejudices against the preaching of the Gospel for hire, he was tempted by the emolument of £150 per annum which was attached to the pastorate. This step coming to the knowledge of the brothers Josiah and Thomas Wedgwood, they hastened to send him a present of £100 to relieve his immediate necessities, and to dissuade him from abandoning poetry and philosophy for the ministry. The cheque was immediately returned by Coleridge with a grateful letter, explaining that the £100 would soon be consumed, and prospectless poverty recur. He therefore proceeded to Shrewsbury, and preached there 'with much acceptance' on the second Sunday of 1798. One of his hearers was William Hazlitt, then a youth of twenty, living with his father, the Unitarian minister at Wem, a village ten miles from Shrewsbury. A quarter of a century afterwards, Hazlitt gave an account of that Sunday which is immortal.[1] He describes how he rose before daylight, and walked ten miles in the mud 'to hear this celebrated person preach.'

When I got there, the organ was playing the 100th Psalm, and, when it was done, Mr. Coleridge rose and gave out his text, 'And He went up into the mountains to pray, *Himself, alone.*' As he gave out this text, his voice 'rose like a steam of rich distilled perfumes,' and when he came to the two last words, which he pronounced loud, deep, and distinct, it seemed to me, who was then young, as

---

[1] *The Liberal*, No. III. (1823): 'My first acquaintance with Poets'—an expansion of an article printed in *The Examiner* for Jan. 12, 1817.

if the sounds had echoed from the bottom of the human heart, and as if that prayer might have floated in solemn silence through the universe. . . . The preacher then launched into his subject like an eagle dallying with the wind. The sermon was upon peace and war : upon church and state—not their alliance, but their separation —on the spirit of the world and the spirit of Christianity, not as the same, but as opposed to one another. He talked of those who had 'inscribed the cross of Christ on banners dripping with human gore.' He made a poetical and pastoral excursion,—and to show the fatal effects of war, drew a striking contrast between the simple shepherd boy, driving his team afield, or sitting under the hawthorn, piping to his flock 'as though he should never be old,' and the same poor country-lad, crimped, kidnapped . . . turned into a wretched drummer-boy . . . and decked out in the loathsome finery of the profession of blood.

The discourse seemed to young Hazlitt as the music of the spheres : 'Poetry and Philosophy had met together, Truth and Genius had embraced, under the eye and with the sanction of Religion.' On the following Tuesday Coleridge came to the manse at Wem, and spent the first two hours in talking to the youth.

His complexion (says Hazlitt) was at that time clear, and even bright. His forehead was broad and high, light as if built of ivory, with large projecting eyebrows, and his eyes rolling beneath them like a sea with darkened lustre. 'A certain tender bloom his face o'erspread,' a purple tinge as we see it in the pale thoughtful complexions of the Spanish portrait-painters, Murillo and Velasquez. His mouth was gross, voluptuous, open, eloquent; his chin good-humoured and round, but his nose, the rudder of the face, the index of the will, was small, feeble, nothing—like what he has done. . . . Coleridge in his person was rather above the common size, inclining to the corpulent, or like Lord Hamlet, 'somewhat fat and pursy.' His hair (now, alas ! gray) was then black and glossy as the raven's, and fell in smooth masses over his forehead.

The day passed off pleasantly, and the next morning Coleridge was to return to Shrewsbury.

When I came down to breakfast I found that he had just received a letter from his friend T. [J.] Wedgwood, making him an offer of £150 a year if he chose to waive his present pursuit, and devote himself entirely to the study of poetry and philosophy. Coleridge seemed to make up his mind to close with this proposal in the act of tying on one of his shoes. It threw an additional damp on his departure. . . . He was henceforth to inhabit the Hill of Parnassus, to be a Shepherd on the Delectable Mountain. Alas! I knew not the way thither.

So mourned Hazlitt—who was but imperfectly consoled by an invitation to Stowey. He accompanied Coleridge part of the way back to Shrewsbury, and 'observed that he continually crossed me on the way by shifting from one side of the footpath to the other. . . . He seemed unable to keep in a straight line.'[1] Hazlitt himself trod on air, for the talk was divine. 'The very milestones had ears, and Harmer Hill stooped with all its pines to listen to a poet.'

The letter which Coleridge had received, and which had been written by Josiah Wedgwood, on his own and his brother Thomas's behalf, was printed in full by Mrs. Sandford.[2] The terms of their offer, then first made public, were contained in these sentences : 'After what my brother Thomas has written [with the present of a hundred pounds], I have only to state the proposal we wish to make to you. It is that you shall accept *an annuity for life of £150, to be regularly paid by us, no condition whatsoever being annexed to it.* Thus your liberty will remain entire. . . . I do not now enter into the particulars of the mode of securing

---

[1] Compare Carlyle in the *Life of Sterling:* 'A lady once remarked that he [Coleridge, at the Grove, Highgate] never could fix which side of the garden-walk would suit him best, but continually shifted, in corkscrew fashion, and kept trying both' (p. 71).

[2] *T. Poole and his Friends*, i. 259-261. The example of the brothers Wedgwood in the disposal of their wealth, seems to be as difficult of imitation as the artistic skill by which, in large measure, the wealth had been acquired by their father :—' My brother and myself are possessed of a considerable superfluity of fortune ; squandering and hoarding are equally distant from our inclinations. But we are earnestly desirous to convert this superfluity into a fund of beneficence, and we have now been accustomed for some time, to regard ourselves rather as Trustees than Proprietors.'

the annuity, etc.—that will be done when we receive your consent to the proposal we are making; and we shall only say that *we mean the annuity to be inde-pendent of everything but the wreck of our fortune.*' [1] Coleridge delayed not a post in accepting the pro-posal, and in announcing this to Poole, on the same day, he wrote [2]: 'High benevolence is something so new, that I am not certain that I am not dreaming.' He adds that he is obliged to remain two Sundays longer at Shrewsbury. 'The congregation is small, and my reputation had cowed them into vast respect-fulness, but one shrewd fellow remarked that he would rather hear me *talk* than *preach.*' On the 19th, Cole-ridge sent in his official resignation of candidature,[3] and on the 29th went off to meet his benefactors at Cote House.[4] With the invitation mentioned in the footnote (4), there went a letter from Daniel Stuart, proprietor of the *Morning Post*, suggesting subjects for contributions in prose and verse, the remuneration for which (as we gather from an allusion in Poole's accompanying letter) was to be a guinea a week. Stuart's letter incidentally reveals the fact that Cole-ridge had been already a contributor to his paper. Poole urges Coleridge to attend at once to Stuart's request, but on the 27th Poole is told that he will be vexed to hear that Coleridge has, so far, written nothing for the *Morning Post*. He has been much

---

[1] It is unaccountable how the unconditional terms of this offer came to be forgotten or ignored by all parties when in 1811 Josiah Wedgwood saw fit to withdraw his half of the annuity. Thomas had died in the meantime, but his half had been secured legally, and was paid regularly until Coleridge's death.

[2] Letter of January 16th, unpublished.

[3] His letter is printed in full in the *Christian Reformer* for 1834, p. 838.

[4] Cottle's *Rem.* p. 172; but Cottle mistakes in supposing the letter there printed to be Coleridge's acceptance of the annuity. It was in reply to an (un-published) invitation from T. Wedgwood dated 'Penzance, January 20,' which had been forwarded by Poole.

fêted at Shrewsbury, he says; and I suspect that
his detention there beyond the date of resignation
was voluntary.    He was certainly unwise in post-
poning both his visit to the Wedgwoods and his contributions to the newspaper.    The introduction to
Daniel Stuart, who had become proprietor and editor
of the *Morning Post* in 1796, must have come from
the Wedgwoods, either directly or through their intimate friend (Sir) James Mackintosh, who in 1789 had
married Stuart's sister Catherine.

I have not detected any of Coleridge's contributions to the *Morning Post* before the beginning of
1798, but between January 8 and the departure for
Germany several poems of various merit appeared.[1]
The magnificent *Ode to France* was by far the most
important of these.    In calling it *The Recantation*,
Coleridge meant, of course, that he recanted his previous deeply-felt and loudly-expressed belief in the
French Revolution as the incarnation of the principle
of Liberty.    The base treatment of Switzerland by
the Revolutionist leaders had opened his eyes.[2]
Though not published till April, the ode and *Frost
at Midnight* are both dated 'February 1798'; *Fears
in Solitude*, 'written during the alarm of an invasion,'
was written two months later.    *The Wanderings of
Cain*[3] and *The Nightingale: a Conversation Poem*
belong to this rich spring and summer, which also saw

---

[1] *Fire, Famine, and Slaughter ; The Raven ; Lewti ; The Recantation* [i.e.
*France : an Ode*] ; and *The Mad Ox* [i.e. *Recantation*].

[2] 'No man was more enthusiastic than I was for France and the Revolution ;
it had all my wishes, none of my expectations. *Before* 1793, *I clearly saw, and
often enough stated in public, the horrid delusion, the vile mockery of the whole
affair*' (*Table Talk*, July 23, 1832).    The editor of *T.T.* quotes stanzas iv. and
v. of *France* in support of Coleridge's imperfect recollection.    It would have
been more useful had he quoted stanzas ii. and iii. in correction of it.

[3] Hazlitt says Coleridge told him the Valley of Stones near Linton was to
have been the scene.    (*My first acquaintance with Poets.*)

the gathering together of the *Lyrical Ballads*.    Before
the end of March *The Ancient Mariner* was ready ; on
the 12th April, Wordsworth tells Cottle he has been
going on ' very rapidly, adding to his stock of poetry.'
The season, he adds, is advancing with extraordinary
rapidity, 'and the country becomes almost every hour
more lovely.'[1]    It was of this season, the splendour
of which has become traditional, that he reminded
Coleridge in the closing lines of *The Prelude* :—

> That summer, under whose indulgent skies,
> Upon smooth Quantock's airy ridge we roved
> Unchecked, or loitered 'mid her sylvan combs,
> Thou in bewitching words, with happy heart,
> Didst chaunt the vision of that Ancient Man,
> The bright-eyed Mariner, and rueful woes
> Didst utter of the Lady Christabel ;
> And I, associate with such labour, steeped
> In soft forgetfulness the livelong hours,
> Murmuring of him who, joyous hap, was found,
> After the perils of his moonlight ride.

The prospect of Wordsworth's enforced quittance of
Alfoxden at Midsummer seems to have produced as
early as March a feeling of unrest among the whole
party. 'We have come to a resolution' (wrote Wordsworth to his friend James Losh[2]), '— Coleridge, Mrs.
Coleridge, my sister, and myself, of going into Germany, where we purpose to pass the two ensuing
years in order to acquire the German language, and to
furnish ourselves with a tolerable stock of information
in natural science.'    As time and discussion went on,
this large scheme underwent some modification.

It was probably in May that Hazlitt paid the visit
to Coleridge which he has brilliantly described in *The
Liberal*.[3]    He heard Coleridge recite ' with a sonorous

[1] *Rem.* p. 175.
[2] Of 'Woodside, near Carlisle.'    Letter of March 11, 1798, quoted in
Knight's *Life*, i. 147.
[3] No. III., 1823, *My first acquaintance with Poets*.

and musical voice the ballad of *Betty Foy.*' He saw Wordsworth, 'gaunt and Don Quixote-like,' in his 'brown fustian jacket and striped pantaloons.'

> Wordsworth read us the story of *Peter Bell*[1] in the open air. . . . There is a *chaunt* in the recitation both of Coleridge and Wordsworth which acts as a spell on the hearer, and disarms the judgment. . . . Coleridge's manner is more full, animated, and varied; Wordsworth's more equable, sustained, and internal. . . . Coleridge has told me that he himself liked to compose in walking over uneven ground, or breaking through the straggling branches of a copsewood. . . . Returning that same evening, I got into a metaphysical argument with Wordsworth, while Coleridge was explaining the different notes of the nightingale to his sister, in which we neither of us succeeded in making ourselves perfectly clear and intelligible. Thus I passed three weeks at Nether Stowey and in the neighbourhood, generally devoting the afternoons to a delightful chat in an arbour made of bark by the poet's friend Tom Poole, sitting under two fine elm trees and listening to the bees humming around us while we quaffed our *flip.*

Coleridge took Hazlitt on a walk to Linton. That the five-and-thirty miles of roughest road was covered in one day — 'our feet kept time to the echo of Coleridge's tongue' — speaks convincingly as to Coleridge's robust condition at this time. In this walk John Chester made a third — 'a native of Nether Stowey,' says Hazlitt, 'one of those who were attracted to Coleridge's discourse as flies are to honey, or bees in swarming time to the sound of a brass pan. . . . He told me his private opinion, that Coleridge was a wonderful man. . . . He afterwards followed [accompanied] Coleridge into Germany.'

Of Coleridge's literary likes and dislikes as pronounced during the walk, Hazlitt gives a tolerably long list. His narrative is not improbably tinged a little by his own prejudices, and distorted by the per-

---

[1] *Peter Bell* was begun on April 20, says Dorothy Wordsworth in her Journal.' Knight's *Life*, i. 143.

spective of a quarter of a century, but it is doubtless
in the main a true account of the vivid impressions he
carried away, and should be read in its entirety.
Another account of the Coleridge of this period has
survived; but as it was written by himself to his
brother George, on whom he was doubtless anxious
to produce a favourable impression, it must be received with due caution.    It is a very long and
deeply interesting letter, and will doubtless be printed
in full in the biography now preparing by the poet's
grandson.   Coleridge begins by saying that he has
been troubled by toothache, and has found relief in
laudanum—not sleep, but that kind of repose which is
as a 'spot of enchantment, a green spot of fountains
and trees in the very heart of a waste of sand.'
He has 'snapped his squeaking baby - trumpet of
sedition,' and given himself over entirely to poetry
and ·philosophical contemplation—but he discreetly
refrains from mentioning the preaching in Unitarian
chapels.   The letter ends by proposing an early walk
down to Ottery.   Had he carried out this intention
he would doubtless have announced the German plan
which was then chiefly occupying his thoughts.

The letter was written in April.   In the same
month, probably, but certainly about this time, came
the rupture with Lloyd ; and, consequent on the painful depression it produced, that famous retirement 'to
a lonely farm-house between Porlock and Linton,' and
resort to 'an anodyne,' of which *Kubla Khan* was the
costly but delightful result.[1]

[1] In the Preface to *Kubla Khan* Coleridge gives the date as 'the summer of
1797,' and in the *Poet. Works* (1893) I have so placed the poem.   But, after
the text of that volume had been printed, a MS. note by Coleridge, dated
Nov. 3, 1810, was discovered, and kindly communicated to me by Mr. Ernest Coleridge.   In this, Coleridge states that the retirement to the farm-house, and the
recourse to opium—he calls it 'the first,' meaning, doubtless, the first recourse

On the 14th May Coleridge's second child was born, and named (but not baptized) ' Berkeley ' in honour of the philosopher, the keystone of whose system was still, in his disciple's eyes, indestructible. In announcing this event to Poole, then waiting by his only brother's death-bed, he claims to be the better able to sympathise with him because of ' sorrows of his own that have cut more deeply into his heart than they ought to have done '—alluding, doubtless, to the rupture with Lloyd, and to his knowledge that Lamb was being alienated from him by Lloyd.

In March there had been talk of a third edition of Coleridge's poems, and on hearing of it Lloyd begged Cottle to ' persuade ' Coleridge to omit his. This caused Coleridge to reply, smilingly, that no persuasion was needed for the omission of verses published at the earnest request of the author ; and that though circumstances had made the Groscollian motto[1] now look ridiculous, he accepted the punishment of his folly. The letter closes with the characteristically sententious reflection—' By past experience we build up our moral being.'[2] The story is much obscured by Cottle. He mixes up with it the Higginbottom Sonnets[3] of November 1797, and omits to supply his documents with dates, but it would seem

for relief from *mental* trouble—were caused by the breach with Lloyd. He goes on to say that the nervous disquietude and misery which he suffered prevented him from finishing *Christabel*. Coleridge is generally unreliable in the matter of dates assigned to particular single events, but I think we may trust him when he synchronises. Besides, it seems far more probable that *Kubla Khan* was composed after *Christabel* (I.) and *The Ancient Mariner*, than that it was the first breathing on his magic flute.

[1] See footnote 5, p. 68 *supra*.

[2] S. T. C. to Cottle, March 8, 1798, in *Rem.* p. 164.

[3] *Poet. Works* (1893), p. 110. These satirical sonnets were printed in Nov. 1797, and one of Lamb's most affectionate letters to Coleridge was written in the following January. (*Letters*, i. 85.)

that by June some sort of reconciliation between
Lloyd and Coleridge had been patched up. 'I love
Coleridge,' wrote Lloyd to Cottle,[1] 'and can forget
all that has happened'; but things must have gone
wrong again, for Lloyd resumed, and too successfully,
his attempt to poison Lamb's mind. On July 28,
Lamb wrote thus to Southey: 'Samuel Taylor Coleridge, to the eternal regret of his native Devonshire,
emigrates to Westphalia. "Poor Lamb" (these were
his last words), "if he wants any *knowledge*, he may
apply to me." . . . I could not refrain from sending
him the following propositions, to be by him defended
or oppugned (or both) at Leipsic or Göttingen'; and
then come the *Theses quædam Theologicæ*.[2] If any
such speech was ever uttered by Coleridge, it must
have been curiously misrepresented to have aroused
in Lamb's gentle spirit the extreme bitterness mani-
fested in the letter[3] he wrote to Coleridge conveying
the *Theses*. In after-years[4] Lamb told Coleridge that
the brief alienation between them had been caused by
Lloyd's tattle, adding that Lloyd's unfortunate habit
had wrought him other mischief.[5] The quarrel must

---

[1] Birmingham, June 7, 1798. In the same letter he mentions that Lamb
had quitted him the day before after a fortnight's visit, and that he will write to
Coleridge (*Rem.* p. 170).

[2] *Letters of Lamb*, i. 88.

[3] *Ib.* i. 321.

[4] *Ib.* ii. 32.

[5] '[Coleridge, in 1821] spoke in the highest terms of affection and consideration of Lamb. Related the circumstance which gave rise to *The Old Familiar
Faces*. Charles Lloyd, in one of his fits, had shown to Lamb a letter, in which
Coleridge had illustrated the cases of vast genius in proportion to talent, and predominance of talent in conjunction with genius, in the persons of Lamb and
himself. Hence a temporary coolness, at the termination of which, or during
its continuance, these beautiful verses were written' (Allsop's *Letters*, etc. p.
141). *The Old Familiar Faces* was first printed in *Blank Verse* (by C. L. and
C. Ll.) 1798, and dated 'January 1798.' As this date is probably correct, the
'friend of my bosom' was certainly Coleridge; the friend whom Lamb had 'left
like an ingrate,' Lloyd,—and Allsop's (or Coleridge's) recollection, therefore, as
regards Lamb's verses, at fault.

have been a source of much pain both to Lamb and
Coleridge—especially to Coleridge, who was conscious
of having thought no evil of Lamb. Coleridge's
feelings had by this time (July 1798) been embittered
by the publication of Lloyd's novel, *Edmund Oliver*,
in which, under the thinnest disguise, and in no
particularly friendly spirit, Coleridge's enlistment
and other adventures had been introduced. The
irritation could not have failed to be increased by the
circumstances, that the book was dedicated to Charles
Lamb, and published by Cottle.

In May, Cottle was invited to Alfoxden and spent
a week there. During this visit, arrangements were
made for the publication of the *Lyrical Ballads*, and
he carried off with him the MS. of *The Ancient
Mariner*. The price of the copyright was fixed at
thirty guineas, payable in the last fortnight of July—
the 'money being necessary to our plan,' wrote Coleridge—the plan being doubtless the German one,
although its details had not then been finally arranged.
It was probably with the view of consulting the Wedgwoods[1] that about the middle of June, Coleridge paid
them a visit at Stoke d'Abernon, near Cobham,[2] during which he learnt that Godwin was anxious to be
*re*introduced to him. Coleridge hopes to see him

---

[1] It may be as well, at this point, to clear away a misunderstanding with
regard to the relations between the Wedgwoods on the one part, and Coleridge
and Wordsworth on the other, in the matter of the cost of the German expedition.   In her very interesting miscellany, *A Group of Englishmen* (1871, p. 98),
Miss Meteyard quotes from the accounts-current between the Wedgwoods and
their Hamburg Agents, P. and O. Von Axen, entries of large payments to Coleridge and Wordsworth during the poets' residence in Germany.   She jumps to
the conclusion, which unfortunately has been accepted by biographers of both,
that (1) Wordsworth's expenses came out of the Wedgwoods' pockets, and (2)
that this was the case also with Coleridge's, *over and above his annuity*.   I
believe the facts to be, that (1) Wordsworth merely banked with the Von Axens,
and (2) all Coleridge's drawings were debited to his annuity, except those made
for account of Chester, whose family paid all his expenses.

[2] *T. Poole and his Friends*, i. 271.

in the following week, but I think the meeting did not
take place until 1800.   On the 3rd August he was
with the Wordsworths at Bristol, and wrote to Poole
that he considered 'the realisation of the [German]
scheme of great importance to his intellectual activity,
and, of course, to his moral happiness.'[1]   He is
doubtful whether Mrs. Coleridge should accompany
him, but inclined to think that as this would involve
borrowing, he had better go alone — at first, at all
events.   He begs for Poole's advice to be laid before
him on his return to Stowey, in a week, after he has
taken a 'dart into Wales.'   The Wordsworths had
quitted Alfoxden at Midsummer, and, after staying
a week with the Coleridges, they walked to Bristol,
where they took lodgings, and superintended the printing of the *Lyrical Ballads*.   Before the end of August
they were in London, in readiness for their journey.

We have no details, but during these weeks it
must have been settled that Mrs. Coleridge and the
two children, Hartley and Berkeley, should remain at
Stowey, under the wing of Poole, and that Coleridge
should take with him the young Stowey man mentioned
by Hazlitt, John Chester.   Coleridge met the Wordsworths in London about the 10th September, and
spent a few hurried days.   He arranged with Johnson
(Cowper's publisher), in St. Paul's Churchyard, for the
printing of the little quarto which contains *Fears in
Solitude*,[2] etc., but unfortunately he found no time for his
most important call—that on Daniel Stuart respecting

---

[1] *T. Poole and his Friends*, i. 272.

[2] FEARS IN SOLITUDE, written in 1798, during the alarm of an invasion.
To which are added, FRANCE, an Ode; and FROST AT MIDNIGHT.   By S. T.
Coleridge.   LONDON : Printed for J. Johnson, in St. Paul's Church-yard.
1798.   Quarto, pp. 23.   'Fears in Solitude' is dated at the end, 'Nether
Stowey, April 20th, 1798.'   Each of the other poems is dated at the end—
'February 1798.'

promised contributions to the *Morning Post*. The party left London on the 14th, and, having taken packet at Yarmouth on the 16th, reached Hamburg on the third day after.

The volume of *Lyrical Ballads, with a few other Poems*, had been published a few days before. It was anonymous, and in the preface ('Advertisement') no hint was given that more than one author was concerned. Coleridge's contributions were:—*The Rime of the Ancyent Marinere; The Nightingale: a Conversation Poem; The Foster-Mother's Tale;* and *The Dungeon*—the two last being overflowings from *Osorio*. The reception accorded to the little volume was far from being enthusiastic, but, everything considered, was not altogether discreditable to the reviewers. If they were shocked by the *Ancient Mariner*, so were Southey and Lloyd, and so, a little, was William Wordsworth. They saw merit in *Goody Blake* and in *The Thorn* and in *The Idiot Boy*, but only Southey, among them all, took the least notice of *Lines at Tintern Abbey*. He was likewise alone in noticing the *Lines left on a Yew-tree Seat;* and not even he was attracted by 'It is the first mild day of March,' or 'Written in Early Spring,' or by the exquisite close of *Simon Lee*—plain evidence of the small extent to which the sweet influences of Cowper and Burns had up to that time affected the dry places of metropolitan criticism. The sale of the volume was slow, but the poets heard nothing at all about it during their absence, except a cheerful report from Mrs. Coleridge that 'the *Lyrical Ballads* are not liked at all by any.'

# CHAPTER V

## GERMANY

### A.D. 1798–1799

THE passage from Yarmouth and the events of the early days spent by the united party at Hamburg, are amusingly described by Coleridge in his 'Satyrane's Letters.'[1] In Hamburg they greatly enjoyed themselves in simple tourist fashion. They met Klopstock and had discussions, of greater length than importance, with him on the literatures of their respective countries. After four days' junketing, Coleridge went off by himself to Ratzeburg, carrying a letter of introduction to the *Amtmann* (Magistrate) of that town, who introduced him to a pastor, with whom he arranged to live (himself and Chester) *en pension*. He then returned to Hamburg, said good-bye to the Wordsworths, and on the 1st October left again for Ratzeburg, remaining there for the next four months. The early separation from the Wordsworths has never

[1] Spenser's Satyrane (*F.Q.* I. vi.)—

Who far abroad for strange adventures sought.

The Letters were first printed in *The Friend* for Nov. 23, Dec. 7, and Dec. 21, 1809. They were reprinted in the *Biog. Lit.* vol. ii. Coleridge, I believe, saw Klopstock only on the first occasion, and the whole of the account of the conversations must have been taken from Wordsworth's notes, for the language used was French, which was practically unintelligible to Coleridge.

been fully explained, and has given rise to unfounded suspicions, such as those which seized on Charles Lamb when he heard the news [1] that the poets had quarrelled. The only allusion to the reasons with which I am acquainted is contained in a letter from Poole,[2] which apparently reflects Coleridge's account of the matter. 'The Wordsworths have left you—so there is an end of our fears about amalgamation, etc. I think you both did perfectly right. It was right for them to find a cheaper situation ; and it was right for you to avoid the expense of travelling, provided you are where *pure German* is spoken.' He adds, ' You will, of course, frequently hear from Wordsworth,'—which shows that the separation took place under no shadow even of momentary unfriendliness. On the day on which the Wordsworths left Hamburg for Goslar (*viâ* Brunswick), William wrote to Poole : 'Coleridge has most likely informed you that he and Chester have settled at Ratzeburg. Dorothy and I are going to speculate further up the country.' They went further only to fare worse, for at Goslar they were nearly frozen to death, saw little or nothing of German society, and learnt little or nothing of the language or literature. Wordsworth, however, did better, for he wrote some of his best poetry, though of course he could have done that under more comfortable circumstances in England. A most cordial correspondence was kept up between the separated friends,[3] and in February Wordsworth and his sister seem to have visited Coleridge at Göttingen.[4] They also

---

[1] Lamb to Southey, Nov. 28, 1798 (*Letters*, i. 98).
[2] To Coleridge, Oct. 8, 1798. *T. Poole and his Friends*, i. 278.
[2] Oct. 3, 1798. Knight's *Life*, i. 178.
[3] Knight's *Life*, i. 184. See also *Hexameters*, and *Ad Vilmum Axiologum*, in *Poet. Works* (1893), pp. 137, 138.
[4] Knight's *Life*, i. 183.

spent a day or two with him, in April, on their way home.[1]

Coleridge's purpose in remaining at Ratzeburg was to acquire a thorough knowledge of German.

> It was a regular part of my morning studies for the first six weeks of my residence at Ratzeburg, to accompany the good and kind old pastor with whom I lived, from the cellar to the roof, through gardens, farm-yard, etc., and to call every, the minutest, thing by its German name. Advertisements, farces, jest-books, and the conversation of children while I was at play with them, contributed their share to a more home-like acquaintance with the language than I could have acquired from works of polite literature alone, or even from polite society.[2]

By the end of those six weeks he 'amazes' his Stowey friends by his report of progress; and vexes them by the accounts of his home-sickness. 'You say you wish to come home!' responds Poole, and advises him to be of good cheer and think of nothing but the accomplishment of the object of his exile. He adds that Stuart is anxiously expecting the promised contributions to the *Morning Post*—contributions which never arrived.[3]

Coleridge certainly wrote warmly affectionate and dolorously home-sick letters to his wife and to Poole, but my impression is that he had distractions. He made little excursions into the adjoining country; the 'nobility and gentry' of the little town paid him much attention, for he was Coleridge, and Englishmen were naturally popular in a town which fired a salute of twenty-one guns in honour of the battle of the Nile. But the mails were very irregular, and he no doubt fretted sometimes—especially when news came that little Berkeley's inoculation had been swiftly followed

---

[1] Knight's *Life*, i. 193.       [2] *Biog. Lit.* 1817, i. 201 *n.*
[3] *T. Poole and his Friends*, i. 282.

by an attack of smallpox which spoiled his fair beauty.
Coleridge tried total abstinence from fermented
liquors, and ate little animal food, but after three
months' experience of the regimen, found that
though his digestion improved and his spirits became
more equable, sleeplessness had been induced. With
what he considered a sufficient stock of German, he
left Ratzeburg on Feb. 6th for Göttingen, where
he arrived on the 12th. He matriculated at the
University, at which he found three Cambridge men,
including two Parrys, elder brothers of the Arctic
explorer. He attended the lectures of Blumenbach
on Physiology and Natural History; those of the
rationalising Eichhorn, on the New Testament,[1] he
studied at second-hand from a student's notes.[2] 'But
my chief efforts were directed towards a grounded
knowledge of the German language and literature,'
and he went deep into the earlier forms of the language—Gothic, etc. All this he did, and, in addition,
'read and made collections for a history of the *belles
lettres* in Germany, before the time of Lessing, and
made very large collections for a life of Lessing.'[3]
'For these last four months,' he adds, 'I have worked
harder than, I trust in God Almighty, I shall ever
have occasion to work again : this endless transcription is such a body-and-soul wearying purgatory. I
shall have bought thirty pounds' worth of books,

---

[1] 'Coleridge, an able vindicator of these important truths [Christian Evi-
dences], is well acquainted with Eichhorn, but the latter is a coward, who dreads
his arguments and his presence. . . . Coleridge is much liked, notwithstanding
many peculiarities. He is very liberal towards all doctrines and opinions, and
cannot be put out of temper. . . . The great fault which his friends lament is the
variety of subjects which he adopts, and the too abstruse nature of his ordinary
speculations, *extra homines positas.*' Parry, in a letter of May 25, 1799, quoted
in Carlyon's *Early Years and Late Reflections,* i. 100 *n.*

[2] *Biog. Lit.* 1817, i. 202.

[3] Letter to J. Wedgwood, May 21, 1799, in Cottle's *Rem.* p. 427.

chiefly metaphysics, and with a view to the one work, to which I hope to dedicate in silence the prime of my life ; but I believe, and indeed doubt not, that before Christmas I shall have repaid myself.'

On the 22nd March Carlyon arrived at Göttingen fresh from Pembroke College (Cambridge) with a travelling fellowship. With him came one or two other young men, so that there was then a friendly little band of Englishmen, with Coleridge for its centre, if not its leader. For he, we are assured, was ' the noticeable Engländer.' From Carlyon's rather dreary farrago of a book, thrown together when he was an old man, we learn that, as at Ratzeburg, so at Göttingen, Coleridge was not without distractions. Of course he talked—he never wearied of talking, and frequently over the heads of his companions, for he tried to make metaphysicians of them. He was the life and soul of an excursion which the Englishmen made to the Harz Mountains, during which he composed the *Lines written in the Album at Elbingerode* and *Home-sick*, and a picturesque letter to Mrs. Coleridge describing his adventures.[1] Carlyon says he contributed the *Home-sick* lines to the Stamm-Buch at the Wermingerode inn. To Poole he sent them in a letter, thus prefacing them :—' O Poole ! I am home-sick. Yesterday, or rather yesternight, I dittied the following hobbling Ditty ; but my poor muse is quite gone—perhaps she may return and meet me at Stowey.'

> 'Tis sweet to him who all the week
>     Through city-crowds must push his way,
> To stroll alone through fields and woods,
>     And hallow thus the Sabbath-day.

---

[1] The letter was printed partially in the *Amulet* for 1829, and completely in the *New Monthly Magazine* for 1835.

And sweet it is, in summer bower,
   Sincere, affectionate and gay,
One's own dear children feasting round,
   To celebrate one's marriage-day.

But what is all, to his delight,
   Who having long been doomed to roam,
Throws off the bundle from his back,
   Before the door of his own home?

Home-sickness is a wasting pang;
   This feel I hourly more and more:
There's healing only in thy wings,
   Thou breeze that play'st on Albion's shore!

*May 26, 1799.*

From Carlyon we learn that Coleridge dressed badly, 'but I have heard him say, fixing his prominent eyes upon himself (as he was wont to do whenever there was a mirror in the room), with a singularly coxcombical expression of countenance, that his dress was sure to be lost sight of the moment he began to talk, an assertion which, whatever may be thought of its modesty, was not without truth.'[1]

He had, however, fits of depression, especially when the intervals between home letters were prolonged. He describes himself as languishing for hours together in vacancy. 'Love,' he cries out, 'is the vital air of my genius,'[2] and in Germany he has seen no

[1] *Early Years*, etc., i. 29.

[2] Letter to Mrs. Coleridge from Göttingen, 'March 12, 1799. Sunday night'—a long and affectionate letter of the highest interest in every respect. It is printed in the *Illustrated London News* for April 29, 1893. He tells his wife that he is 'deeply convinced that if he were to remain a few years among objects for whom he had no affection, he should wholly lose the powers of intellect.' An intense craving for sympathy in all that it produces is one of the concomitants of the artistic nature. But in Coleridge's case the craving was rather for sympathy with *himself.*

    To be beloved is all I need,
    And whom I love, I love indeed,

are the closing lines of *The Pains of Sleep;* and in a letter to Beaumont of the same year (1803) he exclaims : 'Me, who from my childhood have had no avarice, no ambition, whose very vanity, in my vainest moments was, nine-tenths of it, the desire and delight, and necessity of loving and of being loved !' (*Coleorton Letters*, i. 15.)

one to love.    In the first days of April a sad blow fell
on him.    Letters from Mrs. Coleridge and from Poole
reached him with news that little Berkeley was dead.
They were dated March 15, but the child had died
nearly five weeks before.    Poole's letter reveals the
reason of the delay [1]—he feared to disturb Coleridge's
mind, and would have kept him in ignorance until his
arrival in England.    Mrs. Coleridge seems to have
shared Poole's notion, but both must have come to
see that they could not write at all without mentioning
the sad news, and so, in a month, their hand was
forced.    So far from having 'never forgotten herself'
in her sorrow (as Poole, with the kindest of intentions,
feigned), Mrs. Coleridge was distracted with grief,
and her letter to her husband is very touching.    She
adjured him not to fail to return in May as he
had promised.    Coleridge was simply stunned.    So
perfect was his confidence in the love and affection
which had prompted the delay that it drew from him
no word of reproach.    In his letter to Poole he recalls
the lines in *Osorio*—altering them slightly—

> ' Grief, indeed,
> Doth live and dally with fantastic thought,
> And smiling like a sickly moralist,
> Finds some resemblance to her own concerns
> In the straws of chance, and things inanimate !

' But I cannot truly say that I grieve—I am perplexed
—I am sad, and a little thing, a very little thing would
make me weep ; but for the death of the baby, I have
*not* wept.    Oh! this strange, strange, strange scene-
shifter, Death—that giddies one with insecurity, and
so unsubstantiates the living things that one has
grasped and handled ' ; and he goes on to transcribe

---

[1] Poole's letter is peculiarly interesting.    See *T. Poole and his Friends*, i.
290-295.

the 'sublime epitaph' which Wordsworth had sent him some months before—'A slumber did my spirit seal.' He fancies that perhaps the thought of the possibility of Dorothy's death had suggested the lines. A month later (May 6) he writes : 'O my God, how I long to be at home!' The nightingales are singing around him and make him think, he writes, of his own verses, 'only because I thought of Hartley, my *only* child.[1] Dear *lamb*, I hope *he* won't be dead before I get home. . . . I have a strange sort of sensation, as if, while I was present, none could die whom I intensely loved.'[2]

In the same letter Coleridge informs Poole that the Wordsworths had passed through Göttingen [3]—

They were melancholy and hypp'd. W. was affected to tears at the thought of not living near me—wished me, of course, to live in the north of England, near them and Sir F. Vane's great library. I told him that, independent of the expense of removing, and the impropriety of taking Mrs. Coleridge to a place where she would have no acquaintance, two insurmountable objections, the library was no inducement, for I wanted old books chiefly, such as could be procured anywhere better than in a gentleman's new fashionable collection. Finally, I told him plainly that *you* had been the man in whom *first*, and in whom *alone*, I had felt an anchor.

But Wordsworth reiterated that a library was a necessity.[4] Coleridge goes on to say that it is painful to him to think of not living near Wordsworth, 'for he is a *good* and *kind* man, and the only one whom in *all* things I feel my superior.'

On the 24th June Coleridge left Göttingen for

---

[1] *The Nightingale : a Conversation Poem*, in which Hartley is alluded to.
[2] *T. Poole and his Friends*, i. 297.
[3] This visit must have taken place about April 25. See Dorothy Wordsworth's letter to Poole in Knight's *Life of William Wordsworth*, i. 193. There had been a previous visit, 'soon after Coleridge's arrival at Göttingen' (Feb. 12), and previous to March 22. See CARLYON, i. 196.
[4] Up to July the Wordsworths were willing to go to the Stowey neighbourhood if Poole could find them a house. See Knight's *Life*, i. 194.

England.   On the evening before, he and some of his English friends were entertained at supper by Professor Blumenbach.   Coleridge was in the best of spirits, talking away, says Carlyon, 'with the worst German accent imaginable,' and occasionally appealing to his pocket dictionary for a word.   Carlyon and Greenough accompanied Coleridge and Chester as far as Brunswick.   The party paid a second visit to the Harz— again, without finding the Brocken Spectre at home— and spent a day over the Lessing relics at Wolfenbüttel on the way.

# CHAPTER VI

## LONDON—GRETA HALL

### A.D. 1799–1801

COLERIDGE arrived at Stowey at some uncertain date between the 2nd and 29th July, and on the latter day he wrote a friendly letter to Southey, who was at Minehead. Southey seems to have responded tentatively, accusing Coleridge of evil-speaking. Coleridge replied by denying that he had ever accused Southey of anything but enmity to himself, an enmity founded on delusion—and he appealed to Poole. Poole backed up Coleridge, who, he says, had always spoken of Southey with affection. 'As for C. Lloyd,' adds Poole, 'it would be cruel to attribute *his* conduct to aught but a diseased mind.'[1] Southey thus satisfied, brought his wife to Stowey,[2] and there they remained for two or three weeks. It was during this visit that the two poets concocted *The Devil's Thoughts*, after the casual, light-hearted fashion described, long after, by Southey—

> There while the one was shaving
> Would he the song begin,
> And the other, when he heard it at breakfast,
> In ready accord join in.

---

[1] From unpublished correspondence.    [2] *Letters of R. S.* i. 78.

Before the end of August the brothers-in-law and their wives set out from Stowey—the Southeys for Sidmouth, and the Coleridges for Ottery St. Mary, on a visit to the old home. To Poole, Coleridge wrote assurances that he and his wife had been 'received with all love and attention,' and Southey, who was detained a few days at Ottery, gave a lively account of the family party to his friend, John May.[1] 'We were all a good deal amused by the old lady [Coleridge's mother]. She could not hear what was going on, but seeing Samuel arguing with his brothers, took it for granted that he must have been wrong, and cried out, "Ah, if your poor father had been alive, he'd soon have convinced you!"' The visit was prolonged until near the end of September, and Coleridge tells Poole that he had enjoyed himself. Finding that his brothers' opinions, tastes, and creed differed fundamentally from his own, he held his peace, and amiably pledged 'Church and King' when the toast was going round, relieving his feelings occasionally in the company of some friends at Exeter, whose views more nearly coincided with his own—one of them being Hucks, the travelling companion of 1794. On the 30th September he writes to Southey of a rheumatic attack which reminds him of his rheumatic fever at school; and, a fortnight later, of much pain and sleeplessness, with sickness, through indigestion of food taken by compulsion—symptoms, one fears, not without their suggestiveness. Southey was at this time collecting verses for the second volume of his *Annual Anthology*, and Coleridge had promised contributions —even *Christabel*, it would appear, for he promises to set about the finishing of it with all speed, though he

1 *Letters of R. S.* i. 81-83.

doubts if it would make a suitable poem with which to open the volume. He thinks he may go to London.

A week later he went to London—but not directly. He had received alarming accounts of Wordsworth's health, and on the 26th October, in company with Cottle, he arrived at Sockburn, where the Wordsworths were residing with their old friend Tom Hutchinson.[1] Fortunately the cause of alarm had passed away, and almost immediately the three visitors started on a tour of the Lake Country.[2] Cottle having been dropped at Greta Bridge, his place was taken by Wordsworth's sailor brother, John, and the tourists probably penetrated into Gilsland, seeing Irthing Flood, and Knorren Moor, and Tryermaine, and other places whose names give local colour to the second part of *Christabel.* Both poets were strongly attracted by Grasmere, and with Wordsworth it became merely a question of whether he should build a house by the lake-side, or, as he finally decided, to take one which was then available. Before Christmas, he and his sister had taken up their abode in Dove Cottage, which all the world now goes to see.

Coleridge did not go back to Stowey. While in the north he seems to have received a definite proposal to take up his residence in London, and write political articles for the *Morning Post.* In return Stuart seems to have promised to defray all his expenses. To London accordingly he went directly by coach from Sockburn, arriving on November 27. He immediately took lodgings, which at the time he described

---

[1] The brother of Mary and Sarah Hutchinson. It was Coleridge's first meeting with the sisters. Mary was then keeping house for her brother. In October 1802 she became the wife of Wordsworth. Sarah became one of Coleridge's most attached friends.

[2] *Rem.* p. 259. Wordsworth and Coleridge each wrote some account of the tour. See Knight's *Life of Wordsworth*, i. 198-200.

to Poole as 'quiet and healthful,' at 21 Buckingham
Street, Strand;[1] and before the 9th December Mrs.
Coleridge and Hartley had joined him.    He tells
Southey that their *Devil's Thoughts* has been a
great success, and that though he fears he has not
now poetical enthusiasm enough to finish ' Christabel '
for the *Anthology*, he will be ready in time with his
other verses.[2]    As to permanent residence, beyond
the four or five months he will be detained in London,
nothing is decided.    Both for his own and his wife's
sake he should like to fix it near Southey.    To Southey
he says nothing (in any of the letters which have been
printed) of the engagement he had then taken to trans-
late Schiller's *Wallenstein* for Longmans ; but in one
dated Christmas Eve, he says that he 'gives his mornings to the booksellers '—the translation doubtless—
and the time after dinner to Stuart, ' who pays all
expenses, whatever they are '—the earnings of the
morning going towards replacing the annuity-money
he had, by anticipation, spent in Germany.

Before this time he had renewed his intercourse
with Godwin.    On New Year's Eve he wrote to
Poole,[3]—' I work from I-rise to I-set (that is, from
9 A.M. to 12 at night) almost without intermission.'
Up to that time his contributions to the *Morning
Post* had been confined almost entirely to a few
verses ; in January a good many political ' leading

---

[1] The lodging at Howell's in King Street, Covent Garden, mentioned by
Stuart (*Gent. Mag.* May 1838), was occupied not then, but in 1802.

[2] He must have been as good as his word, for the volume contained :—*Lewti*,
*The Mad Ox, Lines at Elbingerode, A Christmas Carol, To a Friend who had
declared his Intention of writing no more Poetry, The Lime-tree Bower my
Prison, To W. Linley, The British Stripling's War-Song, Something childish,
Homesick, Ode to the Duchess of Devonshire, Fire, Famine, and Slaughter,
The Raven, To an Unfortunate Woman at the Theatre*, and a number of
' Epigrams.'

[3] *T. Poole and his Friends*, i. 1.

paragraphs' (as 'leaders' were then called) appeared;[1] in February they dwindled, and on the 14th Coleridge informed Poole[2] that he has given up the *Morning Post*, adding that the editor was 'importunate against it.' He did not give it up all at once, for on the 17th he reported Pitt's speech from long-hand notes made in the House. He tells Wedgwood[3] he has been three times to the House—one of them being 'yesterday,' when he made that famous report. He went to the House on Monday at 7.15 A.M., remained till 3 A.M. on Tuesday, and afterwards wrote and corrected at the newspaper office till 8,—'a good 24 hours of unpleasant activity.' He was very proud of that feat in 'reporting'—in Johnson's manner. To Poole he wrote at the time,[4] 'My report of Pitt's speech made a great noise here,' and in after-years he seems to have told Gillman that it brought Canning next day to the office to inquire of the editor the name of the reporter. On the other hand, Stuart[5] says the report in the *True Briton* was both 'more faithful and more splendid,' and that the story about Canning is 'altogether a romance.' 'I never spoke to Mr. Canning' (he adds) 'until after I had left the *Morning Post*.'

This is a fair specimen of a little controversy which in 1838 arose between Coleridge's biographers and Stuart regarding the connection with the *Morning Post* and the *Courier*. In the *Gentleman's Magazine* for May and June 1838, Stuart printed his version of it,

[1] In 1850 Mrs. H. N. Coleridge collected her father's journalistic productions under the title, '*Essays on his own Times*, being a second series of *The Friend*. By Samuel Taylor Coleridge. Edited by his Daughter.' 3 vols. (paged continuously i.-xciii. 1-1034).

[2] *T. Poole and his Friends*, ii. 6.

[3] Letter printed in Cottle's *Rem.* p. 433.

[4] *Essays on his own Times*, p. 1009.     [5] *Gent. Mag.* May 1838, p. 488.

lest, as he said, some future editor of the *Table Talk*
should 'hold him out as an ungrateful person, who was
rolling about in his carriage while Coleridge, who made
his fortune, was starving in Mr. Gillman's garret.'    In
the *Biographia* (chap. x.) Coleridge asserted that on
Stuart's papers he had 'wasted the prime and manhood
of his intellect,' adding thereby 'nothing to his fortune
or reputation.'    The imputation was naturally resented
by Stuart, who called at Highgate and warmly expressed his feeling, though he refrained from taking
any public notice.    Then, in the *Table Talk* (1835, i.
173—the sentence was suppressed in later editions)
Coleridge is made to say, 'I raised the sale of the
*Morning Post* from an inconsiderable number to 7000
per day in the course of one year.'    To this Stuart
replied with figures showing that the statement had no
foundation.    Only three of Coleridge's contributions,
he says, made any sensation—a paragraph on a state-
paper of Lord Grenville, the 'Character of Pitt' (March
19, 1800), and *The Devil's Thoughts*.    A companion
'Character of Buonaparte' was promised over and
over again, but was never written.    Stuart declares
that he let every one know who wrote the 'Pitt.'
Except for a few months in 1799-1800 Coleridge was
away from London—how could he, asks Stuart, make
the fortune of a daily morning newspaper, the success
of which depends on constant temporary effect?

As regards Coleridge's remuneration, one sees
clearly from his letters that in his own opinion he
had been over-paid.    Nevertheless, it cannot be
doubted that although Coleridge exaggerated his
services, the general reputation of the *Morning Post*
and *Courier* must have been heightened by his
contributions.    Mr. Traill, whose opinion on such

a matter is entitled to the greatest respect, considers that so far from Coleridge's newspaper articles
being tainted with the defects which might have been
looked for—over-rhetorical diction, too much refine-
ment in argument, too much philosophic reflection—
'nothing is more remarkable than their thorough
workmanlike character . . . and the steadiness with
which he keeps his own and his readers' attention
fixed on the special political necessities of the hour.'[1]
In March 1800 Coleridge wrote to Poole[2] :—

> I am not anxious—I am sure, if God gives me health, to make
> all even before the end of the year; and I find that I can without
> any straining gain 500 guineas a year, if I give up poetry—*i.e.*
> original poetry. If I had the least love of money I could make
> almost sure of £2000 a year, for Stuart has offered me half shares
> in the two papers, the *Morning Post* and the *Courier*, if I would
> devote myself with him to them—but I told him I would not give
> up the country and the lazy reading of old folios for two thousand
> times two thousand pounds; in short, that beyond £250 a year I
> consider money as a real evil—at which he stared.

He goes on to say that he will continue writing for
Stuart until he is 'clear'—clear, that must have
been, of advances both from Stuart and the Wedgwoods. Coleridge's statement has been considered
to receive corroboration from a passage in a letter
of Stuart, written long years afterwards to H. N.
Coleridge : 'Could Coleridge and I place ourselves
thirty years back, and he be so far a man of
business as to write three or four hours a day, there
is nothing I would not pay for his assistance. I
would take him into partnership, and I would enable
him to make a large fortune.' I do not think this
statement of contingencies corroborates Coleridge's

---

[1] All that Mr. Traill has to say is valuable. 'English Men of Letters'
series,—*Coleridge*, 1884, pp. 79-86.

[2] The latter part of my extract is printed in the 'Introduction' to *Essays on
his own Times*, p. xci.—'£250' is there misprinted '£350.'

letter to Poole.   On the contrary, I believe that
had Stuart ever offered a partnership, he would
have remembered the circumstance ; and that the offer
would have been communicated to Wordsworth. . In
such case Wordsworth could not have written to Mrs.
H. N. Coleridge : ' So convinced was I of the great
service that your father rendered to Mr. Stuart's paper,
that I urged him to put in his claim to be admitted
a proprietor, but this he declined, having a great
disinclination to any tie of the kind.' [1]   Stuart knew
that regular work for any length of time it was not
in Coleridge's nature to give ; and I have little doubt
that the ' offer ' was a mere affair of ' ifs ' dropped by
Stuart when urging Coleridge to contribute more than
he was doing.[2]   In journalism it was with Coleridge,
as in other matters, ' indolence capable of energies ' ;
and so uniform was Stuart's experience of his friend,
that it is incredible that he should have ever seriously
proposed to take him as a partner.   Except in that
unfortunate passage in the *Biographia*, Coleridge
always acknowledged Stuart's generosity—a generosity which was continued down to the latest months
of the poet's life.

We left Coleridge at Buckingham Street, in the
middle of February, having given up his engagement
with Stuart.   His immediate purpose must have been
to get on more quickly with *Wallenstein*.   Towards
the end of the month Mrs. Coleridge and Hartley left
London, going probably to her mother's house at
Bristol ; Coleridge himself going to the Lambs', who

[1] Introd. to *Biog. Lit.* 1847.
[2] There is a mass of printed matter connected with this controversy, but I do
not think I have omitted anything essential.   See *Gent. Mag.* May, June, July,
and August 1838 ; Introduction to *Biog. Lit.* 1847 ; and editorial introduction and
notes in *Essays on his own Times.*

were then living at Pentonville.  The reconciliation
between these old friends had taken place some time
before.  The first evidence we possess occurs in a
friendly letter from Lamb, dated in all editions ' Jan. 2,
1800,' but which must have been written about the
23rd-27th.  On March 17th Lamb wrote to Manning :
' I am living in a continuous feast.  Coleridge has been
with me now for nigh three weeks, and the more I see
of him in the quotidian undress and relaxation of his
mind, the more cause I see to love him and believe him
a *very good man*, and all those foolish impressions to
the contrary fly off like morning slumbers.  He is
engaged in translations, which I hope will keep him
this month to come.  He is uncommonly kind and
friendly to me. ' [1]

In a letter to Stuart written about this time,
Coleridge graphically describes his situation and
prospects :—

These cursed Plays play the Devil with me.  I have been writing
from morning till night, and almost half the night too, and yet get
on too slowly for the printer. . . . My wife and child leave London
to-morrow ; and I was particularly desirous to have done enough
to have given me some *claim* on him [Longman] for the few pounds,
which I must draw on him for their journey.  These things I
mention, not as justification of my breach of promise, but as
palliations. . . . In about four or five days I shall have finished
the first Play ; and, that being finished, I may go on more leisurely
with the others.  I shall then be able to give you some assistance,
probably as much as you may want.  A certain number of Essays
I consider myself bound to send you AS SOON AS POSSIBLE, in
common honesty.  AFTER these, if it be worth your while, I
will do what I can, only not for any regular *stipend*.  That harasses
me.  I know that hitherto I have received from you much more
than I have earned, and this must not be. . . . I will certainly fill
you out a good paper on Sunday.[2]

How long Coleridge remained with Lamb is

---

[1] *Letters*, i. pp. 113 and 115, respectively.
[2] *Letters from the Lake Poets*, pp. 5, 6.

unknown, for the next glimpse we have of him is in a letter written to Josiah Wedgwood on the 21st April, from Wordsworth's cottage at Grasmere : 'To-morrow morning I send off the last sheet of my irksome, soul-wearying labour, the translation of Schiller.'[1] 'Of its success I have no hope,' he says, 'but with all this I have learnt that I have Industry and Perseverance—and before the end of the year, if God grant me health, I shall have my wings wholly un-birdlimed.' He expects to be back in London in a week. But he went to Stowey[2] instead. To Godwin he writes from Poole's house on May 21st[3] :—

I left Wordsworth on the 4th of this month ; if I cannot procure a suitable house at Stowey, I return to Cumberland and settle at Keswick, in a house of such a prospect, that, if, according to you and Hume, impressions and ideas *constitute* our being, I shall have a

---

[1] WALLENSTEIN.   A Drama in Two Parts.   Translated from the German of Frederich Schiller by S. T. Coleridge.   LONDON : Printed for T. N. Longman and O. Rees, Paternoster-Row, By G. Woodfall, No. 22 Paternoster-Row.   1800.

Octavo.—Titles ; two unpaged leaves ; and pp. 157 : also, an engraved portrait of Wallenstein.   The house of Longmans had acquired a manuscript copy, which Schiller had made expressly for translation into English and publication simultaneously with the original in Germany.   It was attested by him on the 30th September 1799.

The book was almost a complete failure from the publishers' point of view. Most of the copies were probably sold off as ' a remainder ' ; and when, in 1824, Carlyle was writing his *Life of Schiller* in the *London Magazine*, it was unprocurable, and he had to estimate it by quotations.   Judging by these, he says, ' we should pronounce it, excepting Sotheby's *Oberon*, to be the best, indeed the only sufferable translation from the German, with which our literature has yet been enriched.'

And in after years Coleridge himself looked back on his *Wallenstein* with some complacency.   In a note to Essay XVI. of *The Friend* (1818, i. 204—it is suppressed in later editions), he thanks Sir Walter Scott for quoting it (in *Guy Mannering*) ' with applause.'   Elsewhere, Scott said that ' Coleridge had made Schiller's " Wallenstein " far finer than he found it ' (Lockhart's *Life*, iv. 193). About 1820, Coleridge told Allsop that *Wallenstein* was a specimen of his ' happiest attempt, during the prime manhood of his intellect, before he had been buffeted by adversity or crossed by fatality ' (*Letters*, etc., 1864, p. 51).

[2] *Letters from the Lake Poets*, p. 7.

[3] Portions of Coleridge's letters to Godwin were printed in *Macmillan's Magazine* for April 1864.   These, with some additions and some omissions, were reprinted in *William Godwin : his Friends and Acquaintances*, by C. Kegan Paul.   2 vols. 1876.   Vol. ii.   Coleridge and Godwin had become very intimate in the winter of 1799-1800.

tendency to become a god, so sublime and beautiful will be the series of my visual existence. . . . Hartley sends his love to Mary. 'What, and not to Fanny [Imlay]?' Yes, and to Fanny, but I'll have Mary [afterwards Mrs. Shelley]. . . . In Bristol I was much with Davy [afterwards Sir Humphry]—almost all day.[1]

No house was procurable at Stowey, and some time in June Coleridge took his wife and child to Dove Cottage. On the way thither they stayed eight or nine days at Liverpool as the guests of Dr. Crompton (a connection of the Evanses of Darley Abbey), and saw much of the remarkable group of which Roscoe, Rathbone, and Dr. Currie (editor of Burns) were the principal members—all Liberals in politics and religion. The Coleridges remained with the Wordsworths from the 29th June until the 24th July, when they moved into Greta Hall. On the 11th of that month Coleridge writes to Stuart of a sort of rheumatic fever, the result of a cold caught on the journey north, from which he was hardly then recovered, and, making this the excuse for having sent no contributions for two months, promises the second part of 'Pitt' and the 'Buonaparte' immediately. He will at same time say 'whether or no he will be able to continue any species of regular connection with the paper'; and closes by announcing that his address henceforward will be 'Greta Hall.'[2]

On the day on which he entered that famous dwelling, he wrote to J. Wedgwood[3]: 'I parted from Poole with pain and dejection, for him, and for myself in him. I should have given Stowey a decided

---

[1] Davy had been, since October 1798, at Bristol, as principal assistant in Dr. Beddoes's Pneumatic Institution. Coleridge was introduced to him in 1799 before going to London. In January 1800 Coleridge told T. Wedgwood, who took much interest in Davy, that he had 'never met with so extraordinary a *young* man' (Cottle's *Rem.* p. 431).

[2] *Letters from the Lake Poets*, p. 11.

[3] July 24th, 1800; in Cottle's *Rem.* p. 436.

I

preference for a residence . . . but there was no
suitable house, and no prospect of a suitable house.'
Coleridge, however, was by no means inconsolable.
As far back as March, Poole had become jealous of
his friend's ever-growing attachment to Wordsworth—
accusing him even of ' prostration ';[1] and I share Mrs.
Sandford's view, that ' Coleridge would never have been
contented to live in the west of England whilst Wordsworth was living in the north.' Coleridge, no doubt,
believed himself to be sorry for the necessity which
carried him away from Poole, and the two men parted
the best of friends ; and so they continued to be for
some years longer. But Coleridge had always some
one chief friend, generally the one nearest to him, to
whom he gave away so much of himself that he found
it impossible to meet fully other claims which, not the
less, he eagerly and sincerely acknowledged.

There is little need to describe Greta Hall. The
house and its surroundings are well known, and Coleridge's impressions are to be found recounted at length
in many published[2] and unpublished letters. On July
29th he wrote, with a cordial invitation, to Purkis :—

I write to you from the *leads* of Greta Hall, a tenement in the
possession of S. T. Coleridge, Esq. Gentleman—Poet and Philosopher
in a mist. This Greta Hall is a house on a small eminence a furlong
from Keswick in the County of Cumberland. Yes, my dear Sir !
here I am, with Skiddaw at my back ; on my right hand the
Bassenthwait Water with its majestic *case* of mountains, all of
simplest outline—looking aslant over the feather of this infamous
pen, I see the sun setting. My God ! what a scene ! Right before
me is a great *Camp* of single mountains—each in shape resembles
a Giant's Tent ! And to the left but closer to it far than the
Bassenthwait Water to my right, is the lake of Keswick, with its
islands, white sails, and glassy lights of evening—crowned with

¹ *T. Poole and his Friends*, ii. 8, 9.
² To Wedgwood in Cottle's *Rem.* p. 436, etc., and to Godwin in *William
Godwin*, ii. 6-8.

green meadows.    But the three remaining sides are encircled with
the most fantastic mountains that ever earthquakes made in sport,—
as if Nature had *laughed* herself into the convulsion in which they
were made.    Close behind me, at the foot of Skiddaw, flows the
Greta.    I hear its murmuring distinctly ; then it curves round
almost in a semi-circle, and is now catching the purple lights of the
scattered clouds above it directly before me. . . . I have been
grievously indisposed—now, I am enjoying the godlikeness of the
place in which I am settled, with the voluptuous and joy-trembling
nerves of convalescence. . . . Sara Coleridge is well. . . . Hartley
is all health and extacy.    He is a spirit dancing on an aspen leaf,
unwearied in joy—from morning to night, indefatigably joyous.' [1]

He was simply enchanted with everything.    ' I
question if there be a room in England which commands a view of mountains, and lakes, and woods, and
vales, superior to that in which I am now sitting.    I
say this because it is destined for your study, if you
come.'    So he tempted the unlovely Godwin.[2]    To
Poole he wrote, after three weeks' experience :

In gardens, etc., we are uncommonly well-off, and our landlord,[3]
who resides next door in this two-fold house, is already much
attached to us.    He is a quiet, sensible man, with as large a library
as yours, and perhaps larger, well stored with Encyclopedias,
Dictionaries, and Histories, etc.,[4] all modern.    The gentry of the
country, titled and untitled, have all called, or are about to call on
me, and I shall have free access to the magnificent library of Sir
Gilfrid Lawson, a weak but good-natured man.    I wish you could
come here in October, after your harvesting, and stand godfather at the
christening of my child.[5]    We are well, and the Wordsworths are well.
The two volumes of the *Lyrical Ballads* will appear in about a fortnight.

---

[1] Unprinted letter in British Museum.    (Add. MSS. 27, 457, ff., 33, 34.)

[2] *William Godwin*, ii. 8.

[3] Jackson, a retired carrier.    He was the master of Wordsworth's *Waggoner*,
' Benjamin,' and admirable in all relations of life.

[4] To Godwin, he describes Jackson's books as ' almost all the usual trash of
Johnson's, Gibbon's, Robertson's, etc.'

[5] Derwent—born September 14th, 1800, three weeks after the letter was
written.    Coleridge had also asked Godwin (of all men in the world !) to be
godfather, meeting with a refusal.    See a curious passage on Coleridge's then
very unsettled views respecting Baptism, in a letter to Godwin (*W. Godwin*,
ii. 9).    Derwent, when a little baby, was supposed to be dying, ' so,' writes Coleridge to Davy, ' the good people would have it baptized.'    This was doubtless a
private rite.    In November 1803 all three children were publicly baptized—but
only, again, ' to please the good people,' not the father.

But they did not appear for about six months, and in the interval there was much coming and going between Dove Cottage and Greta Hall, as may be seen even in the few extracts from Miss Wordsworth's 'Grasmere Journals,' printed in Prof. Knight's *Life of Wordsworth*.  The interchange of visits was so frequent that the friends seem to have thought little more of the twelve miles which lay between Grasmere and Keswick, than they had of the three between Stowey and Alfoxden.  Having left Dove Cottage on the 24th July, Coleridge was back again on the 31st, bringing with him the second volume of Southey's *Annual Anthology*.[1]  The party spent two days walking, rowing on the lake, and reading one another's poems 'in the breeze and the shade,' and, on the 2nd August, the two poets walked back to Greta Hall, Wordsworth returning home on the 6th.  Two days after, Wordsworth and his sister went over on a week's visit.  As it has been said that Coleridge *never* went to church, one may oppose to that scandalous report Miss Wordsworth's entry for Sunday, August 10th : 'Very hot.  The C.'s went to church.  We sailed upon Derwent in the evening.'  Three Sundays later, Miss Wordsworth records : 'At 11 o'clock Coleridge came when I was walking in the still, clear moonshine in the garden.  He came over Helvellyn. . . . We sate and chatted till half-past three . . . Coleridge reading a part of *Christabel*.'  On the 4th October 'Coleridge came in while we were at dinner, very wet.  We talked till twelve o'clock.  He had sate up all the night before writing essays for the newspaper. . . . Extremely delighted with second part of *Christabel*.  5th October. — Coleridge read

[1] See footnote 2 at p. 106 *supra*.

*Christabel* a second time ; we had increasing pleasure.
. . . 6th October. — After tea read *The Pedlar*
[*Excursion*]. Determined not to print *Christabel* with
the *L*[*yrical*] *B*[*allads*].[1]   7th October.—Coleridge
went off at 11 o'clock.' Ten days later Miss Wordsworth records that 'Coleridge had done nothing for
*L.B.*'; but on October 22nd he was back at Dove
Cottage again reciting *Christabel.* 'We were very
merry. . . . William read *Ruth*, etc.' Stoddart was
with them, and went to Greta Hall with Coleridge. It
may have been then that Stoddart received the copy
of *Christabel* which he read to Scott.[2]   In November
and December the Wordsworths and Coleridge continued to go and come, but no extracts from the
*Journals* are printed between December 9, 1800 and
October 10, 1801.   The volumes of *Lyrical Ballads*

---

[1] The MS. (or part of it) had been sent to the printers, but on the 15th
September, Wordsworth countermanded the printing of *Christabel*, 'for the
present.' On the 20th he sent to the printer the Preface, which comprised the
following paragraph :—

'For the sake of variety, and from a consciousness of my own weakness, I
have again requested the assistance of a friend who contributed largely to the
first volume, and who has now furnished me with the [*long and beautiful*—these
words erased] Poem of CHRISTABEL, without which I should not yet have
ventured to present a second volume to the public.'

Three weeks passed without any fresh 'copy' being forwarded to the printers,
and on the 10th of October, they are told to cancel the above paragraph
and substitute another, which is to tell the reader that the 'Friend' who supplied
*The Ancient Mariner*, etc., 'has also furnished me with a few of those poems in
the second volume which are classed under the title of " Poems on the Naming
of Places." If any sheets of *Christabel* have been printed, they are to be
cancelled ; other poems will be forwarded, and henceforth the printers may
depend on a constant supply of "copy."' What poems of Coleridge's were
meant for substitutes does not appear ; we know only that nothing new of his
appeared in the first, and nothing at all in the second volume of any of the
editions of the *Lyrical Ballads*.

For these new facts I am indebted to the courtesy of Mr. T. Norton Longman,
grandson and successor of the publisher of the *Lyrical Ballads*. Mr. Longman
possesses the MSS. and proof-sheets of these, and of other volumes of Wordsworth's Poems. Coleridge wrote most of the instructions to the printer of the
edition 1800, but signed them all with Wordsworth's name, and much of the
transcription of poems is in the hand of Dorothy Wordsworth. In some cases
all three hands appear in the same document.

[2] Lockhart's *Life*, 1837, ii. 23.

which bear the date, ' 1800,' on the title-page were
published in January 1801.

On November 1, 1800, Coleridge tells Wedgwood
how his labours on *Christabel* had been interrupted[1]—

> In the meantime (he adds) I had got myself entangled in
> the old sorites of the old sophist—procrastination.   I had suffered
> my necessary businesses to accumulate so terribly that I neglected to
> write to any one, till the pain I suffered from not writing made me
> waste as many hours in dreaming about it as would have sufficed
> for the letter-writing of half a life.

He goes on in this extremely interesting letter to
declare that although his situation at Keswick is delightful, he feels the loss of Poole's society, and of
opportunities of meeting with the Wedgwoods.   Yet
when he revises the step he has taken, he cannot see
how it could have been avoided.

> You will in three weeks see the letters on *The Rise and Condition
> of the German Boors*.   I found it convenient to make up a volume
> out of my journey, etc., in North Germany, and the letters (your
> name of course erased) are in the printer's hands.   I was so
> weary of transcribing and composing, that when I found those more
> carefully written than the rest, I even sent them off as they were.

The volume never reached ' the printer's hands.'
Certain asterisks which follow probably represent a
demand for money, for twelve days later Coleridge
thanks his correspondent for his ' kind letter with the
£20,' adding that he believes he has ' anticipated on
the next year to the amount of £30 or £40, probably
more.'   He still complains of trouble in his eyes.
I am much afraid that apart from spasmodic efforts
to complete *Christabel*, Coleridge had been simply
idling—so far, at least, as a poet and philosopher
whose eye and mind are in a state of activity can be
said to idle.   But he was also a bread-winner, and

[1] Cottle's *Rem.* p. 439.

well as it may be for such to 'gather in summer' it
is unwise to 'sleep in harvest.' The volume about
'German Boors,' though not a myth, might as well
have been one, for he 'suspended' it for months, and
then tried to get Longmans to accept in its place a
metaphysical work, which they probably suspected
would come to no better result. Another book, on
which he had received an advance from Sir Richard
Phillipps, was also abandoned, and the money refunded.
The newspaper articles of which he told the Wordsworths in October were, save the introductory paper,
Poole's.[1] After these Stuart received nothing for a
whole year, except some satirical verses on his brother-
in-law, Mackintosh,[2] who was Coleridge's rival in the
good graces of the Wedgwoods—a production therefore which, brilliant as it was, he might more judiciously
have retained for private consumption, or, at most,
private circulation. His letters for the earlier part
of the winter are full of 'work for the booksellers' in
arrear, yet he seems to make no effort to rescue it
from that always crowded limbo of his. But he talks
of 'undertaking' a huge geographical school-book of
' 12 or 1400 pages' (!) if Godwin does not decide on
doing it himself.[3] Eight days later he tells Thelwall
that he 'amuses' himself by studying the most
ancient forms of the Northern Languages, his
'serious' occupation being a metaphysical investiga-
tion of the laws by which our feelings form affinities
with each other, with ideas, and with words. As to

---

[1] *Essays on his own Times*, pp. 413 and 1020, 1021.

[2] *The Two round Spaces on the Tombstone.* Stuart, in 1838, believed that
he had detected the purpose of the verses, and refused to publish them—a piece
of forgetfulness which tends to invalidate to some extent all that he put forward
solely on the authority of his recollections, in the controversy respecting Coleridge's services to the *Morning Post* and *Courier* (*Gent. Mag.* May 1838, p. 486).

[3] *William Godwin*, ii. 14 (Letter of Dec. 9, 1800).

Poetry, he has abandoned it, 'being convinced that he never had the essentials of a poet's genius.'

Before the end of the year he seems to have had an illness of some severity—rheumatic fever, followed by other troubles. The illness was intermittent, but before the end of January he reports himself as quite well again. He was, however, in serious pecuniary straits—owing money to Wordsworth and Lamb and Poole, and behind with his annual allowance of £20 to his mother-in-law, while a considerable part of his annuity for 1801 had been drawn in advance. Poole came to the rescue as regards one or two of the most pressing obligations. How the others were met, if met at all, there is no record. Coleridge proposes to publish his tragedy 'as a poem,' and also *Christabel*. The £60 he 'hoped' to get for these cannot have been received, for they did not go to the printers. 'A drama and a sort of farce,' 'works written purposely vile' for the theatre, are supposed to be available 'if aught good come of them'; but Coleridge must have known he was romancing, for he adds—'that is a dream.' The only bright spot in the letters of this time is that wife and children are well—Derwent 'a fine, fat fellow,' and Hartley 'an universal darling,' 'a fairy elf.'

As soon as Coleridge recovered, he gave himself up entirely to metaphysics, 'thinking with intense energy'—the outcome being a series of letters addressed to the Wedgwoods, attacking Locke, Descartes, and Hobbes, but mainly Locke, whom he declares to be a mere plagiarist.[1] The intensity of the study is not relaxed until the middle of March, when he takes 'a week's respite, that he may make *Christabel* ready for the press . . . in order to get rid of his

---

[1] *T. Poole and his Friends*, ii. 31.

engagements to Longman.'   One of the engagements,
'the German book,' he has put aside owing to metaphysical preoccupations, although he confesses that
'poverty is staring him in the face.'   The distress
throughout the country—the Birmingham poor-rate,
Wedgwood tells Poole, is fifty shillings in the pound—
shocks Coleridge.   His distaste for 'booksellers' work'
grows in intensity ; he thinks he will go to America ;
then, he will not, until he is starved out of his native
land.  Such is the burthen of his letters for months.  Yet
all the time his bread and butter were secured to him
in the annuity ; he had books to write for which the
publishers were waiting, and Stuart would gladly have
paid for the copious remarks on the 'condition of
England question' which he spent much of his time
inditing in the form of letters to his unpaying corre-
spondents !  With the best will in the world to extend
nothing but sympathy towards a dear friend and a
man of genius beating his wings against the realities
of life, even Poole found it difficult to be quite patient
with Coleridge's perplexities.

With Coleridge's schemes at this period it is impossible to keep pace.   To Thelwall he says he has
for ever renounced poetry for metaphysics ; to Poole
and Davy he announces the resumption of *Christabel ;*
to Davy [1] he further intimates a determination to take
up immediately the serious study of chemistry, aided
by a laboratory to be set up by Wordsworth's friend
Calvert ; all this, in addition to the devotion of four
or five months to what his heart '*burns* to do,'
an essay 'Concerning Poetry, and the nature of the
Pleasures derived from it'—a work which 'would
supersede all the books of metaphysics, and all the

---

[1] Letter of Feb. 3, 1801, in *Fragmentary Remains*, p. 86.

books of morals too.' He is 'proud of himself' on
account of the results, which will some day be visible,
of his vigorous thinking during his illness.

On the 18th April, at the end of a very long letter
to Poole on the 'oppressed state of the Country,'
Coleridge speaks of his own complex troubles. For
ten days he has kept his bed. His complaint he can
scarce describe.

It is a species of irregular gout . . . it flies about me in
unsightly swellings of my knees, and dismal affections of my stomach
and head. What I suffer in mere *pain* is almost incredible, but
that is a trifle compared with the gloom of my circumstances. . . .
If the fine weather continues, I shall revive, and look around me,
and before the Fall of the year make up my mind to the important
question—'Is it better to die, or to quit my native Country, and live
amongst strangers!' Another winter in England would *do for me*.
Besides, I am rendered useless and wretched—not that my bodily
pain afflicts me—God forbid! Were I a single man and independent, I should be ashamed to think myself wretched, merely because
I suffered pain. . . . It is not my bodily pain, but the gloom and
distresses of those around me for whom I ought to be labouring and
cannot.[1]

Poole replied [2] sympathetically, but almost ignored
the account of the bodily pain. On the 17th May
Coleridge responded by another long letter recounting
his sufferings during the previous months. He does
not regret the metaphysical studies, which he fears
broke him down again after his January fever.

In the course of these studies I tried a multitude of little
experiments on my own sensations and on my senses, and some of
these (too often repeated) I have reason to believe did injury to my
nervous system. However this be, I relapsed, and a devil of a
relapse it has been. . . . The attacks on my stomach and the
nephritic pains in my back, which almost alternated with the stomach
fits—they were terrible! The disgust, the loathing, that followed
these fits, and no doubt in part, too, the use of the brandy and
laudanum which they rendered necessary!

---

[1] Partly printed in *T. Poole and his Friends*, ii. 43, 44.
[2] May 7, 1801. *Ib.* ii. 44-47.

On Monday, May 4th, he recovered all at once, and
went over to Wordsworth, improving every day until
the 12th, when a walk of six miles brought on a sleep-
less night and a swollen knee. He is now at home, he
says, and recovering, and proposes (*D.V.*) to spend the
next winter at St. Michael's, one of the Azores.[1]

I think there can be no doubt that this letter gives
the true account of the beginning of what Coleridge,
in after-years, was accustomed to call his 'slavery' to
opium. It fully confirms his reiterated contention that
it was begun as a relief from pain, and not in a search
after unholy pleasure. ' My sole sensuality was *not*
to be in pain.'[2] That there was in Coleridge a notable
disposition to resort to opium, not only for relief from
pain, but also from mental depression, we have already
seen. It is therefore not at all surprising that he
should have resorted to it under the double pressure
of mental and bodily distress in the winter of 1800-1.
In 1804, 1814, 1820, and in 1826, Coleridge made
various statements regarding the immediate cause
of his beginning to take opium. They all agree,
almost literally, in stating that the relief was sought
from rheumatic affections and knee-swellings which
had kept him almost bed-ridden for six months. The
'six' months is an immaterial exaggeration, but it is
clearly to the illness and the sudden temporary cure
described to Poole, that Coleridge was referring.[3]

---

[1] Parts of these letters are printed in *T. Poole and his Friends*, ii. p. 48.

[2] 'Note from Pocket-Book [Malta] December 23, 1804,' quoted in Gillman's
*Life*, p. 246. See also Coleridge's statement of 'April, 1826,' *ib.* p. 247 ; Letter
to Cottle, April 26, 1814, in *Rem.* p. 366 ; and letter to Allsop, July 31, 1820,
in *Letters*, etc., i. 41.

[3] Coleridge's dates were not generally well assorted in his memory, but this
one may probably be taken as substantially accurate. The passage has much
significance as to the duration of the opium-eating as well as to the date of its
beginning : ' I now write to say that if God . . . hath worked almost a miracle
of grace in and for me by a sudden emancipation from a thirty-three years'

The account given to Cottle (1814) speaks of a
'medical journal' which recommended 'laudanum,'
internally and externally, for swelled knees.   'It acted
like a charm, like a miracle!   I recovered the use of
my limbs, of my appetite, of my spirits, and this continued for near a fortnight.   At length the unusual
stimulus subsided, the complaint returned—the supposed remedy was recurred to—but I need not go
through the dreary history.'   In the Gillman memorandum (1826) the account is the same, except that
for the plain 'laudanum' a mythical 'Kendal Black
Drop'[1] is introduced as working all the woe, with
a suggestion that he did not know it to be a preparation of opium.   To Allsop (1820) Coleridge makes no
mention of any medical journal, but blames 'unhappy
quackery' and 'that most pernicious form of ignorance,
medical half-knowledge,'—whether his own or some
one else's is not clear,—for his being '*seduced* into the
use of narcotics.'   In all these accounts—which are
essentially true accounts, in spite of the alloys pardon-
ably introduced for apologetic purposes—much is made
of the 'ignorance' which 'seduced' him into the use
of the opiate, and of the openness with which the use
was proclaimed to all and sundry.   Here, I fear,
Coleridge's memory served him badly, for long before
1799 he well knew the good and the bad effects of
opiates ; while, so far as I can learn, his correspondence of this period, full as it is of his sufferings, contains no allusions to opiates, excepting only the passing

[1832 – 33 = 1799] fearful slavery, if God's goodness should come home, and so
far perfect my convalescence as that I should be capable of resuming my literary
labours [etc.].'   S. T. C. to Rev. H. F. Cary, 'Highgate, April 22, 1832,' in
*Memoir of H. F. C.* 1847, ii. 194.
    [1] Locally named 'Black Drops' were common enough then, and before and
after ; but all except the most uneducated users must have known them to be
preparations of opium.

mention in that one letter to Poole. I doubt if any of Coleridge's friends knew, until his return from Malta, of his habitual and excessive addiction to opium. De Quincey says he made confession to him in 1807, and the statement seems, though only on the surface, to be confirmed by the Gillman memorandum of 'April 1826,' but Cottle declares that he heard of opium first in 1814. I do not think there is any more to be said of Coleridge's 'slavery.' All that De Quincey has written on the subject may wisely be disregarded; and this applies generally to his numerous stories about Coleridge. So many of them are demonstrably inaccurate, that the credit of all is vitiated. I do not for a moment mean to suggest that De Quincey consciously misrepresented anything, but long before he began to write about Coleridge his own indulgence in opium-eating had deprived him of the power of distinguishing between facts and fancies.

# CHAPTER VII

## GRETA HALL

WE have seen that about the middle of May Coleridge thought of seeking a renewal of health in the Azores. Health improved, and the idea was abandoned. The end of June brought a relapse, and the idea was resumed. Of course there was a money difficulty. On July 1 he asked Poole's advice, and proposed to raise money by getting an advance from a publisher. About the same time, Wordsworth, who was in much anxiety about Coleridge, also wrote to Poole[1] putting the case; he disapproved strongly of Coleridge's plan of raising funds, and suggested that Poole might be disposed to advance £50, and if more should be needed, to procure it from other friends in the west. On July 21 Poole replies, to both letters, in one addressed to Coleridge, full of sympathy, but regretting that the multiplicity of claims on him at the time disable him from advancing more than £20, and suggesting that certain other friends might make up the rest. Coleridge was deeply hurt. He allowed six weeks to pass before replying; and though his letter is not free

---

[1] See the whole of this interesting correspondence, with valuable editorial elucidations, in *T. Poole and his Friends*, ii. 56-65.

from bitterness, it concludes with assurances of affection, and some details as to his ill-health and the
impossibility of 'staying in this climate.'    He has
asked John Pinney if he may go and stay for a while
on his estate in Nevis (West Indies).    'My spirits are
good, I am generally *cheerful*, and when I am not, it
is because I have exchanged it for a deeper and more
pleasurable tranquillity'—a periphrasis, one fears, for
opium-dreams.    A fortnight after this Coleridge tells
Godwin [1] he has had to give up going abroad for want
of money, and if a last effort to reach Mr. John King's
estate in St. Lucia fail, 'he may perhaps go up to
London and maintain himself as before, by writing for
the *Morning Post*.'    Poole was 'painfully affected' by
Coleridge's letter of September 7, though it had been
followed quickly by one of affectionate sympathy on
the occasion of his mother's death.    Coleridge replied
by an epistle in which honey and gall are mingled in
almost equal proportions.    Poole, whose temper was
as warm as his heart, thought both letters 'outrageous,'
but friendship stood the strain, and he lent Coleridge
£25 to enable him to pay a visit to London and
Stowey.    Coleridge promised not to stay at Stowey
less than two months; the remainder of the time till
March he would pass with the Wedgwoods and other
friends in the west country.

The plan, one need hardly say, was not fully
accomplished.    Coleridge arrived in London on the
15th November.[2]    He tells Davy [3] he means to stay a
fortnight there, and Godwin that he 'planned a walk
into Somersetshire,' but he remained in London until
Christmas, first with Southey and then at a lodging in

---

[1] Letter of September 22, 1801.    *William Godwin*, ii. 81.
[2] *William Godwin*, ii. 83.                          [3] *Frag. Rem.* p. 92.

Covent Garden.[1] On December 14 he wrote to Poole[2]: 'I am writing for the *Morning Post*, and am reading in the old libraries, for my curious metaphysical work, but I hate London.' He left for Stowey on Christmas Day,[3] returning to Howell's about January 21st.[4] Thomas Wedgwood had been his fellow-guest at Poole's during the visit. Poole went to London with Coleridge, and both attended Davy's popular lectures[5] at the Royal Institution, Coleridge saying that his object was 'to increase his stock of metaphors.'[6] On February 6, 1802, Southey informs W. Taylor[7] that T. Wedgwood and Mackintosh are hatching a great metaphysical work, to which Coleridge has promised as preface, 'a history of metaphysical opinion,' for which he is reading Duns Scotus and Thomas Aquinas. But during all this time Coleridge was writing 'heart-rending' accounts of his health to the Wordsworths,[8] and on 19th March, 'on a very rainy morning,' he appeared at Dove Cottage.[9] 'His eyes,' says Dorothy, 'were a little swollen with the wind. I was much affected by the sight of him, he

---

[1] 'I took a first floor for him in King Street, Covent Garden, at my tailor's, Howell's, whose wife was a cheerful good housewife, of middle-age, who I knew would nurse Coleridge as kindly as if he were her son. . . . My practice was to call on him in the middle of the day, talk over the news, and project a leading paragraph for the next morning. In conversation he made a brilliant display . . . but I soon found he could not write daily on the occurrences of the day' (D. Stuart in *Gent. Mag.* May 1838, p. 487). He does not say here that Coleridge gave him hardly any contributions, but in *Essays on his own Times* there is nothing between December 3, 1801, and September 21, 1802.

[2] See also *T. Poole and his Friends*, ii. 73.

[3] Unprinted letter to Poole of Christmas Eve ; also undated and misplaced letter to Stuart in *Letters of Lake Poets*, p. 7.

[4] *Ib.* p. 24, and Knight's *Life of Wordsworth*, i. 288.

[5] *T. Poole and his Friends*, ii. 102.

[6] Paris's *Life of Sir H. D.* i. 138.

[7] *Mem. of W. T.* i. 398. A week after this Coleridge informs Poole that his 'health has been on the mend ever since Poole left town, *nor has he had occasion for opiates of any kind*' (*T. Poole and his Friends*, ii. 77).

[8] See Miss Wordsworth's Journals in Knight's *Life of Wordsworth*, i. 288 *et seq.*

[9] *Ib.* i. 302.

seemed half-stupified.'    Next day the party 'had a
little talk of going abroad.'    'William read *The Pedlar*.
Talked about various things—christening the children,
etc. etc.'    When Coleridge had gone, his hosts 'talked
about' him, as they paced the orchard walk.

We may be sure that when, on the 19th March,
Coleridge walked over to Dove Cottage, he had not
been long at Greta Hall.    He was in sad case of
body and mind, and sought Dove Cottage as naturally
as the thirsty hart seeks the water-brooks.    What he
thought of himself and of Wordsworth at this time we
may read in '*Dejection: an Ode*, written on April 4,
1802.'[1]    But let the ode be read in its original
form,[2] before the frosts of alienation had withered
some of its tenderest shoots.    For it was addressed to
Wordsworth, and, before printing, addressed to him
by name.    No sadder cry from the depths was ever
uttered, even by Coleridge, none more sincere, none
more musical.    Health was gone, and with it both the
'natural joy' which had been his in rich abundance,
and that rarer kind which, as he tells us, dwells only
with the pure ; nor was this all, for he discovered that
he had lost control of his most precious endowment,

---

[1] *Poet. Works*, 1893, p. 159, and 'Note 162,' p. 626.
[2] As printed in *Morning Post*, Oct. 4, 1802—Wordsworth's wedding day.
See *Poetical Works*, 1893, Appendix G. p. 522.    See Lamb's Latin letter to
Coleridge, Oct. 9, 1802 (*Letters*, i. 185, 331-333).    April 4 was probably the
day on which the poem was completed.    The Wordsworths were at Greta Hall
on the 4th and 5th, and doubtless it was read to them.    At the close of the
original version Wordsworth was thus addressed :—

> O William, friend of my devoutest choice,
> O rais'd from anxious dread and busy care,
> By the immenseness of the good and fair
> Which thou see'st everywhere,
> Joy lifts thy spirit, joy attunes thy voice,
> To thee do all things live from pole to pole,
> Their life the eddying of thy living soul !
> O simple spirit, guided from above,
> O lofty Poet, full of life and love,
> Brother and friend of my devoutest choice,
> Thus may'st thou ever, evermore rejoice !

K

his 'shaping spirit of imagination.' He felt that
poetically he was dead, and that if not dead spiritu-
ally, he had lost his spiritual identity.

> There was a time when, though my path was rough,
>     This joy within me dallied with distress,
> And all misfortunes were but as the stuff
>     Whence Fancy made me dreams of happiness :
> For hope grew round me, like the twining vine,
> And fruits, and foliage, not my own, seemed 'mine.
> But now afflictions bow me down to earth :
> Nor care I that they rob me of my mirth ;
>     But oh ! each visitation
> Suspends what nature gave me at my birth,
>     My shaping spirit of Imagination.
> For not to think of what I needs must feel,
>     But to be still and patient, all I can ;
> And haply by abstruse research to steal
>     From my own nature all the natural man—
>     This was my sole resource, my only plan :
> Till that which suits a part infects the whole,
> And now is almost grown the habit of my soul.

I make no more quotations, for the ode is a whole,
and must be read as a whole. But it is incomplete as
a statement of Coleridge's condition and circumstances.
The symptoms of the disease are described with great
and deeply-affecting fulness, but the causes are only
vaguely hinted at. In addressing Wordsworth, there
may have been no need for more. Besides the bodily
ailments, there were at least two causes—fatal indulgence in opium, and growing estrangement between his
wife and himself. If the excessive indulgence in opium
was unknown to the Wordsworths, it may have been
suspected, and Coleridge may have known that it was
suspected. The domestic trouble must have been
known to them. In these earlier days the discord
was not constant ; there were intervals of peace,[1] but
even then Coleridge had accustomed himself to seek

---

[1] 'I am at present in better health than I have been, though by no means
strong and well—*and at home all is Peace and Love*' (original underlined).
S. T. C. to Estlin, 26th July 1802, in *Estlin Letters*, p. 82.

happiness, or, at least, relief from cares, elsewhere than in the house which should have been his home.   By the end of this year the estrangement had made considerable progress, and Greta Hall knew—

> those habitual ills
> That wear out life, when two unequal minds
> Meet in one house, and two discordant wills.

If there be any mystery here, I shall not attempt to fathom it ; but I doubt if there be any.   The marriage had not been made in Heaven ; it had been brought about by the meddlesomeness of third parties —we have seen Southey's statement as to his own share — whose interference it is easier, perhaps, to understand than to justify.   Attachment between Coleridge and his wife there had been, and the links had proved strong enough to bear some strain : if there had been love, its roots had found no sustenance, and when it withered away, root and branch, there remained no bond of community of mind and tastes —nothing but the unsheathed material fetters which galled, and which, when the galling became intolerable, were laid aside.   There is nothing in this simple theory inconsistent with the view that Coleridge was a difficult man to manage, and that his wife was unequal to the task.   It is doubtless a correct view, but it does not go deep enough.   Coleridge's many faults as a husband have been made patent enough, perhaps more than enough ; of Mrs. Coleridge's as a wife, I have heard of none save that sometimes she was 'fretful.'   Had she not fretted, and often, it would have been a miracle, for she had provocation in abundance ; but 'fretting' is a habit which often brings about consequences that seem disproportionate, and which is apt rather to increase than to abate the provocation.

Although evidence of Coleridge's undue indulgence in opium, and of some of its consequences, comes earlier than that of conjugal estrangement, I am inclined to believe that both began about the same time. Of each the predisposing cause had long been latent, but whether the quickening of the one brought the other to life, and if so, which was cause, and which effect, it would now be idle to inquire. What may be considered as certain is, that each acted and reacted to the aggravation of both. I have thought it best to deal somewhat fully with these painful matters at their first appearance, seeing that as they coloured Coleridge's subsequent life so must their existence be assumed (for I shall mention them as seldom as possible) in what remains of this narrative. The winter of 1801-1802 was a turning-point in Coleridge's life.

After his home-coming about the middle of March, Coleridge spent much of his time at Dove Cottage,[1] and when he was not there intercourse by correspondence was incessant. On the night of April 29th Wordsworth could not sleep after reading a letter from his friend. On May 4th Coleridge looked well and parted from his friends 'cheerfully'—evidently an exception which proves the rule. On the 9th Wordsworth began his verses 'about C. and himself,'[2] on the 11th he finished

---

[1] Knight's *Life*, i. 302 *et seq.*

[2] *Stanzas written in my pocket copy of Thomson's Castle of Indolence*, in which Coleridge is thus described :—

> A noticeable Man with large gray eyes,
> And a pale face that seem'd undoubtedly
> As if a blooming face it ought to be ;
> Heavy his low-hung lip did oft appear,
> Depressed by weight of musing Phantasy ;
> Profound his forehead was, though not severe ;
> Yet some did think that he had little business here:
>
> Sweet heaven forbid ! his was a lawful right ;
> Noisy he was, and gamesome as a boy ;

them, but they were not sent to Coleridge until June 7. On May 15th 'a melancholy letter from Coleridge' took kind Dorothy over to Greta Hall, but four days later he was able to walk half-way back with her. On the 22nd he met the Wordsworths at a favourite trysting-place, and they 'had some interesting, melancholy talk' about his private affairs. When the Wordsworths left Dove Cottage for Gallow Hill on their way to the Continent, they spent the first two nights at Greta Hall, and when they left (July 11) Coleridge walked with them six or seven miles. 'He was not well,' writes Dorothy in her 'Journal,' 'and we had a melancholy parting after having sate together in silence by the roadside.' The friends were not to meet again until the middle of October, Wordsworth's marriage taking place in the meantime.

Reverting to the beginning of May, we find Coleridge answering a friendly letter from Poole.[1] It is only a month since the *Dejection* ode, but he is in better health and spirits, promising that by the end of

> His limbs would toss about him with delight
> Like branches when strong winds the trees annoy.
>
> .     .     .     .     .     .     .
>
> He would entice that other Man to hear
> His music, and to view his imagery :
> And, sooth, these two did love each other dear,
> As far as love in such a place could be ;
> There did they dwell—from earthly labour free,
> As happy spirits as were ever seen.

I think with Canon Ainger (*Macmillan's Magazine*, June 1887, p. 87) that Wordsworth may possibly have had Coleridge rather than himself in view when, in the same week, he added these lines to *The Leech Gatherer* :—

> My whole life I have lived in pleasant thought,
> As if life's business were a summer mood ;
> As if all needful things would come unsought
> To genial faith, still rich in genial good ;
> But how can He expect that others should
> Build for him, sow for him, and at his call
> Love him, who for himself will take no heed at all ?

[1] *T. Poole and his Friends*, ii. 79.

the year he will have disburthened himself of all metaphysics, and that the next year will be devoted
to a long poem! His small poems are about to be
published as a second volume [which did not appear],
but he will not write many more of that order. . He
has had an offer from a bookseller to travel on the
Continent, for book-making purposes, but, on account
of his ignorance of French, has declined, in spite of
many temptations to acceptance—'household infelicity,'
for one. He sees by the papers that a portrait of him
is in the Exhibition, and supposes it must be [John]
Hazlitt's.[1] 'Mine,' he says, 'is not a picturesque face.
Southey's was made for a picture.' Then there follows an intimation that on the 4th April last he had
written to Poole a letter in verse, but thinking it 'dull
and doleful,' had not sent it. He meant, no doubt, a
transcript of the ode *Dejection*. Soon after this, Poole
went on his travels in France and Switzerland, and
he did not return until December. From a letter of
Southey[2] we gather that in August Coleridge was full
of projects, and in September–November he sent a
few miscellaneous contributions to the *Morning Post*.[3]
August was cheered by an unexpected visit from
Charles and Mary Lamb—unexpected, because time, as

[1] 'Hazlitt's does look as if you were on your trial, and certainly had stolen
the horse ; but then you did it cleverly,—it had been a deep, well-laid scheme,
and it was no fault of yours that you had been detected.' Southey to S. T. C.
(*Life and Corr.* ii. 291.)

[2] R. S. to S. T. C., August 4, 1802 :—'As to your essays, etc. etc., you
spawn plans like a herring ; I only wish as many of the seed were to vivify in
proportion. . . . Your Essays on Contemporaries I am not much afraid of the
imprudence of, because I have no expectation that they will ever be written ; but
if you were to write, the scheme projected on the old poets would be a better
scheme' (*Life and Corr. of R. S.* ii. 190).

[3] Including the comparison between Imperial Rome and France ; 'Once a
Jacobin, always a Jacobin' ; the letters to Fox ; the account of The Beauty of
Buttermere, whose story fills so large a space in De Quincey's article on Coleridge (*Works*, 1863, ii. 81); and the *Ode to the Rain* (p. 168). The last
recorded contribution to the *M.P.* is dated November 5, 1802. See *Essays on
his own Times*.

Lamb tells Manning,[1] did not admit of notice. 'Coleridge received us with all hospitality in the world, and gave up his time to show us all the wonders of his country. . . . Here we stayed three full weeks, in which time I visited Wordsworth's cottage, where we stayed a day or two with the Clarksons . . . and saw Lloyd. The Wordsworths were gone to Calais.' The greater part of the months of November and December were spent in a tour in South Wales[2] with Thomas and Miss Sarah Wedgwood, the tour being followed by visits at country-houses of the Wedgwoods and their connections. Coleridge seems to have made himself very popular, and the tour was a great success, but Tom Wedgwood was a dangerous companion, for he was an amateur in narcotics, and just then in hot pursuit of Bang[3]—'the Nepenthe of the Ancients,' as Coleridge, who helped to procure a supply, delighted to remember.

On December 24 Coleridge and Wedgwood called at Dove Cottage on their way to Greta Hall, when Coleridge learnt from the Wordsworths that a daughter had been born to him on the previous morning.[4] The Grasmere Journals, unfortunately, have been printed only as far as January 11, on which day Coleridge is reported as 'poorly, in bad spirits.' He was still anxious to go abroad; so was Tom Wedgwood, and in Coleridge's company; but though Coleridge was unwilling, he did not like to refuse outright, and until February professed to be at Wedgwood's call.[5]

---

[1] Letter of September 24, 1802 (*Letters*, i. 181). *The Picture, or The Lover's Resolution*, was written during Lamb's stay, and published soon after in the *Morning Post*.

[2] *A Group of Englishmen*, pp. 159-166; also p. 208.

[3] *Ib.* p. 215; Paris's *Life of Davy*, i. 173; and Cottle's *Reminiscences*, pp. 459 and 464.

[4] Miss Wordsworth's Journals (Knight's *Life of W. W.* i. 359).

[5] Letters of January 9 and 14, 1803, in Cottle's *Rem.* pp. 450, 454.

On January 9th he describes graphically a foolish adventure in a storm in Kirkstone Pass, which resulted in his 'feeling unwell all over.' He 'took no laudanum or opium,' but ether (Scylla and Charybdis), and recovered at once. Only temporarily, however, for on the 14th[1] a relapse is described, from which he had recovered (again an exception which proves the rule) 'without any craving after exhilarants and narcotics.' But eleven days later, existence at Greta Hall having again become intolerable, Coleridge is once more at Cote House,[2] ready, professedly, to go anywhere with Tom Wedgwood.[3] But Wedgwood was in low spirits, and undecided, and by February 4 Coleridge was with Tom Poole. On the way, he had spent a few days at Bristol with Southey,[4] who found him 'a poor fellow, who suffers terribly from this climate.' At Stowey, Coleridge's health improved, but not, he thinks, sufficiently to permit of his travelling with Wedgwood.[5] If Coleridge

---

[1] One of Coleridge's finest letters : 'I never find myself alone, within the embracement of rocks and hills, a traveller up an alpine road, but my spirit careers, drives, and eddies, like a leaf in autumn ; a wild activity of thoughts, imaginations, feelings, and impulses of motion rises up from within me ; a sort of bottom-wind, that blows to no point of the compass, comes from I know not whence, but agitates the whole of me ; my whole being is filled with waves that roll and stumble, one this way, and one that way, like things that have no common master. I think that my soul must have pre-existed in the body of a chamois-chaser. The simple image of the old object has been obliterated, but the feelings, the instinctive habits, and incipient actions, are in me, and the old scenery awakens them. The further I ascend from animated nature, from men, and cattle, and the common birds of the woods and fields, the greater becomes in me the intensity of the feeling of life. Life seems to me then an universal spirit, that neither has nor can have an opposite ! "God is everywhere," I have exclaimed, "and works everywhere, and where is there room for death?" . . . I do not think it possible that any bodily pains could eat out the love of joy, that is so substantially part of me, towards hills, and rocks, and steep waters ; and I have had some trial' (Cottle's *Rem.* p. 454). This shows an immense recovery from the *Dejection* of nine months before.

[2] Unprinted letter to T. Poole, Feb. 2, 1803.

[3] Cottle's *Rem.* pp. 458-461.

[4] *Life and Corr. of R. S.* ii. 201. In a letter of February 6, 1803, he writes to W. Taylor : 'I am grieved that you never met Coleridge : all other men whom I have ever known are mere children to him, and yet he is palsied by a total want of moral strength' (*Mem of W. T.* i. 455).

[5] Cottle's *Rem.* p. 459.

travelled, it must be alone, and this being the case, Wedgwood had to cross the Channel with a hired companion.
Coleridge's mythical ' History of Metaphysics' is still
dangled before his friends' eyes.   ' I confine myself to
facts in every part of the work, excepting that which
treats of Mr. Hume: *him* I have assuredly besprinkled
copiously from the fountains of Bitterness and Contempt.'[1]   After a visit to Gunville (Josiah Wedgwood's
Dorsetshire place), Coleridge returned to Keswick,
*viâ* London.   Davy gives a sad account of him.[2]
' During his stay in town I saw him seldomer than
usual ; . . . generally in the midst of large companies,
where he is the image of power and activity.   His elo-
quence is unimpaired; perhaps it is softer and stronger.
His will is probably less than ever commensurate with
his ability.   Brilliant images of greatness float upon
his mind like the images of the morning clouds upon
the waters . . . agitated by every breeze, and modified
by every sunbeam.   He talked, in the course of one
hour, of beginning three works, and he recited the
poem of *Christabel*, unfinished, as I had before heard it.'

During this visit it was arranged that Lamb should
see a reprint of Coleridge's poems (1796 and 1797)
through the press, and the volume was published in
the summer.[3]   At the beginning of June, Coleridge
informs Godwin [4] that his health is ' certainly better
than at any former period of the disease,' and asks
him to find a publisher for a work of six hundred

---

[1] Letter to Purkis, Stowey, February 17, 1803, in Paris's *Life of Davy*,
i. 173.
  [2] Letter to Poole, May 1, 1803, *ib.* i. 176.
  [3] POEMS, by S. T. Coleridge.   [Motto from *Statius* as in 1796.]   Third
Edition.   LONDON : Printed by N. Biggs, Crane Court, Fleet Street, for T. N.
Longman and O. Rees, Paternoster-Row.   1803.
  Duodecimo, pp. xi. ; 202.   See Lamb's letter to Coleridge, March 20, 1803
(*Letters*, i. 199).
  [4] Letter to Godwin, June 4, 1803, in *William Godwin*, ii. 92.

pages octavo, the half of which can be ready for the
printer at a fortnight's notice.   'I entitle it "Organum
verè Organum, or an Instrument of Practical Reasoning in the Business of Real Life"; to which will be
prefixed (1) a familiar introduction to the common
system of Logic, namely, that of Aristotle and the
Schools; (2) . . .' and so on for a full page of close
print.   When this work is fairly off his hands—more
and more metaphysics to follow; not a word of the
poetry, with the promise of which he pleased Poole.
(Meantime, as a little relaxation, if Godwin will find
a publisher for Hazlitt's abridgment of Search's—
Tucker's—'Light of Nature pursued,' Coleridge will
write a preface and see the sheets through the press.)
I suppose Godwin knew as well as Coleridge that this
newer *Organum* had not and never would pass beyond
the stage of synopsis, and acted accordingly.

At Greta Hall, Coleridge remained with his 'mind
strangely shut up'[1] until Sunday the 14th August,
when in company with William and Dorothy Wordsworth he set out on a Scotch tour.[2]   Incidentally we
learn that an Irish jaunting-car, drawn by a jibbing old
screw, carried the party (when the road happened to
be level or not very steep on either grade), and that
poor Coleridge did not enjoy the bumping so much as
his robuster companions enjoyed the scenery.   In a
fortnight, on the day after the meeting with that
'sweet Highland girl, ripening in perfect innocence,'
by the Inversnaid ferry-house, Coleridge parted from
his friends, professing to be very unwell, and unable to

---

[1] Letter to T. Wedgwood, September 16, 1803, in Cottle's *Rem.* p. 466 :
'For five months past my mind has been strangely shut up.'
[2] See *Recollections of a Tour made in Scotland*, A.D. 1803, by Dorothy
Wordsworth.   Edited by J. C. Shairp.   1874.   A charming book.   Coleridge's
partial account is printed in *Memorials of Coleorton*, 1887, i. 6-8 ; and Wordsworth's *Ib.* i. 35.

face the wet in an open carriage. He sent on his
trunk to Edinburgh, and said he would follow it[1]—
and this he did though somewhat circuitously, for he
travelled *via* Argyllshire, Perthshire, and Aberdeenshire.
On arriving at Tyndrum,[2] a week after the parting, the
Wordsworths were astonished to learn that Coleridge,
'who we had supposed was gone to Edinburgh, had
dined at this very house . . . on his road to Fort-
William . . . on the day after we parted from him'—
but the kindly Dorothy has no word of reproach for her
errant friend. I suppose Coleridge had found the close
companionship incompatible with that free indulgence
in narcotics which had become to him a necessity of
pleasurable or even tolerable existence. In his solitude, as he told Beaumont and Poole, he walked to
Glencoe, on to Cullen (between Fochabers and Banff),
back to Inverness, and thence over the moorland, by
Tummel Bridge to Perth,—doing ' 263 miles in eight
days, in the hope of forcing the disease into the ex-
tremities,—and so strong am I, that I would undertake
at this present time to walk 50 miles a day for a week
together. In short, while I am in possession of my
will and my reason, I can keep the fiend at arm's-
length ; but with the night my horrors commence.
During the whole of my journey, three nights out of
four, I have fallen asleep struggling and resolving to
lie awake, and awaking have blest the scream which
delivered me from the reluctant sleep.'[3] At Perth,

---

[1] *Tour*, p. 117.        [2] *Ib.* p. 184.

[3] *Mem. of Coleorton*, i. 7. Coleridge goes on to tell Beaumont that nine
years ago he had 'a three months' visitation of this kind'—a statement in the
highest degree improbable, and entirely uncorroborated. A fortnight later (Oct.
3) he recites his Scotch night-horrors to Poole (but without the reminiscence
of nine years before), and adds a poetical version, which afterwards formed lines
18-32 of *The Pains of Sleep*. De Quincey relates similar experiences in a cancelled passage of his *Confessions*, which is printed only in the notes to Dr. Garnett's edition of that work (*Parchment Library* ed. 1885, p. 263). Coleridge

Coleridge received a summons to greet the Southeys
who had arrived at Greta Hall on the visit which
ended only with their lives.   Taking coach *viâ* Edinburgh, he reached home on the 15th September.   A
week later he informs Beaumont that he .is doing
*translations* from his (Beaumont's) drawings, and will go
on and make a volume of them.   None of these ' translations' have been traced.   On October 1 he writes of
the continuance of the night-horrors, and fears that a
change of climate will prove to be his only medicine.
He sends, too, a copy of the *Chamouni* poem.[1]

At this time kind Beaumont, having 'a most
ardent desire to bring Wordsworth and Coleridge
together, purchased a small property at Applethwaite,
a mile or two west of Greta Hall, . . . and presented
it to Wordsworth, whom, as yet, he had not seen';[2] but

had returns of these 'visitations' long after he was supposed to have abandoned
the abuse of opium.  See, for instance, a letter of July 31, 1820, and another of
March 4, 1822, in Allsop's *Letters*, etc. (pp. 42 and 169, respectively).   *The
Visionary Hope*, which was probably written after *The Pains of Sleep*, bewails
the 'obscure pangs' which 'made curses of his dreams.'

[1] *Hymn before Sunrise, in the Vale of Chamouni*.   The text differs from that
finally adopted (see *Poet. Works*, 1893, Appendix F., p. 521, for the version
sent to Beaumont).   Neither to Beaumont, nor to the public, did Coleridge ever
acknowledge his considerable obligations to Frederica Brun's poem of the same
name, which she addressed to Klopstock.   On the contrary, the remarks with
which he prefaced the poem when it was printed in the *Morning Post* (Sep.
11, 1802) are calculated to convince the reader that it had been written at
Chamouni, or with the impressions of the scenery fresh in his mind's eye.   The
plagiarism (there is unfortunately no other word for it) was pointed out by De
Quincey in *Tait's Magazine* for 1834, where he honestly grants that Coleridge
had 'created the dry bones of the German outline into the fulness of life.'   The
expression 'dry bones,' however, is hardly fair to Frederica Brun, thé text of
whose poem is reprinted in the note to the *Hymn* in Coleridge's *Poet. Works*,
1893, p. 629, taken from the first edition of *Table Talk* (1835) where an
apology is attempted for Coleridge's action.

[2] *Mem. of Coleorton*, i. xii.  See also Wordsworth's sonnet *At Applethwaite*—

> Beaumont, it was thy wish that I should rear
> A seemly cottage in this sunny dell ;
> On favoured ground, thy gift, where I might dwell
> In neighbourhood with one to me most dear,
> That undivided we from year to year
> Might work in our high calling—a bright hope
> To which our fancies, mingling, gave free scope
> Till checked by some necessities severe.

the 'severe necessities' which soon drove Coleridge
from the neighbourhood prevented further action.[1]   At
the end of November[2] Southey describes Coleridge
as 'quacking himself for complaints that would tease
anybody into quackery.'   Coleridge himself had made
up his mind to go to Malta 'immediately.'

A fortnight later he 'is going to Devonshire,'
—anywhere, apparently, away from Greta Hall.
Climate had, no doubt, something to do with this
voluntary exile; probably domestic infelicity had even
more.   Poole was at this time temporarily established
at a lodging in Abingdon Street, Westminster, and on
the 20th December, Coleridge started for London that
he might consult him.   But on the way he went to
Dove Cottage, where he fell ill.   By the middle
of January he had been, by the tender care of Mrs.
and Miss Wordsworth, nursed into sufficient wellness
to permit of his journey being continued, and after
resting a week at Liverpool he arrived at Poole's
lodging about the 23rd.   He did not, however, remain
long at Abingdon Street; before the 18th February,
he had taken up his quarters with Tobin[3] in Barnard's
Inn, and there he remained until he sailed for Malta.
In February, he paid a short visit to the Beaumonts
at Dunmow, their place in Essex.   He saw much of
Davy (then the spoilt child of society), of Sotheby,
of Godwin, of John Rickman[4]— Lamb's 'pleasant
hand'—and, above all, of Lamb himself.   And he

---

[1] 'The "severe necessities" that prevented this arose from Coleridge's
domestic situation' ('Fenwick-note' to the sonnet).

[2] R. S. to Miss Barker, November 27, 1803, in *Letters of R. S.* i. 253,
where it is misdated '1804.'

[3] Whether John, the solicitor and dramatist, or his 'dear brother Jim,' so
unceremoniously dismissed from 'We are seven,' I know not ; but, I believe, the
former.   See Wordsworth's *Memoirs* i. 109.

[4] Secretary to Speaker Abbott, and a famous statistician.   He planned and conducted the first regular Census of Great Britain, on the lines now universally adopted.

was not idle, for, though Mrs. H. N. Coleridge has failed to trace any contributions of that period, during part of his stay he was at the *Courier* office from nine till four.[1]  He saw Mackintosh, who was about to go to Bombay, and who offered to take Coleridge with him and provide him with a place.  Judging from a letter to Poole (Jan. 26, 1804), Coleridge treated the offer with amused scorn.  He met George Burnett— *ci-devant* Pantisocrat, and the only one who had taken the craze seriously enough to be greatly affected by its abandonment.  Poor Burnett had become almost a waif, and Coleridge tells Rickman with the prettiest air of sympathetic innocence, that George's eyes look like those of 'an opium-chewer,' though he hopes to Heaven he may be mistaken.

There were schemes, too, for publishing great works.  One of them was to be entitled ' *Consolations and Comforts from the exercise and right application of the Reason, the Imagination, and the Moral Feelings, addressed especially to those in Sickness, Adversity, or Distress of Mind, from Speculative Gloom, etc.*'[2]

---

[1] So he tells Rickman in a letter of Feb. 25.  All the references to Rickman here, and some of the facts, are taken from unpublished correspondence which has been kindly entrusted to me by his representatives.  In one letter Coleridge seems to allude to writings in the *Courier:* 'As soon as my Volunteer Essays and whatever of a *Vindiciæ Addingtonianæ* I can effect by simple attack on the antagonists of the Ministers are published, they shall be sent to you without fail.'

[2] I take this from an unpublished letter to Poole, but there is a shorter title and a fuller account of the 'book' in a letter to Beaumont.  In the latter Coleridge gives a prospectus of another great work to follow, and states, that while at present he is giving only a quarter of his time to poetry, one half shall be devoted to it as soon as 'Consolations' is off his hands (*Mem. of Coleorton*, i. 44-48).  The title of the projected work recalls one of the subjects to be treated in the *Friend* (see the prospectus of that work, 1809).  In the unrevised version of the prospectus the phrase, 'speculative gloom,' occurs.  It was abandoned at Francis Jeffrey's instance, and here Coleridge apologises to Poole in these words: 'I put that last phrase, though barbarous, for your information.  I have puzzled for hours together and could never hit off a phrase to express that idea, that is at once neat and terse, and yet good English.'  (See *Illustrated London News*, June 10, 1893.  Art. 'Unpublished Letters of S. T. Coleridge.' *Athenæum* for Sep. 19, 1893.  Art. 'Coleridge on Quaker Principles.')

—materials for which, as he believed, had occupied his mind for months past.  But with all these projects and other distractions, Coleridge was steadily looking out for a ship to carry him to Malta.  Malta, however, was then looked on merely as the most convenient stepping-stone for Sicily, Catania being the desired haven.  Rickman's aid was sought, and it was he who, some time before March 5, found him a vessel, the 'Speedwell,' to sail with a convoy at some uncertain but not distant date.  Almost the last thing Coleridge did before leaving England was to sit for his portrait to Northcote, of which Southey wrote to the victim, that it 'looks like a grinning idiot ; and the worst is, that it is just like enough to pass for a good likeness, with those who only know your features imperfectly.'  On the 27th March he went to Portsmouth, but it was the 9th April ere the winds permitted the 'Speedwell' and her companions to set sail.  Of passengers she carried, besides Coleridge and his fortunes, two, whom he describes respectively as a liverless half-pay lieutenant, and 'an unconscionably fat woman who would have wanted elbow-room on Salisbury Plain.'  From the *Memorials of Coleorton* (i. 41-43), we learn that the ways and means for carrying out this expedition were provided by a loan of £100 from Wordsworth, and a gift of the same amount from Sir George Beaumont.  Mrs. Coleridge was left free of debt, and with liberty to draw the full amount of the Wedgwood annuity of £150.  Out of the annuity had to come £20 for Mrs. Fricker, and taxes amounting to about £15.

# CHAPTER VIII

## MALTA AND ITALY

### A.D. 1804-1806

GIBRALTAR was reached in ten days, and Coleridge greatly enjoyed the short stay on shore. On April 25th, the convoy set sail again, but so baffling were the winds, that it was the 18th May when the 'Speedwell' reached Valetta harbour. The passage from England had been to Coleridge a time of much activity of mind, but also of much home-sick brooding, while the want of exercise had told unfavourably on his health.[1] His first letter was to his wife, and was dated from 'Dr. Stoddart's,[2] July 5, 1804,'[3] no earlier opportunity of despatching letters having occurred. There was a pleased flutter in the kindly coterie over

---

[1] Many details of the passage, and of his impression of Gibraltar, are given to Stuart in a letter of April 21, 1804, printed in *Letters from the Lake Poets*, pp. 33-41.

[2] Stoddart was then not, as is commonly stated, Chief Justice of Malta, but King's Advocate (Attorney-General), and he enjoyed besides good private practice in the Vice-Admiralty Court. He became Chief Justice, but many years later. His sister Sarah became the first wife of William Hazlitt.

[3] The letter is printed in full in the *Illustrated London News* for June 10, 1893. It begins 'My dear Sara,' and ends, 'while I live your comforts will be always thought of by me as my first duties. Again and again may God bless you and our dear children, and S. T. COLERIDGE.' He reports that he had been miserably ill on the passage, and that though, since his arrival, free from 'such sharp illnesses as in England,' he has suffered from 'dreadful languor, weight on my breath,' etc. Since the very hot weather had set in he had been feeling better.

the news of 'the forlorn wanderer,' as Mary Lamb
styled Coleridge in thanking her constant correspondent, Sarah Stoddart, for the tidings, and for the
kindness extended to him. But he did not for long
remain the guest of Stoddart, mention of whom became so rare in the poet's letters to Lamb, that Mary
felt suspicious, and asked, 'Did your brother and Col.
argue long arguements, till between the two great
arguers there grew a little coolness?' Before the
6th July he had become the honoured guest, and in
some measure the private secretary, of the Governor
(his official title was 'Civil Commissioner'), Vice-
Admiral Sir Alexander John Ball, who had been one
of Nelson's captains, and to whom Coleridge had
carried letters of recommendation. 'Sir A. Ball is,
indeed, in every respect as kind and attentive to me
as possible,' he writes, and, so far, he is quite satisfied
of the wisdom of leaving England and its 'inward
distractions.' This was written on July 6th[1] to
Stuart, to whom he sends 'some Sibylline Leaves
which he wrote for Sir A. B., who has sent them
home to the ministry.' 'They will give you,' he
adds, '*my ideas* on the importance of the island,' and
Stuart may publish them, 'only not in the same words.'
He considers himself 'a sort of diplomatic under-
strapper hidden under the Governor's robes,' so that
Stuart must be discreet. Early in August, the demon
of restlessness drove him to Sicily, with the intention
of returning to Malta in the late autumn. He accordingly left Malta under convoy of Major Adye (who
was carrying despatches to Gibraltar),[2] for Syracuse,

---

[1] *Letters from the Lake Poets*, p. 41. A letter to the same effect was written
to Sir G. Beaumont on Aug. 1 (see *Mem. of Coleorton*, i. 70). In neither is
Stoddart mentioned.

[2] Major Adye also undertook to forward a series of letters which Coleridge

where he remained till the beginning of November.[1]
Sir Alexander Ball proposed to make some use of
Coleridge in Sicily.   On the 24th August he wrote
thus to the English representative at Syracuse, Mr.
Leckie :—

> You have admirably described the leading features of my friend
> Coleridge, whose company will be a delightful feast to your mind.
> We must prevail on him to draw up a political paper on the revenue
> and resources of Sicily, with the few advantages which His Sicilian
> Majesty derives from it, and the danger he is in of having it seized
> from him by the French.   We should then propose to his Majesty
> to transfer his right of that island to Great Britain upon condition
> that she shall pay him annually the amount of the present revenue.[2]

In a letter to Stuart, dated 'Syracuse, Oct. 22,
1804,' Coleridge writes: 'I leave the publication of
THE PACQUET which is waiting for convoy at Malta for
you, to your own opinion.   If the information appear
new or valuable to you, and the letters themselves
entertaining, etc., publish them; only do not sell the
copyright of more than the right of two editions to
the booksellers.'   What this '*pacquet*' may have been,
I do not know.   It probably never reached Stuart.
Coleridge adds that he has drawn on Stuart for £50
to the order of Stoddart.   By the 22nd November
Coleridge was back in Malta, occupying a 'garret in
the Treasury,' and acting as Private Secretary to Sir
Alex. Ball.   In a despatch[3] of Jan. 2, 1805, to the
Secretary of State, the Governor, in referring to a

---

says he had written to Beaumont, but these were destroyed at Gibraltar among
Adye's papers on his death by the plague, four days after his arrival (Letter to
Stuart in *Letters from the Lake Poets*, p. 47).

[1] Coleridge frequently alluded to his 'ascents of Etna,' but it is improbable
that he went much higher than the village of Nicolosi, mentioned in a note to
*Table Talk*, July 25, 1831.

[2] The whole letter ('Naples, 24th August, 1804') which is unprinted, is
very curious.   Ball proposes for Sicily just what in our own time has been done
with Cyprus.

[3] The extract from the official copy of the despatch in the archives at Malta
was kindly procured for me by a friend there.

commission issued by him to Captain Leake, R.A., to proceed to the Black Sea to buy oxen, etc., says that he takes with him 'a Mr. Coleridge'—an intimation which shows that there was good foundation for certain rumours which reached Coleridge's friends, probably through Stoddart's letters.[1] But a better appointment prevented the *ci - devant* 'Watchman' from aiding the prosecution of Pitt's wicked wars in the character of Assistant-Commissary. On the 18th January, Mr. Alex. Macaulay, the Public Secretary, died somewhat suddenly, and Coleridge received the acting appointment, pending the absence of Mr. E. T. Chapman, for whom the office was destined. The full salary attached to it was £1200, and in accordance with custom Coleridge was promised the half, £600 a year. It is vastly amusing to think of him 'having the honour to be the obedient humble servant' of the 'infamous Castlereagh,' who at this time happened to be the Secretary of State for War and Colonies. But few traces of Coleridge's official life remain at Malta, for some years ago the records of the Chief Secretary's office previous to 1851 were burnt. A collection of State papers, however, which was printed not long ago, contains a good many documents signed or countersigned by 'S. T. Coleridge, Pub. Sec. to H.M. Civ. Commissr.'; and the mere routine work must have been very considerable, for there lies before me a highly unimportant document —'Affidavit of the Paymaster of the Maltese Artil-

---

[1] 'Coleridge is confidential secretary to Sir A. Ball, and has been taking some pains to set the country right as to Neapolitan politics, in the hope of saving Sicily from the French. He is going with Capt. —— into Greece, and up the Black Sea to purchase corn for the Government. Odd, but pleasant enough, if he would but learn to be contented in that state of life into which it has pleased God to call him—a maxim which I have long thought the best in the Catechism' (Southey to Rickman, Feb. 16, 1805, in *Life and Corr.* ii. 315). See also *A Group of Englishmen*, p. 305.

lery,' sworn before, and signed by Coleridge as Public
Secretary, on March 13, 1805.[1]

In a letter to Stuart (May 1, 1805) he complains
of overwork, and 'wishes to Heaven he had never
accepted his office as Public Secretary, or the former
one of Private Secretary, as, even in a pecuniary point
of view, he might have gained twice as much and improved his reputation.' He adds : ' I have the title
and the palace of the Public Secretary, but not half
the salary, though I had promise of the whole. But
the promises of one in office are what every one knows
them to be, and Sir A. B. behaves to me with real
personal fondness, and with almost fatherly attention.'
In this letter, as in one of April 27th,[2] Coleridge bewails the irregularity of the opportunities of communication. He gets few letters, and his own go to the
fishes. It is, he believes, a judgment on him for
former 'indolence and procrastination' that now when
all his gratification is in writing letters to England, he
has seldom a chance of despatching them. On April
27th it is his ' intention to return home overland by
Naples, Ancona, and Trieste, etc., on or about the 2nd
of next month.' On May Day his 'heart is almost
broken ' that he cannot go by this convoy ; Chapman
has not arrived to relieve him, and he may not come
till July. He begs Stuart to ' write to Mrs. Coleridge
and say that his constitution is, he hopes, improved by
the abode here, but that accidents, partly by an excess
of official labour and anxiety, partly from distress of
mind at his not hearing from his friends, and knowledge that they could not have heard from him, etc.

---

[1] He seems also to have acted as a magistrate.   See the amusing story in the
additional ' Omniana' in *Lit. Remains*, 1836, i. 335.

[2] *Letters from the Lake Poets*, p. 46.

etc. etc., have produced an alteration in him for the
worse,' and that he hopes to get away, homewards, by
the end of May.   In February the Wordsworths lost
their sailor brother, John, to whom Coleridge was
much attached, and when the news reached Malta,
Coleridge was so much affected that, as he wrote to
his wife, he ' kept his bed for a fortnight.'   The fear
of similar consequences prompted Mrs. Coleridge to
refrain from informing him of the death of his friend,
Thomas Wedgwood, which took place in July 1805.[1]
In the same letter Mrs. Coleridge says that she has
received one from her husband of July 21, informing
her that he cannot leave until Mr. Chapman arrives ;
' he is unhappy in the extreme, not having received
above three or four letters from home during his
residence in the island.   I myself have only had four
from him.'[2]

Mr. Chapman arrived on Sep. 6, and Coleridge
quitted Malta on the 21st.   He left for Rome in company with a gentleman, unnamed, who paid all expenses,
meaning to stay only a fortnight, and then *return
for the winter* to Naples, where Coleridge had left
most of his clothes and all his letters of credit, manu-
scripts, etc.   He had not been ten days in Rome when
' the French torrent rolled down on Naples,' and return thither, or receipt of anything thence, was equally
impossible.[3]   This shows that Coleridge must have

---

[1] Mrs. S. T. C. to J. Wedgwood, Oct. 13, 1805, in *A Group of Englishmen,*
p. 303, an admirably expressed letter.

[2] In his notes to ' Unpublished Letters ' in the *Illustrated London News,* Mr.
E. H. Coleridge says that only fourteen letters written from Malta have come
under his notice.   Opportunities of writing were doubtless few, but during his
stay in the island, Coleridge ' made copious entries in his journals and diaries,
and of these only a few fragments have been published.'   A specimen of great
interest follows (*I. L. N.* June 10, 1893).

[3] Letter to Stuart, ' [London] Aug. 18, 1806.'   Its narrative stops abruptly
at the point above (*Letters from the Lake Poets,* p. 56).

lingered long at Naples. We know that he was there
at the end of October when the news of Trafalgar
reached the city; Gillman quotes[1] an entry from his
diary there, dated Dec. 15th; the French entered
Naples early in February 1806, so that Coleridge cannot have arrived at Rome much before the end of
January. He remained until the 18th of May—the
second anniversary of his arrival at Malta.

Of his doings in Rome we know little or nothing.
Soon after reaching England he wrote thus to Stuart :
'If I recover a steady though imperfect health, I
perhaps should have no reason to regret my long
absence; not even my perilous detention in Italy; for
by my regular attention to the best of the good things
in Rome, and associating almost wholly with the artists
of acknowledged highest reputation, I acquired more
insight into the Fine Arts in three months than I could
have done in England in twenty years.'[2]  He made
many new acquaintances—among others Baron W.
von Humboldt[3] (then Prussian Minister at the Papal
Court) and Ludwig Tieck[4]—and one friend, Washington Allston,[5] the American painter.  Of his leaving
Rome and Italy, of the reasons which led to it, and of

---

[1] *Life*, p. 179.

[2] *Letters from the Lake Poets*, p. 60.   Gillman (*Life*, p. 179) makes a statement much to the same effect.   See also an interesting letter on his Italian art-
studies which Coleridge addressed to Samuel Rogers in 1815 (*Rogers and his
Contemporaries*, by P. W. Clayden, 1889, i. 191).

[3] In *The Friend* (1818, etc., Sect. II. Essay xi.) Coleridge says he then read to
him Wordsworth's *Ode on the Intimation of Immortality*.   This poem was not completed until 1806 ; but some incomplete draft of it may have been sent to him at
Malta.   He had with him a MS. copy of the earlier portion of the *Prelude*.   See
also an allusion to Humboldt in *Table Talk*, Aug. 28, 1833.

[4] He renewed acquaintance with Tieck in London in 1817.   See p. 230
*infra*.

[5] He began a portrait of Coleridge at Rome, but, though well advanced, it
was not finished when Coleridge left.   It is now in the possession of Allston's
niece, Miss R. Charlotte Dana, of Boston, U.S.A.   The same painter's portrait
of Coleridge, now in the National Portrait Gallery, was taken at Bristol in 1814.
See the recently published *Life* of Allston, by Flagg, p. 105.

the manner of it, Coleridge is reported to have given several accounts which are not altogether consistent.[1] The only points common to them all are that he was warned to get away from Rome and Italy as quickly as possible, because Napoleon had ordered his arrest for having, years before, written certain articles in the *Morning Post;* and that he instantly fled to an Italian port, whence he found passage to England. The details attributed to him, besides being inconsistent, are mostly trivial, and probably owe much of both qualities to their reporters. It is not improbable that Napoleon ordered the arrest of the English in Italy ; possible, even, that he marked Coleridge down individually ; and the poet may have been warned, and his escape assisted, by influential acquaintances ; but we know nothing of the circumstances from Coleridge directly. He certainly did not go direct to Leghorn and sail directly, or go to Leghorn and skulk about *incognito* until he secured a passage—as is variously alleged. He probably went direct to Leghorn,[2] and, after arranging for a passage in an American vessel, left again ; but at all events he wrote a letter[3] to Washington Allston (then at Rome) on June 19 from some town unnamed, where he had then been for more than a fortnight :—

---

[1] Gillman, *Life*, pp. 179-181 ; Cottle's *Rem.* pp. 310-313 ; and (through John Sterling) in Caroline Fox's Journals. I cannot learn that any Englishmen were then arrested at Rome, or that there was any general exodus of our country-men.

[2] 'Coleridge has been daily expected since the 1st of May last year. The last accounts were dated in the May of this—he was then at Leghorn, about to embark for England' (Unprinted portion of letter of Southey to Cottle, Aug. 11, 1806, in *Life and Corr.* iii. 51). See also Southey's letter to Danvers (*Letters of R. S.* i. 377).

[3] This letter was partly and incorrectly printed in *Scribner's Mag.* for Jan. 1892. The publishers most kindly sent me a corrected and completed transcript, from which I quote. With other letters of Coleridge, it appears in Mr. Flagg's *Life of Allston.* Mr. Russell was an artist, an Exeter man, and Coleridge's fellow-passenger from Italy to England.

I have been dangerously ill for the last fortnight; . . . about ten days ago when rising from my bed I had a manifest stroke of palsy along my right side and right arm.   My head felt like another man's head, so dead was it. . . . Enough of it—continual vexations and preyings upon the spirit.   I gave life to my children, and they have repeatedly given it to me, for, by the Maker of all things, but for them I would try my chance.   But they pluck out the wing-feathers from the mind.   I have not recovered the sense of my side or my hand, but have recovered the use.   I am harassed by local and partial fevers.   This day at noon we set off for Leghorn: all passage through the Italian states and Germany is little other than impossible for an Englishman, and Heaven knows whether Leghorn may not be blockaded.   However, we go thither, and shall go to England in an American ship. . . . On my arrival at Pisa . . . I will write a letter to you, for this I do not consider as a letter. Nothing can surpass Mr. Russell's kindness and tenderheartedness to me.

# CHAPTER IX

A.D. 1806–1810

WHEN Coleridge's ship arrived at the quarantine
ground off Portsmouth on the 11th August, he was ill,
and possibly for that reason wrote to no one. Mr.
Russell, however, wrote to his own friends at Exeter,
who wrote to the Coleridges at Ottery, who wrote to
Mrs. Coleridge—the news reaching her on the 15th.
Coleridge arrived in London on the 17th, and on the
following day, having taken up his quarters with
Lamb, wrote to Stuart and to Wordsworth. In both
letters[1] he described himself as much better since he
landed, but in neither did he say anything about going
home. He did not write to Wedgwood for ten
months, and when he did, he described himself as
having arrived from Italy 'ill, penniless, and worse
than homeless.' Almost his first words to Stuart were,
'I am literally afraid, even to cowardice, to·ask for
any person, or of any person.' Spite of the friendliest
and most unquestioning welcome from all most dear to
him, it was the saddest of home-comings, for the very

---

[1] *Letters from the Lake Poets*, p. 54; *Mem. of Coleorton*, i. 157. These
books are the main authorities for this period.

sympathy held out with both hands induced only a
bitter, hopeless feeling of remorse—a

> Sense of past youth, and manhood come in vain ;
> And genius given, and knowledge won in vain ;—

of broken promises,—promises to friends and promises
to himself ; and above all, sense of a will paralysed—
dead perhaps, killed by his own hand.

Wordsworth, whose family had outgrown Dove
Cottage, was then looking for a house close to Keswick, that he might be near Coleridge, should Coleridge decide on living at Greta Hall.  He would do
nothing until that was settled, but no answer came to
his repeated inquiries by letter.  Coleridge seems
soon to have left Lamb's chambers for a room at the
*Courier* office (348 Strand), and to have settled down
as assistant to Stuart and to his editor, Street.  He
had been sent for by Lord Howick (Foreign Secretary),
but had been repulsed by the hall porter, and doubted
whether the letter on the state of affairs in the Medi-
terranean which he had left had ever reached his
Lordship.  A few days after Fox's death (Sep. 13)
he promised Stuart a 'full and severe critique' of that
statesman's latest views.  About the same time,
through Davy or William Smith, M.P. for Norwich,
or both, he undertook to deliver a series of lectures on
'Taste' at the Royal Institution.  On Sep. 16—just
a month after his landing—he wrote his first letter
to his wife, to say that he might be expected at
Greta Hall on the 29th.  Before this, Wordsworth
had informed Sir George Beaumont that Coleridge

---

dare not go home, he recoils so much from the thought of
domesticating with Mrs. Coleridge, with whom, though on many
accounts he much respects her, he is so miserable that he dare not
encounter it.  What a deplorable thing !  I have written to him to

say that if he does not come down immediately I must insist upon seeing him somewhere. If he appoints London I shall go. I believe if anything good is to be done for him it must be done by me.[1]

It was Wordsworth's letter, doubtless, which drew Coleridge to the North. Dorothy's letter to Lady Beaumont,[2] written on receipt of the announcement of Coleridge's home-coming, goes copiously and minutely into the reasons for the estrangement between the poet and his wife. Miss Wordsworth still had hopes of an improvement.

We have long known (she writes) how unfit Coleridge and his wife were for each other; but we had hoped that his ill-health, and the present need his children have of his care and fatherly instructions, and the reflections of his own mind during this long absence, would have so wrought upon him that he might have returned home with comfort, ready to partake of the blessings of friendship, which he surely has in an abundant degree, and to devote himself to his studies and his children. . . . Poor soul! he had a struggle of many years, striving to bring Mrs. C. to a change of temper, and something like communion with him in his enjoyments. He is now, I trust, effectually convinced that he has no power of this sort. . . . But suppose him once reconciled to that one great want, an utter want of sympathy, I believe he may live in peace and quiet. Mrs. C. has many excellent properties, as you observe; she is unremitting in her attentions as a nurse to her children, and, indeed, I believe she would have made an excellent wife to many persons. Coleridge is as little fitted for her as she for him, and I am truly sorry for her.

Of Coleridge during the next three months, the only glimpses we have are in the correspondence of distracted friends who cannot draw a word of reply to the letters they address to him. Josiah Wedgwood is the most persistent inquirer—he craves for the long-promised material for the *Life* of his brother Thomas, then being prepared by Sir James Mackintosh.[3] On

---

[1] Knight's *Life*, ii. 74.     [2] *Mem. of Coleorton*, i. 162.
[3] Sir James Mackintosh was more diplomatic than Coleridge, for he proved as faithless to his trust and his promises, without sharing the just displeasure of the Wedgwood family.

Nov. 10th, Wordsworth (who had taken his family to Coleorton farm-house) wrote: 'Alas! we have had no tidings of Coleridge—a certain proof that he continues to be very unhappy.' The truth of the presentiment was soon confirmed. Before the 10th December, the Wordsworths had received four letters from Coleridge, in all of which he 'spoke

with the same steadiness of his resolution to separate from Mrs. C., and she has fully agreed to it, and consented that he should take Hartley and Derwent and superintend their education, she being allowed to have them at the holidays. I say she has agreed to the separation, but in a letter which we have received to-night he tells us she breaks out into outrageous passions, and urges continually that one argument (in fact the only one which has the least effect upon her mind), that this person and that person, and everybody will talk.'[1]

Wordsworth at once wrote and begged Coleridge to come to Coleorton and bring the two boys with him, and on December 21 Coleridge arrived, bringing, however, only Hartley.[2] On Christmas Day, Miss Wordsworth described him to Lady Beaumont as tolerably well and cheerful, and 'already begun with his books.' He seemed 'more like his old self,' and 'contented in his mind, having settled things at home to his satisfaction.'

It was early in the following month that Wordsworth recited to Coleridge the great autobiographical poem which we know as *The Prelude*. He had

[1] Miss Wordsworth to Lady Beaumont in *Mem. of Coleorton*, i. 182. 'Dec. 10, 1806,' is the post-mark. The date printed at the head of the letter, 'Nov. 16,' is an impossible one.

[2] Two days previous Miss Wordsworth wrote thus to Lady Beaumont: 'He [Coleridge] writes calmly and in better spirits. Mrs. C. had been outrageous; but for the last two or three days she had become more quiet, and appeared to be tolerably reconciled to his arrangements. I had a letter from her last week—a strange letter! She wrote just as if all things were going on as usual, and we knew nothing of the intentions of Coleridge. She gives but a very gloomy account of Coleridge's health, but this in her old way, without the least feeling or sense of his sufferings.' *Mem. of Coleorton*, i. 187.

carried with him to Malta a transcript of the first five
'Books,' but the poem had been slowly built up and
completed during his long absence, and was addressed
to himself. How deeply the recital impressed him
may be gathered from the touching and beautiful
response [1] made while the sound of his friend's voice
was still vibrating. The picture which Coleridge
draws of himself is too sacred for comment—the
companion-portrait of his friend is drawn in lines even
more strongly contrasting than those which had been
used in *Dejection*.

[1] *To a Gentleman* [William Wordsworth], *composed on the night of his recitation of a Poem on the growth of an Individual Mind.*

I quote from the original version chiefly for the sake of including the seventeen lines beginning 'Dear shall it be to every human heart,' which were first
printed in the *Mem. of Coleorton*, i. 215. The original version is given entire
in *Poet. Works*, 1893, Appendix H, p. 525.

> O Friend! O Teacher! God's great gift to me!
> Into my heart have I received that lay
> More than historic, that prophetic lay
> Wherein (high theme by thee first sung aright)
> Of the foundations and the building up
> Of thy own Spirit thou hast loved to tell
> What *may* be told, by words revealable :
> .    .    .    .    .    .
>                      Thy work
> Makes audible a linkèd song of Truth—
> Of Truth profound a sweet continuous song,
> Not learnt, but native, her own natural notes!
> Dear shall it be to every human heart,
> To me how more than dearest! me, on whom
> Comfort from thee, and utterance of thy love,
> Came with such heights and depths of harmony,
> Such sense of wings uplifting, that its might
> Scatter'd and quell'd me, till my thoughts became
> A bodily tumult ; and thy faithful hopes,
> Thy hopes of me, dear Friend, by me unfelt!
> Were troublous to me, almost as a voice,
> Familiar once, and more than musical ;
> As a dear woman's voice to one cast forth,
> A wanderer with a worn-out heart forlorn,
> Mid strangers pining with untended wounds.
>
> O Friend, too well thou know'st, of what sad years
> The long suppression had benumb'd my soul,
> That, even as life returns upon the drown'd,
> The unusual joy awoke a throng of pains—
> Keen pangs of Love, awakening, as a babe
> Turbulent, with an outcry in the heart!
> And fears self-will'd, that shunn'd the eye of Hope ;
> And Hope that scarce would know itself from Fear ;

On January 27, 1807, Miss Wordsworth reports
Coleridge as pretty well, 'though ailing at some
time in every day. He does not take such strong
stimulants as he did, but I fear he will never
be able to leave them off entirely.' On February
17 he is still at Coleorton, but it must have been
soon after this that he took Hartley up to London
on a visit to Basil Montagu. It was probably while
then in town that he made preliminary arrangements
through Davy for the delivery of the course of lectures
which had been spoken of in 1806, for in August we
find Davy endeavouring to get a definite answer on
the subject.[1] Some time in May, Coleridge and
Hartley joined Mrs. Coleridge and the two younger
children at Bristol (where they had been since the
end of March), and on the 6th June the whole
family became the guests of Poole at Stowey. The
visit was planned for but a fortnight, after which
the Coleridges were to have gone to Ottery[2] to stay
with his brother George, but the visit had to be aban-

> Sense of past youth, and manhood come in vain,
> And genius given, and knowledge won in vain ;
> And all, which I had cull'd in wood-walks wild,
> And all which patient toil had rear'd, and all
> Commune with THEE had open'd out—but flowers
> Strew'd on my corse, and borne upon my bier,
> In the same coffin, for the self-same grave !

But the 'orphic song' brought to the listener something more wholesome than
despairing remorse—it brought, for the moment at least, hope, and something
else which could not be defined. 'Thought was it ?' he asks himself, 'or
aspiration ? or resolve ? '—

> The tumult rose and ceas'd : for peace is nigh
> Where Wisdom's voice has found a list'ning heart.
> Amid the howl of more than wintry storms,
> The halcyon hears the voice of vernal hours
> Already on the wing !

[1] *Frag. Rem.* p. 98.
[2] 'In less than a week I go down to Ottery, with my children and their
mother, from a sense of duty as it affects myself, and from a promise made to
Mrs. Coleridge as far as it affects her, and indeed as a debt of respect to her, for
her many praiseworthy qualities.' (*Unpublished Letter of S. T. C.*)

doned, owing, it was said, to illness in the house.
The true reason was, that when George Coleridge was
made aware of the proposed separation of S. T. Coleridge from his wife, he refused to receive them into
his house.    This proved a lasting rupture with Ottery.
The Coleridges remained on with Poole—Mrs. Coleridge and the children until the end of July, when
they returned to Bristol ; Coleridge himself until the
end of September.    There is much of the doings of
this period in Mrs. Sandford's book.    It appears to
have been on the whole a happy time for all parties,
and it would seem as if, probably through Poole's good
offices, some kind of reconciliation, or at least some
resolution to 'try again,' had been patched up between
Coleridge and his wife, for when Mrs. Coleridge left
Stowey for Bristol it had been arranged that she
should there be joined by her husband, and that the
family party should return intact to Greta Hall.
Coleridge appears to have been cheerful enough while
he basked in the sunshine of old associations and old
friendships, but when his host and constant friend
urged him to exert himself in preparing for the proposed lectures at the Royal Institution, poor Coleridge could only respond with a sigh—

> Let Eagle bid the Tortoise sunwards soar,
> As vainly Strength speaks to a broken Mind ![1]

Poole succeeded, however, in overcoming Coleridge's
reluctance to resume communication with Josiah
Wedgwood.    While on a visit from Poole's to his old
neighbour, Mr. Brice of Aisholt, Coleridge wrote the
letter[2] which contains the statement already quoted as
to his having returned from Italy 'ill, penniless, and

---

[1] *T. Poole and his Friends*, ii. 195.
[2] To Josiah Wedgwood, June 27, 1807, in *A Group of Englishmen*, pp.
324-328.

worse than homeless.' It is a sad letter, differing however but little from many which Coleridge was called on to write—a medley of confessions, promises, projects, and pleas self-justificatory. The. long-promised contributions to the estimate of Thomas Wedgwood's philosophical views, and the more recently demanded contribution to the memoir (supposed to be preparing by Sir James Mackintosh), were both among the 'effects which have been most unkindly or injudiciously detained by Stoddart' at Malta. If Josiah Wedgwood only knew Coleridge's grief for the loss of his friend Thomas, and his 'own bad state of health and worse state of mind,' he would pity rather than wonder at the 'day after day procrastinating.' 'The faultiest parts of my conduct (he urged) have arisen from qualities both blameable and pitiable, but yet the very opposite of Neglect or Insensibility.' He flatly denies an accusation of having abused Mackintosh to his (M.'s) relations. 'I am at present,' he adds, 'on the eve of sending two volumes of poems to the press,[1] the work of past years.' *Christabel*, the most greatly admired, has been, he is told, 'anticipated as far as all originality of style

---

[1] In Cottle's *Early Recoll.* (ii. 130, but not in his *Rem.*) is printed an extract from a letter written by Coleridge to Wade at this time. Its exact date cannot now be ascertained, for of the original only a fragment remains, but it must belong to the early days of September 1807. Some unprinted passages indicate that Coleridge's poems were being transcribed for the press by Mrs. Coleridge at Bristol, that he was under contract with Messrs. Longman for a book (possibly these poems), and that he had received the offer of a regular engagement on some provincial newspaper, and had declined it, under the belief that its acceptance would displease the Wedgwoods. In the same letter he describes himself as under unfulfilled obligations to Wade : 'penniless, resourceless, in heavy debt, his health and spirits absolutely broken down, and with scarce a friend in the world '—an obvious exaggeration, seeing that in Wordsworth and Poole alone he had a host, and that he had been reconciled to Wedgwood. Cottle, as usual, darkens knowledge by garbling the extract he gives. Coleridge did not write ' *I have* too much reason' to fear the loss of the annuity ; but that at a previous time, when another grief was weighing on him, he *had had* reason to fear for the continuance of the annuity.

and manner goes by a work[1] which he has not read.' If this be true, it is 'somewhat hard, for [Scott] had, long before the composition of his own poem, publicly repeated *Christabel.* Besides' (he goes on), 'I have finished a Greek and English grammar on a perfectly new plan, and have done more than half of a small but sufficiently complete Greek and English Lexicon, so that I can put both to press whenever I can make just terms with any bookseller.'[2] Nothing is said about lectures. Of this apologia, Wedgwood wrote to Poole : 'His letter removed all those feelings of anger which occasionally, but not permanently, existed in my mind towards him.'[3]

It was in the following month that De Quincey appeared on the scene. On the 26th of July, Cottle wrote a letter of introduction[4] for that 'Gentleman of Oxford, a scholar and man of genius' (so he described De Quincey) to Poole, which contained a request that he might be introduced to Coleridge. The Opium-eater's story[5] is too well known to require more than brief mention here. When he arrived at Stowey, Coleridge was at Bridgwater, and thither the neophyte pursued him. He found Coleridge standing in reverie, under his host's gateway : 'In height he might seem to be about five feet eight (he was in reality about an

---

[1] He is referring to Scott, and *The Lay of the Last Minstrel.*

[2] One of these statements had some foundation, for it was from a Greek grammar of his own making that Coleridge taught his little boys. The projects —they were never more—are mentioned again, a year and a half later, in a letter to Davy : 'As soon as I have a little leisure I shall send my Greek accidence and vocabulary of terminations to the press with my Greek-English Lexicon, which will be followed by a Greek Philosophical grammar' (*Frag. Rem.* p. 106).

[3] *T. Poole and his Friends*, ii. 185.

[4] *Ib.* ii. 190.

[5] It began to appear in *Tait's Magazine* for Sep. 1834, two months after Coleridge's death ; and has been reprinted (with many alterations) in De Quincey's collected *Works* (1863, ii. 38-122). The whole article bristles with blunders of every description. Even the portions which relate the author's own experience and observation require a large allowance for refraction.

inch and a half taller) . . . his person was broad and
full, and tended even to corpulence; his complexion
was fair, though not what painters technically call fair,
because it was associated with black hair; his eyes
were large and soft in their expression; and it was
from the peculiar appearance of haze or dreaminess
which mixed with their light, that I recognised my
object.'

As soon as it had been arranged that De Quincey
should join a dinner-party which Coleridge's host, Mr.
Chubb, was to entertain on that evening, Coleridge
began to talk 'in a continuous strain of eloquent dissertation,' which, after about three hours, was arrested
by the entrance of Mrs. Coleridge. 'She was in
person full and rather below the common height;
whilst her face showed, to my eye, some prettiness
of rather a common order.' When De Quincey had
been 'frigidly' introduced, Mrs. Coleridge retired,
and no doubt the dissertation was resumed. But
with all this copious talk, De Quincey declares that
'never had he beheld so profound an expression of
cheerless despondency' as that which sat on the
talker's countenance. At the large dinner-party in
the evening, Coleridge seemed to talk with an
effort, and to give no heed when his hearers misrepresented what he said. At ten, — dinner had
probably begun at five or six, — De Quincey left
the party, and 'feeling that he could not easily go
to sleep after the excitement of the day, and fresh
from the sad spectacle of powers so majestic already
besieged by decay,' he mounted his horse, and through
the divine calm of the summer night rode back to
Bristol. He states that in the course of their conversation 'Coleridge told him of the over-clouding

of his life' by the abuse of opium, and warned him
against forming the habit, with so 'peculiar an
emphasis of horror' as to impress upon the young
man's mind ' a feeling that he never hoped to liberate
himself from the bondage.' As to this alleged confession, I feel almost persuaded that De Quincey's
memory deceived him, and that he learned the secret
and received the warning at some later period. Such
a lapse in groping back through a past of seven-and-
twenty years, is much more probable than that Coleridge should have divulged to a perfect stranger a
hitherto jealously-guarded secret. It struck the generous young man that Coleridge might be hampered
in many ways by pecuniary difficulties. Immediately
after his return to Bristol, he learned that such was
the case, 'and in consequence' (he says) 'of what I
heard, I contrived that a particular service should be
rendered to Mr. Coleridge, a week after, through the
hands of Mr. Cottle.'

Such is De Quincey's delicate way of telling the
story of his own impulsive generosity. Cottle's
account[1] is familiar. De Quincey proposed to give
Coleridge five hundred pounds, but Cottle prudently
induced the young man to make the sum three
hundred. The gift was professedly accepted as an
unconditional loan, which (as he told Cottle) Coleridge trusted to be able to restore in two years,

---

[1] *Rem.* pp. 341-344. The narrative is, as usual, full of inaccuracies—as
is shown by a comparison with the correspondence printed in *De Quincey's
Memorials* (2 vols. 1891), but the latter gives no new complexion to the *conduct*
of the parties. Both De Quincey and Cottle write as if the transaction had been
carried through at once, but the correspondence explains how it came to drag on
from July till November. This was not De Quincey's fault, for he found difficulties in raising the whole of the money at once. Cottle prints Coleridge's
receipt : 'November 12, 1807—Received from Mr. Joseph Cottle the sum of
Three hundred pounds, presented to me, through him, by an unknown friend.
S. T. Coleridge, Bristol.'

and as removing the pecuniary pressures which alone stood in the way of the completion of works, which, if completed, would make him easy. In one year he hopes to ask the name of his bene-factor, that he may show him good fruits of the 'tranquillity of mind which his kindness' has rendered possible.[1] I do not doubt the perfect sincerity with which this letter was written, but in view of the events which followed, it can only be read with a pang. Of the use to which De Quincey's gift was put by Coleridge, nothing, I believe, is known. One hopes that part went to repay Wordsworth's loan of £100 made in 1804 ; but, at all events, soon afterwards, it was all gone. 'Heaven knows, of the £300 received through you,' wrote Coleridge to Cottle in 1815, 'what went to myself!'

Coleridge left Stowey for Bristol about the 12th September. On the 11th he had written a long letter to Davy[2] in reply to an urgent message regarding the proposed lectures. He is better, and his 'will acquir-ing some degree of strength and power of reaction.'

I have received such manifest benefit from horse exercise, and gradual abandonment of fermented, and total abstinence from spirituous, liquors, and by being alone with Poole, and the renewal of old times, by wandering about my dear old walks of Quantock and Alfoxden, that I have seriously set about composition with a view to ascertain whether I can conscientiously undertake what I so very much wish, a series of Lectures at the Royal Institution.

He has, however, changed his mind as to the subject. If he lectures, it will not be on 'Taste,' but on 'the Principles of Poetry,' and he will 'not give a single lecture till he has in fair writing at least one-half of the whole course, for as to trusting anything to immediate

---

[1] S. T. C. to Cottle (n.d.), *Rem.* p. 342.        [2] *Frag. Rem.* p. 99.

effort, he shrinks from it as from guilt, and guilt in him it would be.' He concludes by asking Davy to await his final decision, at the end of the month. During the months (September–November) which Coleridge spent in Bristol, he seems to have given himself up very much to talk about religion, surprising his friends there with the change which had taken place in his beliefs. A long and deeply interesting letter[1] printed by Cottle shows that he was no longer a Unitarian— he probably never had been one, in the strictest sense —but a fully-developed Trinitarian. In a letter[2] to Poole from 'Keswick, Dec. 28, 1807,' Mrs. Coleridge says that when her husband joined her at Bristol, 'in such excellent health and improved looks, she thought of days "lang syne," and hoped and prayed it might continue.'

Alas! (she adds), in three or four days it was all over. He said he must go to town *immediately*, about the Lectures, yet he stayed three weeks without another word about removing, and I durst not speak lest it should *disarrange* him. Mr. De Quincey, who was a frequent visitor to C. in College Street, proposed accompanying me and the children into Cumberland, as he much wished to pay Wordsworth and Southey a visit. . . . Towards the end of October, accordingly, I packed up everything, C.'s things (as I thought, for London) and our own, and left Bristol.[3] . . .

[1] *Rem.* pp. 314-325. I have not seen the original, but it was, no doubt, carefully revised by Cottle before printing. The reports of conversations on these topics are more completely given in Cottle's *Early Recoll.* ii. 99-124. These are, even more than the letter, open to the suspicion of severe editing. Southey wrote thus to W. Taylor, July 11, 1808 : 'Had Middleton been now at Norwich, it is possible that you might have seen Coleridge there, for M. called upon him in London. It has been his humour for [some] time past to think, or rather to call, the Trinity a philosophical and most important Truth, and he is very much delighted with Middleton's work on the subject. Dr. Sayers would not find him now the warm Hartleyan that he has been ; Hartley was ousted by Berkeley, Berkeley by Spinoza, and Spinoza by Plato ; when last I saw him Jacob Behmen had some chance of coming in. The truth is that he plays with systems, and any nonsense will serve him for a text from which he can deduce something new and surprising' (*Mem. of W. T.* i. 215).

[2] Partly printed in *T. Poole and his Friends*, ii. 202-204.

[3] For De Quincey's account of the journey, see *Works* (1863, ii. 128) ; Art. 'William Wordsworth.'

I left him (as I thought) ready to jump into the mail for London.
Lo! three weeks after I received a letter from him from White Horse
Stairs, Piccadilly; he was just arrived in town, had been ill, owing
to sitting in wet cloaths, had passed three weeks at the house of a
Mr. Morgan, and had been nursed by his wife and her sister in the
kindest manner.   C. found Davy very ill.   The Lectures on that account were postponed.   Stuart had insisted on his being at the *Courier*
office during his stay in town. . . . Wordsworth obtained a few lines
from him ten days ago.   Davy was better, and the Lectures were to
commence in a fortnight.   Since then we have heard nothing.   Dr.
Stoddart is arrived from Malta.   He has brought with him C.'s papers.
C. wrote to him to expostulate with him for having detained them so
long.   He received an abusive answer, saying he would deliver up
the papers to a person properly documented, with £50 for expenses,
etc.   C. has since found that he [Stoddart] is writing a book himself. . . . Southey is enraged at his [Stoddart's] conduct, and fore-
told this about the book, and gave it as a reason why C.'s documents
were not forthcoming. . . . He [Coleridge] has published a poem
in the *Courier* lately—*The Wanderer's Farewell*.[1]

This very interesting letter of Mrs. Coleridge
gives a succinct account of her husband up to the end of
1807.   It will be observed that it contains no mention
of De Quincey's bounty.   He, of course, would say
nothing to Mrs. Coleridge, and Coleridge himself had
evidently been equally reticent.   His detention at
Bristol, we may assume, was not unconnected with
the delay in receiving the three hundred pounds
which was paid on November 12, at least a fortnight
after Mrs. Coleridge's departure.

Coleridge returned to his old quarters at the top of

---

[1] 'To Two Sisters : A Wanderer's Farewell' printed in the *Courier*, Dec.
10, 1807.   The signature was *Siesti*, but this disguise of ESTEESI proved too thin
for Mrs. Coleridge's jealous eyes.   'The wanderer' was Coleridge, and the
'two sisters' were Mrs. J. J. Morgan, and Miss Brent, and Mrs. Coleridge was
highly displeased.   Coleridge wrote :—

> Even thus did you call up before mine eyes
> Two dear, dear Sisters, prized all price above ;

and Mrs. Coleridge well knew that these were not herself and Mrs. Southey.
The poem in its integrity was first reprinted in *Poet. and Dram. Works*, 1877-80.
It will be found also in *Poet. Works*, 1893, p. 179.   A few lines adapted from
it were published in ed. 1834 (and after) with the heading, 'On taking leave of
——, 1817 ' (the date a misprint for ' 1807 ').

the *Courier* building in the Strand. ' He sits up in
a two pair of stairs room at the *Courier* office and
receives visitors,' writes Lamb to Manning (Feb. 28) ;
and De Quincey, in his *Lake Poets*, gives a dismal
account of Coleridge's situation at this period :—

> I called upon him daily, and pitied his forlorn condition. There
> was no bell in the room, which for many months answered the
> double purpose of bed-room and sitting-room. Consequently I
> often saw him picturesquely enveloped in night-caps surmounted by
> handkerchiefs indorsed upon handkerchiefs, shouting . . . down
> three or four flights of stairs, to a certain ' Mrs. Brainbridge,' his
> sole attendant, whose dwelling was in the subterranean regions of
> the house [the *Courier* office].

His sole duty being to prepare his lectures, he gave
much time to the assistance of Stuart and Street in
the conduct of their newspaper. Of this, the first[1]
course of lectures delivered by Coleridge, but a scanty
and fragmentary record remains.[2] Lamb writes to
Manning on February 26, 1808 : ' Coleridge has
delivered two lectures at the R.I. ; two more were
attended,[3] but he did not come. It is thought he
has gone sick upon them. He ain't well, that's certain.
Wordsworth[4] is coming to see him.' This sounds a
little unfeeling, as coming from Lamb ; but it was
mainly a letter from Mary Lamb,[5] which was bringing

---

[1] It was really the first, notwithstanding statements by Coleridge and his
editors to the contrary.

[2] The following is a list of all the lectures of this course, of which there is
any general or particular record, printed and unprinted : I. Jan. 12, 1808 ; II.
Feb. 5 ; III. and IV. before April 3. At least three more were given before
May 15, and several more in the course of the succeeding five or six weeks.
Notes of four were made by H. Crabb Robinson—see his *Diary*, etc., 1872, i.
140 ; and Mrs. H. N. Coleridge's *Notes and Lectures on Shakespeare* [by S. T.
C.] 1849. These are not included in *Lectures and Notes on Shakspere and other
English Poets*, by S. T. C., now first collected by T. Ashe (Bell, 1883), a useful,
and in many respects an excellent compilation.

[3] To the confusion of the sense, this word has hitherto been printed ' intended.' I quote from the original letter.

[4] On this, see *Mem. of Coleorton*, ii. 35.

[5] Coleridge had been ill and better again in December 1807 (*Mem. of Coleorton*, ii. 41). On Feb. 18, 1808, he reports to Beaumont that he has been ' very

Wordsworth to town.   I gather that Lamb suspected
opium to be largely responsible for his friend's illness, and that Wordsworth's moral influence would be
more powerful than his own.   Wordsworth came, and
Southey followed; and during their stay in town
Coleridge recovered, and before Wordsworth left on
the 3rd April he had heard two lectures, which (he
says) 'seemed to give great satisfaction,' although
Coleridge ' was not in spirits, and suffered much during
the week both in body and mind.'[1]   About this time
Coleridge reviewed his friend Clarkson's ' History of the
Abolition of the Slave-trade' in the *Edinburgh*.  He had
begged Jeffrey to be merciful to an imperfect book for
the sake of the almost perfect character of the author;
on which Jeffrey asked Coleridge to be himself the
critic.   Coleridge afterwards complained of gross mutilation of his MS. and of inversion of some of his
sentiments, especially as regards Pitt, whose sincerity
in the matter of Abolition, he had asserted.[2]   He

---

ill' for many weeks, with only two 'day-long intervals.' He has been able to
do nothing except to write 'a moral and political defence of the Copenhagen
business,' which requires only a concluding paragraph.   This no doubt was for
the *Courier* (see H. C. Robinson's *Diary*, etc., 1872, i. 138).   'I shall disgust
many friends,' he adds, but I do it from my *conscience*.   What other motive have
I?' (*M. of C.* ii. 47).   There is not a word about lectures.

[1] *Mem. of Coleorton*, ii. 48.

[2] Allsop's *Letters*, etc., p. 185.   The article was printed in the *Edinburgh
Review* for July 1808.   In a letter to Jeffrey (printed in the *Illustrated London
News* for June 10, 1893), dated 'Grasmere, Dec. 8, 1808,' Coleridge expresses his
thanks for the insertion of the article as an act of personal kindness and attention to
the request of one a stranger except by name, and says that the 'pecuniary remuneration' he had received was a surprise to him.   He mildly points out that the
alterations the article had undergone have not been very skilfully made; and complains of the inversion of the remarks on Pitt's favourable attitude towards Abolition.
Coleridge declares that 'such is his detestation of that pernicious minister, such
his contempt of the cowardice and fatuity of his measures, and his Horror at the
yet unended Train of their direful consequences, that if obedience to Truth could
ever be painful to him, this would have been.'   He acted well in praising Pitt,
but was pleased that Jeffrey 'acted equally well in altering' the passage 'according to his convictions.'   The only explanation of Coleridge's far-stretched complaisance is that he was at the time endeavouring to enlist Jeffrey's aid in getting
subscribers for *The Friend*, and meekly accepted two out of three emendations
in the phrasing of the Prospectus, which Jeffrey had suggested.

proposed to republish his review, corrected and aug-
mented, but he did not, and it has never been reprinted.[1] In May, Coleridge writes[2] of himself as
correcting and revising Wordsworth's *White Doe of
Rylstone*, then ready for the press. He is hampered
by 'the heat and bustle of these disgusting lectures,'
the next of which will be his first on 'Modern Poetry,'
to be followed, later on, by one on Wordsworth's
'System and Compositions.' The lectures came to an
end late in June.[3] De Quincey's statements[4] respecting Coleridge's condition during the period of the
lectures, and of his *frequent* failure to appear at
Albemarle Street, have much appearance of exaggeration. They are in no way corroborated by
Crabb Robinson, and the two failures reported by
Lamb were probably all that took place.

When the lectures were over, Coleridge went to
Bury St. Edmunds on a visit to the Clarksons. Mrs.
Clarkson was one of his most devoted and sympathetic friends, and one whose high qualities of mind
and heart were greatly appreciated by him. It was
no doubt owing to her good influence that he at this
time relinquished laudanum, or at least the abuse of it.
The abuse was no longer a secret from his intimates,
for soon after this visit he wrote thus to Stuart :—

I am hard at work, and feel a pleasure in it which I have not
known for years ; a consequence and reward of my courage in at

---

[1] *Letters from the Lake Poets*, p. 180 ; Allsop's *Letters*, etc., p. 185 ; *Frag.
Rem.* p. 102.

[2] Knight's *Life of W. W.* ii. 100.

[3] Whether he delivered the full contract number of sixteen, I know not, but
it seems probable he did, for he received the full fee of a hundred pounds—£40
advanced in October 1808 and £60 in March 1809. In April 1808 he had applied for the £60, and been refused. This lack of confidence was much resented
by him, and he immediately borrowed £100 from Stuart, part of which was
required to pay the premium on his life-policy (*Gent. Mag.* June 1838, p. 581 ;
*Letters from the Lake Poets*, p. 135).

[4] *Works* (1863), ii. 99.

length overcoming the fear of dying suddenly in my sleep, which, Heaven knows, alone seduced me into the fatal habit, etc. . . . If I entirely recover I shall deem it a sacred duty to publish my cure, tho' without my name, for the practice of taking opium is dreadfully spread.[1]

This was written from 'Allan Bank,' Wordsworth's recently-entered and very uncomfortable house at Grasmere. 'Coleridge has arrived at last' (wrote Southey to his brother Tom, September 9, 1808), 'about half as big as the house. He came with Wordsworth on Monday, and returned with him on Wednesday. His present scheme is to put the boys to school at Ambleside and reside at Grasmere himself.'[2] At Stowey, a year before, some such arrangement had been discussed as a contingency, but up to June 1808 nothing further had been said regarding it to Mrs. Coleridge. She was anxious, 'on the children's account,' that Greta Hall might be decided on, and the landlord, Jackson, was seconding her efforts by building some additional accommodation, fearing that, owing to the presence of the Southey family, Coleridge found too little privacy. On December 4, Miss Wordsworth writes from Allan Bank to Mrs. Marshall : 'At the time of the great storm, Mrs. Coleridge and her little girl[3] were here, and Mr. Coleridge is with us constantly. . . . Mr. Coleridge and his wife are separated, and I hope they will both be the happier for it. They are upon friendly terms, and occasionally see each other. In fact, Mrs. Coleridge was more than a week at Grasmere [Allan Bank] under the same roof with him. Coleridge intends to

---

1 *Letters from the Lake Poets*, p. 181, where the passage appears to be given incompletely.

2 *Life and Corr.* iii. 16.

3 See Sara Coleridge's recollections of this visit, printed in her *Memoirs* (1873), i. 17-20. The two boys had been placed at school at Ambleside.

spend the winter with us. On the [other] side of this paper you will find the Prospectus of a work which he is going to undertake; and I have little doubt but that it will be well executed if his health does not fail him; but on that score (though he is well at present) I have many fears.'[1]

The 'prospectus' was, of course, that of *The Friend*. Coleridge and his associates of this period must have used up a ream or two of it in their correspondence—one fly-leaf of the foolscap sheet having been left blank expressly for this advertising purpose. Early in December Coleridge wrote of his project to Davy[2]: 'My health and spirits are improved beyond my boldest hopes. A very painful effort of moral courage has been remunerated by tranquillity—by ease from the sting of self-disapprobation. I have done more for the last ten weeks than I had done for three years before. . . . I would willingly inform you of my chance of success in obtaining a sufficient number of subscribers, so as to justify me prudentially in commencing the work, but I do not possess grounds even for a sane conjecture. It will depend in a great measure on the zeal of my friends.' To Stuart and to Poole he wrote in the same strain, and to them he added an intimation that he had consulted a physician. To Poole he says he is now feeling 'the blessedness of walking altogether in the light,' which, taken in conjunction with the letter to Davy, we may interpret as meaning that opium-eating had been suspended for a time.[3]

---

[1] Knight's *Life*, ii. 120.

[2] *Frag. Rem.* p. 101.

[3] In all these letters of December, Coleridge writes of *The Friend* as of something of which they had been previously aware. Can it have been to some such project that Coleridge alluded in a mutilated passage of his letter to Wordsworth of May 1808? He has been writing of Wordsworth's pecuniary anxieties, and

The 'prospectus' mentioned by Miss Wordsworth was sent out without consultation with any one,[1] and the first number was announced for 'the first Saturday in January 1809,' 'in case of a sufficient number of subscribers being obtained.'

Of course *The Friend* did not appear on January 7. On January 18, Southey told Rickman: 'Meantime a hundred difficulties open upon him [Coleridge] in the way of publication, and doubtless some material changes must be made in the plan. . . . [*The Friend*] is expected to start in March.' At first *The Friend* was to be printed and published in London; next, in Kendal; but in February Coleridge arranged with 'a clever young man,' Mr. John Brown, to print and publish for him in Penrith. Then it was discovered that this clever young man had not type enough, and Coleridge had to buy £38 worth. On the 23rd March, Wordsworth, who had become very anxious, thus wrote to Poole[2]: 'I give it to you as my deliberate opinion, founded upon proofs which have been strengthening for years, that he neither will nor can execute anything of important benefit to himself, his family, or mankind'; all is 'frustrated by a derangement in his intellectual and moral constitution. In fact, he has no voluntary power of mind whatsoever, nor is he capable of acting under any *constraint* of duty or moral obligation.' *The Friend* may appear, 'but it cannot go on for any

goes on : 'Indeed, before my fall . . . I had indulged the hope that, by division of labour, you would have no occasion to think about . . . [*sic* in *Life*] as, with very warm and zealous patronage, I was fast ripening a plan which secures from £12 to £20 a week (the prospectus, indeed, going to the press as soon as Mr. Sotheby and Sir G. Beaumont had read it).' Knight's *Life*, ii. 102.

[1] *Letters of R. S.* ii. 120. See an interesting letter from Coleridge to Thomas Wilkinson (Wordsworth's friend of the 'Spade') Dec. 31, 1799, on the prospectus of *The Friend* in the *Friend's Quarterly Examiner* for July 1893—Art. 'S. T. Coleridge on Quaker Principles'; and *Athenæum* for Sept. 16, 1893— Art. 'Coleridge on Quaker Principles.'

[2] Knight's *Life of W. W.* ii. 124.

length of time.   I am *sure* it cannot.   C., I understand,
has been three weeks at Penrith,' and will answer no
letters.   And then he calls on Poole to come to the
rescue—in summer, for it is of no use to attempt to
stop Coleridge *now*.   A week later (March 30)
Wordsworth wrote again to Poole—Coleridge, he says,
has not been at Grasmere for a month.   He is now at
Keswick, 'having had a great deal of trouble about
arranging the publication of *The Friend*. . . . I cannot say that Coleridge has been managing himself
well.'   Probably he had heard from Southey that
opium was again in the ascendant.   Poole, Stuart,
Montagu, and Clarkson were advancing money for the
stamped paper.[1]   It was sent, unfortunately, by the
wrong route and did not arrive till May 8.   At last, but
not until June 1st, *The Friend* No. I. appeared.[2]   'The
mode of payment by subscribers will be announced in
a future number,' promised Coleridge, and in No. II.
this promise was fulfilled—characteristically, by a vague
proposal that payment should be made 'at the close of
each twentieth week.'   The third number will be de-
ferred for a fortnight (instead of a week) to allow lists of
subscribers to come in, and arrangements to be made
for mode of payment.   Nothing more was said about
the matter until after the issue of the twentieth number,
at the end of the year.

Having seen No. II. despatched on June 8, Cole-

---

[1] The stamp on each number was 3½d., but there were discounts which reduced the cost to little more than 3d.

[2] 'THE FRIEND ; a Literary, Moral, and Political Weekly Paper, excluding
Personal and Party Politics and Events of the Day.   Conducted by S. T. Coleridge of Grasmere, Westmoreland.   Each number will contain a stamped sheet
of large Octavo, like the present ; and will be delivered free of expence, by the
Post, throughout the Kingdom, to Subscribers.   The Price each Number One
Shilling. . . . Penrith : Printed and Published by J. Brown.'   The continuity
of issue was frequently broken—thus there were eight blank weeks between II.
and III. ; three between III. and IV. ; one between XI. and XII ; one between
XX. and XXI. ; and one between XXVI. and XXVII. and last.

ridge returned from Penrith to Grasmere and wrote to
Stuart[1]: 'I printed 620 of No. I. and 650 of No. II.,
and so many more are called for that I shall be forced
to reprint both as soon as I hear from Clarkson [re-
garding fresh stocks of paper].[2] The proof-sheet of
No. III. goes back to-day, and with it the "copy" of
No. IV., so that henceforth we shall be secure of
regularity.' Alas! No. III. appeared on August 10—
seven weeks late; and No. IV. on September 7—
again three weeks late. And no wonder. The conditions were impossible. There was Coleridge himself; there were the imperfect arrangements for
supplies of paper; and, as if these hindrances were
not enough, there were the relative situations of
Grasmere and Penrith. The mere distance, 28 miles,
was nothing; but there was no direct post, and Kirkstone Pass lay, a veritable lion, in the path. The
defective postal system was only ameliorated by the
passage of chance chaises either way, but once when
the printing-house rats had devoured a page-long
motto from Hooker, and two fresh transcripts were
entrusted by Coleridge to two drivers, both failed of
delivery to the printer; and No. VIII. was, in consequence, issued a week after due date. Then the
subscription-list plan proved a bad one, as Coleridge
publicly confessed in after years.[3] In January 1810
he made the same confession in a letter to Lady
Beaumont[4]—many subscribers withdrew their names,

---

1 *Letters from the Lake Poets*, p. 166. 'June 13.'

2 A collation of a set of stamped, with the set of unstamped, numbers issued
with a title-page in 1812, shows that the first twelve numbers in the volume were
*revised reprints* done in 1809.

3 *Biog. Lit.* 1817, i. 162. The real facts of the story there given about 'the
gentleman who procured nearly a hundred names' will be found in *Mem. of
Coleorton*, ii. 99. A comparison of the two versions will repay the curious
student.

4 *Mem. of Coleorton*, ii. 96-108.

and many of those who did not, withheld the money.
Nearly all complained that the contents were too dull,
and an attempt was made to enliven the pages by
printing 'Satyrane's Letters.' These, with contributions in prose and verse from Wordsworth, practically
filled up the numbers from November 23 to January
25 (1810), when the 'Sketches and Fragments of the
Life and Character of the late Sir Alexander Ball'[1]
began—a series, too long indeed, but destined never
to be completed.

While *The Friend* was being abandoned to
Satyrane and Wordsworth, Coleridge was contributing a series of letters to the *Courier*[2] 'On the
Spaniards,' with the view of exciting British sympathy
in the struggles of that nation against Napoleon. His
own feelings were thoroughly roused—'for this' (he
wrote) 'is not a quarrel of Governments, but the war
of a people against the armies of a remorseless invader,
usurper, and tyrant.' 'Coleridge's spirits have been
irregular of late,' wrote Miss Wordsworth to Lady
Beaumont at the beginning of March 1810.[3] 'He
was damped after the twentieth number by the slow
arrival of payments,[4] and half persuaded himself that
he ought not to go on. We laboured hard against
such a resolve, and he seems determined to fight onwards.' And she proceeds to describe how, from the
commencement, *The Friend* had been produced by fits

---

[1] It is commonly stated, on what authority I know not, that Coleridge and
Ball had got on very badly, and that the laudation in *The Friend* was insincere. All
the evidence derivable from Coleridge's correspondence and diaries of the period
points in the opposite direction. I suspect that Stoddart spread reports about
Coleridge which were coloured by his resentment of real or imaginary injuries.

[2] No. I. appeared on December 7, 1809, and No. VIII. and last on January
20, 1810. Reprinted in *Essays on his own Times*, pp. 593-676.

[3] *Mem. of Coleorton*, ii. 109-115.

[4] 'Of the small number who have paid in their subscriptions, two-thirds,
nearly, have discontinued the work.' S. T. C. to Lady Beaumont, January 21
1810 (*Mem. of Coleorton*, ii. 97).

and starts—sometimes a number in two days, sometimes not a line composed for 'weeks and weeks';
the papers being generally dictated to Miss Sarah
Hutchinson, and never retranscribed.[1]   In the same
letter Miss Wordsworth announces that Miss Hutchinson's prolonged visit was to come to an end in a
fortnight.   'Coleridge most of all will miss her, as she
has transcribed almost every paper of *The Friend* for
the press.'   So much did Coleridge miss his devoted
secretary, that *The Friend* came to an end with her
visit to Allan Bank—flickering out with 'No. XXVII.,
Thursday March 15, 1810'—the last printed words,
'(To be concluded in our next number),' referring to
the articles about Ball.

So perished, one cannot say untimely, a work which
Hazlitt not inaptly described as 'an enormous title-page
. . . an endless preface to an imaginary work.'   But
it was, like all that came from Coleridge, an integral
part of himself, and therefore a heap of ore rich in
finest metal.   *The Friend* of Highgate and 1818,
which he himself described as a '*rifacimento*'
of the original, was practically a new work.   The
original would bear reprinting, for it is now unknown
except to the curious book-collector.

During the long period of Coleridge's domestication with the Wordsworths a good deal of friendly
intercourse was kept up between Allan Bank and
Greta Hall; and the Coleridge boys, who were at
school at Ambleside, spent most of their weekly
holidays with the Wordsworths.   The following
passage from a letter[2] of Mrs. Coleridge to Miss
Betham is pleasant reading, not only for the tone in

[1] The MSS. with some correspondence therewith connected are preserved
in the Forster Collection at South Kensington.
[2] Unprinted.   'Greta Hall, December 19, 1809.'

which her husband and the Wordsworths are mentioned, but as showing that Coleridge and Lloyd no
longer shunned each other. 'Brathay' was Lloyd's
home. 'My dear friend, I know it will give you
[pleasure] to hear that I was very comfortable during
my visits in Westmoreland. C[oleridge] came often to
Brathay, before I went to Grasmere, and kindly ac-
ceded to my wish of taking my little daughter home
again with me after she had passed a fortnight with
him at Allan Bank. His first intention was to keep
her with him until Christmas, and then to bring her
home with her brothers.· . . . C. is to spend the last
week of the boys' holidays here, and take them back
with him [to Ambleside]. . . . I hope you will soon
come again to see us, and I will introduce you to C.,
and *he* to his invaluable friends.'

Coleridge's movements after the cessation of *The
Friend* in the middle of March are not easy to trace.
On the 15th April he wrote to Lady Beaumont
from Ambleside, excusing himself for inattention to
a letter which had arrived at Grasmere when his depression of spirits 'amounted to little less than absolute
despondency.' He had only that day found courage
to open the letter, which contained an 'enclosure.'
He must not accuse himself of idleness, for he has
been 'willing to exert energy, only not in anything
which the duty of the day demanded.' The next
glimpse is in a letter from Mrs. Coleridge to Poole,
dated October 3.[1] The poor wife knows not 'what to
think or what to do.' Coleridge has been at Greta
Hall for four or five months 'in an almost uniform
kind disposition towards us all.' His spirits have been

---

[1] *T. Poole and his Friends*, ii. 241. The date is printed 'August 3,' but the
month must have been October.

better than for years, and he has been reading Italian to both the Saras—only, he has been doing nothing else. 'The last number of *The Friend* lies on his desk, the sight of which fills my heart with grief and my eyes with tears,' and the writer never ceases to pray that ' Mr. Poole were here.'

# CHAPTER X

## LONDON

In October, Basil Montagu, with his wife and her little daughter (Anne Benson Skepper, afterwards Mrs. B. W. Proctor), called at Greta Hall on his way south from a tour in Scotland. There was a vacant place in the chaise, and this Coleridge took, the party arriving at Montagu's residence (55 Frith Street, Soho), on the 26th October. Coleridge was to have been a guest there for an indefinite period, but within a few days the visit came to an abrupt and painful end. When the chaise halted at Allan Bank, and Wordsworth learnt that Coleridge was to become an inmate of the Montagu household, he expressed to Montagu, in confidence, a fear that some of Coleridge's ways would prove inconvenient in a well-ordered town establishment. This he did with the kindest motives, and no doubt in the kindest terms, thinking that prevention was better than cure—if Coleridge and Montague became housemates they would quarrel, which would be a misfortune for both, especially for Coleridge. Three days after arrival in London, Montagu informed Coleridge that he had been commissioned by Wordsworth to say to him that certain of his (Coleridge's)

habits had made him an intolerable guest at Allan Bank,
and that he (Wordsworth) had 'no hope for him.'  Unfortunately Coleridge believed this monstrous story, and,
soon after, he left Montagu's roof, taking refuge with
the Morgans, then living at Hammersmith.  He was
heart-broken that Wordsworth could have said such
things of him,—much more, that he should have commissioned Montagu to repeat them.  But for a long
time he said nothing.  The breach between the two
poets remained open until May 1812, when a reconciliation was effected by the good offices of Crabb
Robinson.  It turned out, of course, that Wordsworth
had neither used the wounding (even coarse) language
attributed to him with regard to Coleridge's personal
habits, nor said anything in the spirit attributed to him ;
nor had he commissioned Montagu to repeat to Coleridge anything whatever—very much the contrary.
He confessed to having said (or implied) to Montagu
that he had 'little or no hope' of Coleridge, and expressed deep regret that he had said anything at all to
so indiscreet a man as Montagu.[1]  Letters declared to
be 'mutually satisfactory' were exchanged by the two
poets, and the troubled air was stilled ; but each was
conscious that it was also darkened, and that in their
friendship there could never be 'glad confident
morning again.'

To return to the winter of 1810.  It was on the
3rd November that Coleridge began his visit to the
Morgans at No. 7 Portland Place, Hammersmith—a

---

[1] Southey's deliverance was as follows, in an unprinted letter of April 25,
1812, to Miss Betham : 'My own opinion is . . . that Montagu has acted with
a degree of folly which would be absolutely incredible in any other person ; that
W. is no otherwise blameable than as having said anything to such a man which
he would have felt any dislike to seeing in the *Morning Post* ; that I do not
wonder at C.'s resentment.'  The story of the quarrel between Coleridge and
Montagu as told by De Quincey (*Works*, 1863, ii. 120) is no better founded than
the accompanying statement that the quarrel was never made up.

visit which, with few and short interruptions, lasted until 1816, when the still longer one to the Gillmans began. Wordsworth and Montagu had broken down —and even, to some extent, Poole; but without a moment's delay, there presented itself to the perplexed traveller another of those 'perpetual relays' (to use De Quincey's words) 'which were laid along Coleridge's path in life.' As at Bristol in 1807, the family which now gave him shelter consisted of Mr. and Mrs. Morgan and Miss Charlotte Brent, the sister of Mrs. Morgan. For some months Coleridge seems to have done nothing but go about among his friends and talk to them divinely. Henry Crabb Robinson first met him at Lamb's on the 14th November, and for some time thenceforward became his Boswell, writing down in his diary [1] summaries of Coleridge's discourse. Lamb describes his old friend at this time in a fashion not altogether reassuring: 'Coleridge has powdered his head, and looks like Bacchus, Bacchus ever sleek and young. He is going to turn sober, but his clock has not struck yet; meantime he pours down goblet after goblet. . . .' [2] On November 28 he tells Hazlitt that Coleridge is writing or going to write in the *Courier* against Cobbett, and is in favour of paper-money; but so far as can be traced his connection with the *Courier* did not begin until April. In February, Mrs. Coleridge informed Miss Betham [3] that since his departure from Greta Hall, Coleridge 'had not *once*

---

[1] *Diary, Reminiscences and Correspondence of H. C. Robinson.* Selected and edited by Thomas Sadler, Ph.D. 3 vols. 1870. My references are to the 'third edition, with corrections and additions,' in two volumes, 1872.

[2] Letter to Miss Wordsworth dated '[August 1810],' but it must have been written in November or December. *Letters*, i. 262.

[3] Letter printed in *Fraser's Magazine*, July 1878, p. 75. ' *P.S.*—This very day Coleridge left us four months ago; he had been here five months in better health, spirits, and humour than I had seen him for any great length of time for years before. I fear he has been different since he left us' (Feb. 16, 1811).

addressed any of his northern friends,' and that she had only just heard, and by chance, of her husband being domiciled with the Morgans, and that he had been applying for advice from Dr. Abernethy. 'I wish C. would write!' exclaims the sorely-tried wife, 'both Southey and myself have written often to him' —letters which, as we know, the recipient had felt himself incapable of opening.

In March, Coleridge wrote what he calls an unnecessarily long letter to Robinson—'long enough for half a dozen letters,' 'when to have written to half a dozen claimants is a moral (would it were a physical) necessity. The moral obligation is to me so very strong a stimulant, that in nine cases out of ten it acts as a narcotic. The blow that should rouse, *stuns* me.' [1] This was merely his own way of putting Hazlitt's saying that Coleridge was capable of doing anything which did not present itself as a duty. In this letter Coleridge says that he has been extremely unwell. George Burnett's death—in the hospital of Marylebone workhouse—has upset Mary Lamb, and her illness 'has almost overset me.' Robinson, however, attributed Mary Lamb's illness to the excessive stimulation produced by too much of Coleridge's company. In April he proposed to Stuart [2] to become a sort of assistant to Street, the editor of the *Courier*.

If it were desirable I could be at the office every morning by half-past nine, to read over all the morning papers, etc., and point out whatever seemed valuable to Mr. Street; that I might occasionally write the leading paragraph when he might wish to go into the City or to the public offices; and, besides this, I would carry on a series of articles, a column and a half or two columns each, independent of small paragraphs, poems, etc., as would fill whatever room there was in the *Courier*, when there was room.

---

[1] *Diaries*, i. 189.    [2] *Letters from the Lake Poets*, p. 191.

He humbly urges that he would make 'no pretence
to any control or intermeddlement,' and begs to be
allowed 'a month's trial.'   Stuart referred him to
Street, and on May 5 Coleridge informed Stuart that
from Street he had had 'a warm assent.'   'As to weekly
salary he said nothing, and I said nothing, except that
he would talk with you.'   Coleridge would therefore
begin next morning at half-past eight.   He would
come up by the stage which passed Portland Place at
7.20.   He adds that he has 'written to Keswick to
calm Mrs. Coleridge's disquietudes concerning the
annuity'—by which he means the premium of £27
a year on his life-policy for £1000, taken out in 1803.
Money for this he had just borrowed from Stuart.
He also proposes to 'finish off the next number of
*The Friend*, which will contain a full detail of the plan
of a monthly work including *The Friend*'—a work
which had been suggested to him by Baldwin, the
publisher.   Nothing came of the 'monthly work,' but
Coleridge began at once in the *Courier*, doing a good
deal of work both as a sub-editor and as a contributor [1]
during the ensuing five months.   His connection with
the paper nearly broke down in July.   An article he
had written on the Duke of York was printed on the
12th, but the Government having heard of it, procured
its suppression at the sacrifice of about 2000 copies
which had been struck off.[2]   This mightily offended
Coleridge, whose suspicions that the *Courier* was not
altogether independent were now confirmed, and he
moved Crabb Robinson to endeavour to get him an
engagement on the *Times*.   Robinson's endeavours

---

[1] The contributions of 1811 reprinted in *Essays on his own Times* begin
with April 19 and end with September 27, filling pp. 733-938.   Mr. Traill considers them as in all respects much inferior to the early work in the *Morning Post*.
[2] *Diaries of H. C. R.* i. 177, and *Essays on his own Times*, pp. 850, 1027.

failed, however, and Coleridge went on with the
*Courier* until the end of September.

About this time he seems to have thought of
resuming his old *rôle* of lecturer; and before the end
of October he issued a prospectus of a course of fifteen
lectures to be given in the rooms of the 'London
Philosophical Society, Scots Corporation Hall, Crane
Court, Fleet Street (entrance from Fetter Lane).'
The lectures were to be 'on Shakespeare and Milton
in illustration of the Principles of Poetry, and their
application as grounds of Criticism to the most popular
works of later English Poets, those of the living
included.' The prices of the tickets were two guineas
for the single and three for the double. The first
lecture was delivered on the day appointed, 18th
November, and the others followed in due succession,
on Mondays and Thursdays, until January 27, 1812—
seventeen in all. Coleridge did not write out his
lectures, but delivered them extemporaneously, de-
claring that even the notes he held in his hand
hampered him.[1] Two unfortunate consequences resulted—the lecturer was frequently desultory and
digressive, and the lectures have come down to us
only in fragmentary reports. The fragments, however, which have been recovered from contemporary
newspapers, from Crabb Robinson's diaries, and from
J. P. Collier's note-books,[2] suffice to show that Cole-

[1] The Morgans complained that Coleridge *would* not look into his Shakespeare, which they were continually putting in his way; and that, as if spellbound, he would make no preparation for his lectures except by occasional
reference to an old MS. commonplace book.

[2] *Lectures and Notes on Shakspere and other English Poets.* By S. T.
Coleridge. Now first collected by T. Ashe. London 1883.—Much unnecessary
doubt was cast on the authenticity of Collier's shorthand notes when he printed
them in 1856 (*Seven Lectures on Shakespeare and Milton*, etc.), by critics who
forgot that Collier was quite incapable of inventing what he put forward as
Coleridge's. More extended reports of the first eight lectures, by a Mr. Tomalin,
have recently been discovered and may yet be published.

ridge's audiences probably heard the finest literary criticism which has ever been given in English. Writing after the fourth lecture, Robinson says that Coleridge has had 'about 150 hearers on an average.' From Byron's correspondence [1] we learn that Rogers attended on several occasions, on one of which he heard Campbell attacked by name, and himself 'indirectly.' 'We are going in a party' (wrote Byron) 'to hear the new Art of Poetry by the reformed schismatic'; and again on December 15 he writes: 'To-morrow I dine with Rogers and am to hear Coleridge, who is a sort of rage at present.' On January 20, Robinson saw Byron and Rogers among the audience. On that day week the course 'ended' (says Robinson) 'with *éclat*. The room was crowded, and the lecture had several passages more than brilliant.'

Immediately after this Coleridge set off for Greta Hall, picking up on the way and carrying home with him his two boys from their school at Ambleside. During the weeks he remained with Mrs. Coleridge, she received many letters and messages from Miss Wordsworth begging her to urge Coleridge to write to her, and on no account to leave the Lake country without seeing them. It was all in vain. But 'the Grasmere business,' wrote Coleridge to Morgan (March 27, 1812), 'has kept me in a fever of agitation. Wordsworth has refused to apologise, and has thus made his choice between me and Basil Montagu. I have been in such a fever about the Wordsworths, my reason deciding one way, my heart pulling me the contrary; scarcely daring to set off without seeing them. Brown, the printer of *The Friend*, who had £20 or £30 of mine and £36 worth

[1] Moore's *Life*, one-vol. ed. pp. 147, 148.

of types, about 14 days ago ran off and absconded.'[1]
It was probably a hope of saving something out of the
wreck of Brown's estate that caused Coleridge to take
Penrith on his way back to London, but it hardly
excuses him for staying there a whole month without
communicating with his wife or any of his friends,
who had begun to feel great anxiety long before he
reappeared in town towards the end of April. An
unpublished letter of Mrs. Coleridge describes her
husband as 'cheerful' during his stay at Greta Hall.
He talked of settling with her and the children in
London, after a year—a proposal which Mrs. Coleridge listened to gravely, suggesting that until the
children's education was completed, it was better she
and they should remain in the country; after which
she would willingly follow his amended fortunes. So
this scheme was settled, and Coleridge promised that
he would write regularly, and that never, never again
would he leave his wife's, or the boys', or Southey's
letters unopened. It was probably during this visit—
the last he ever paid to the Lake country—that Coleridge contributed his quota—meagre in quantity, but
in quality far out-weighing the other—to *Omniana*,[2]
which was published in the following October—
'Coleridge,' wrote Southey in November, 'kept the
press waiting fifteen months for an unfinished article,
so that at last I ordered the sheet in which it was
begun to be cancelled, in despair.'[3]

On his arrival in London, Coleridge returned to
the Morgans, who were now living at 71 Berners Street,

---

[1] Letter printed in the Catalogue of Mr. Locker-Lampson's collection at
Rowfant, p. 200. The month is there misprinted as 'May.'

[2] 'OMNIANA, or *Horæ otiosiores*.' 2 vols. 1812. An interesting selection
from the commonplace books of Coleridge and Southey.

[3] November 5, 1812. *Letters of R. S.* ii. 299.

Oxford Street, and immediately issued a prospectus for a series of lectures 'on the Drama of the Greek, French, English, and Spanish stage, chiefly with reference to the works of Shakespeare.' They were to be delivered at Willis's Rooms, 'on the Tuesdays and Fridays in May and June, at 3 o'clock precisely,' beginning on May 12th. 'An account is opened at Messrs. Ransom, Morland, & Co., Bankers, Pall Mall, in the names of Sir G. Beaumont, Bart., Sir T. Barnard, Bart., and W. Sotheby, Esqre., where subscriptions will be received and tickets issued.' Coleridge made his first appearance on the new platform just a week behind time; a delay attributable probably to the negotiations then being carried on by Robinson for the reconciliation with Wordsworth.[1] These negotiations began on May 3, and ended happily, as already described, on the 11th. Of this course, the only record with which I am acquainted is contained in Robinson's diary.[2] Wordsworth attended one of the lectures. At what proved to be the last, on June 5, Coleridge announced a further course to take place in the winter, for which the money would be taken at the doors—a change in business arrangements which seems to show that the array of fine names and a Pall Mall banking-house had not proved a success.

---

[1] See p. 180 *supra*.

[2] *Diaries*, i. 200-203. On May 3, Robinson, who was one of the few Englishmen who then knew anything about the German Philosophers, records that Coleridge told him in conversation that from Fichte and Schelling 'he had not gained any one great idea. To Kant his obligations are infinite, not so much from what Kant has taught him in the form of doctrine, as from the discipline gained in studying the great German philosopher. Coleridge is indignant at the low estimation in which the post-Kantians affect to hold their master.' Again, on May 29, Coleridge said that 'he adheres to Kant, notwithstanding all Schelling has written, and maintained that from the latter he has gained no new ideas. All Schelling has said, Coleridge [asserts that he] has thought [for] himself or found in Jacob Boehme.' One wonders whether Robinson has reported accurately?

On August 7 he expressed to Stuart[1] a wish to rejoin the *Courier*, but only as an occasional contributor, proposing to send in within the next fortnight some twenty articles on current Church and State politics. His finances have been thrown behindhand by the rewriting of his play, and by composing the second volume of *The Friend*, but he hopes before another eight days have passed to submit the tragedy to the theatre-people, and if they will not have it, to accept Gale & Curtis's offer to publish it. He has also been consulting a new doctor.

Some time before the beginning of October Coleridge's 'rewritten play,' with its new title of *Remorse*, had been, through the influence of Lord Byron, accepted by the Drury Lane Committee,[2] whose new theatre was about to be opened. In October there was issued a 'Syllabus of a Course of Lectures on the Belles Lettres, to be delivered by S. T. Coleridge, Esqre., at the Surrey Institution.' Lecture I. was to be on the right use of words; II. and III. on the Evolution of the Fine Arts; IV. on Poetry in general; V. on Greek Mythology; VI. on the connection between the diffusion of Christianity and the formation of modern languages; VII. on Shakespeare; VIII. a philosophical analysis of *Romeo and Juliet* and of *Hamlet;* IX. on *Macbeth* and *Othello;* X. on Shakespeare; and XI. and XII. on *Paradise Lost.* I have summarised the somewhat lengthy syllabus from the unique copy preserved by Crabb Robinson. It has no dates, price of tickets, or the like; but I have elsewhere found that the lectures were given on consecutive

---

[1] *Letters from the Lake Poets*, p. 213.

[2] 'Do you see or hear anything of Coleridge? Lamb writes to Lloyd that C.'s play has been accepted. Heaven grant it success' (Wordsworth to Stuart, *Letters from the Lake Poets*, p. 359).

Tuesday evenings; and that Robinson attended the
first on Nov. 3. He says it was a repetition of former
lectures, and dull. As the two men walked away
from the lecture-room together, they talked of Spinoza,
and Coleridge projected a series of lectures on Education, 'each to be delivered in a state in which it may
be sent to the press.'[1] Robinson seems to have
attended seven of the lectures. Of the earlier of those
heard by him, he gives a poor account, but the twelfth
he describes as a very eloquent and popular discourse
on the general character of Shakespeare (the subject
announced was 'Milton'), and of the concluding lecture (Jan. 26) he says that Coleridge was 'received
with three rounds of applause on entering the room,
and very loudly applauded at the close. . . . He this
evening, as well as on three or four preceding nights,
redeemed the reputation he lost at the commencement of the course.' So far as I am aware, Robinson's
jottings form the only record of these lectures.

On Dec. 6, Robinson found Coleridge at Morgan's,
in good spirits, and determined to devote himself to
the Drama—chiefly to Melodrama and Comic Opera.
On the following day he wrote to Robinson requesting
the loan of Goethe's *Theory of Colours*, and repeating
his determination respecting the drama—expecting
to profit by Goethe's happy mode of introducing
incidental songs.[2] He mentions another little project,
'one steady effort to understand music.'

On December 22, Coleridge informs Stuart[3] that
his play is in rehearsal, and that he finds the repeated
alterations rather a tedious business. The managers
are more sanguine than he is, and with one exception

---

[1] *Diaries*, etc. i. 209.          [2] *Diaries*, i. 222.
[3] *Letters from the Lake Poets*, p. 217.

the performers are pleased and gratified with their parts. On the 23rd January 1813, *Remorse* was first produced at Drury Lane. All the accounts which have come down to us describe the performance as, on the whole, a great success.[1] The best evidence, however, is the fact that it ran for twenty nights, and that Coleridge received for his share £400—the contract being that he was to get £100 each for the 3rd, 6th, 9th, and 20th night. For the pamphlet[2] of the play he received from the publisher two-thirds of the profits, and as it ran into a third edition, the author's share may have been something considerable. In a long letter to Southey,[3] written while *Remorse* was still on the boards, Coleridge speaks of the praise it had extorted from a hostile press—notably the *Examiner*, Leigh Hunt's paper, to which Hazlitt was a regular contributor. These critics, he says, as a matter of course temper their praise of the play by general accusations of 'sentimentalities, puerilities, whinings, and meannesses, both of style and thought'

---

[1] H. C. Robinson's *Diaries*, etc., i. 212; *Autobiographical Recollections of C. R. Leslie, R.A.*, by T. Taylor, 1860, ii. 32-34. Newspaper notices collected in OSORIO : *a Tragedy*. London: Pearson, 1873; *Reminiscences* (1826) of Michael Kelly, who composed the very successful incidental music.

[2] REMORSE, a Tragedy in five Acts. By S. T. Coleridge.

> Remorse is as the heart, in which it grows :
> If that be gentle, it drops balmy dews
> Of true repentance ; but if proud and gloomy,
> It is a poison-tree, that pierced to the inmost
> Weeps only tears of poison !
>                                        ACT I. SCENE I.

LONDON : Printed for W. Pople, 67 Chancery Lane. 1813. Price Three Shillings. Octavo, pp. xii.; 72.

The 'Second Edition' differs materially from the first. The 'Third Edition' is a mere reprint of the 'Second,' and copies sold slowly. (Lamb's *Letters*, i. 274.) Charles Lamb supplied the 'Prologue'—it was an adaptation, not very skilfully executed, of his 'Rejected Address' for the opening of Drury Lane—and Coleridge supplied the 'Epilogue.' See Notes to REMORSE in *Poet. Works*, 1893.

[3] 'Tuesday, Feb. 8. 1813, 71 Berners Street.' Printed in the *Illustrated London News* for June 24, 1893—a letter of great and varied interest.

in his former writings, but 'without one single quotation or reference in proof or exemplification.' As far
as his own judgment goes,

the two best qualities of the tragedy are, first, the simplicity and
unity of the plot, in respect of that which of all the unities is
the only one founded on good sense—the presence of a one all-
pervading, all-combining Principle. . . . The second good quality is
I think the variety of metres according as the speeches are merely
transitive, or narrative, or passionate, or (as in the Incantation),
deliberate and formal poetry. It is true they are all, or almost all,
Iambic blank verse, but under that form there are five or six perfectly distinct metres. As to the outcry that the *Remorse* is not
pathetic (meaning such pathos as convulses in *Isabella*, or *The
Gamester*), the answer is easy. True ! the poet never meant that it
should be. It is as pathetic as the *Hamlet* or the *Julius Cæsar*. . . .
As to my thefts from *Wallenstein*, they came on compulsion from
the necessity of haste, and do not lie on my conscience, being
partly thefts from myself, and because I gave Schiller twenty for one
I have taken. . . . The house was crowded again last night, and the
Manager told me that they had lost £200 by suspending it on the
Saturday night that Jack Bannister came out.

Coleridge says nothing of the less admirable
qualities he must have detected in the tragedy, and
which are the more prominent to the student of to-day.
His partiality for the only offspring of his pen which
earned pudding as well as praise, is not surprising, but
there was another reason not so apparent. In 1820,
Coleridge told Allsop that *Remorse* was still a great
favourite of his, 'the more so as certain pet abstract
notions of mine are therein expounded.'[1] Whatever
we may think of *Remorse* as play or poem, we must
rejoice that it hit the taste of playgoers of the period,
and that its good fortune served to cheer the poet.

When Poole heard of his old friend's success,
he was prompted to send him congratulations, and
these, says Mrs. Sandford, 'drew forth an instant
response penetrated with all the old tenderness.' In

[1] *Letters*, etc. p. 51.

the same letter to Poole there followed 'an out-
pouring of grief and difficulties, with some allusion at
the end to the withdrawal of the Wedgwood pension, and to the "year - long difference" between
Wordsworth and himself, compared with the sufferings of which, he writes, "all former afflictions of
my life were less than flea - bites." They were
reconciled, indeed, " but — aye there remains the
immedicable But." ' [1]

The reference in this letter is one of the earliest I
have found as to the withdrawal by Josiah Wedgwood
of his half of the pension of £150 granted in 1798.
As already explained,[2] the total pension was granted
to Coleridge for life, and absolutely free from conditions
except 'the wreck of the Wedgwoods' fortune.' Josiah
Wedgwood's present action is unaccountable save on
the assumption that he had entirely forgotten the
terms of his letter of Jan. 10, 1798. But this assumption is hardly tenable, for as a man of the strictest
business habits, he must have kept an accurately filed
copy of so important a letter. Even had this been
lost, or mislaid, Josiah Wedgwood cannot have been
unaware that his brother's half-share had been at the
time secured legally to Coleridge for life, and this fact
was of itself proof, *prima facie*, that the whole had been
granted on the same terms. Very reluctantly, for
Josiah Wedgwood had otherwise shown himself to be
just and generous, I am driven to the conclusion that
the withdrawal was a high-handed proceeding, and
that Coleridge, though he must have been aware of

---

[1] *T. Poole and his Friends*, ii. 244.
[2] See p. 83 *supra*. The withdrawal must have taken place at the end of
1812. Miss Meteyard's unsupported statement (*Group of Englishmen*, p. 378)
that it took place in 1811, has hitherto been accepted. Her justification of
Wedgwood was written in ignorance of the unconditional terms on which the
pension had been granted.

this, made no complaint,[1] owing to a painful consciousness that the benefaction had not been used for the
high purposes which had led both to the granting and
to the acceptance of it. Practically, Mrs. Coleridge
was the sufferer by the withdrawal of the half, for the
whole had been for many years at her disposal.
Neither did she, disheartened though she was by the
loss of income, at a time when sorely tried by the
increasing expenses, actual and prospective, of the
children, bring any accusation against Wedgwood.

On the 1st December 1812 a shadow was cast on
Wordsworth's household by the death of his little son,
Thomas. It seemed to them as if their sun had gone
down, and Coleridge was deeply moved. As soon as
the sad news reached him he wrote to Wordsworth
a long letter overflowing with affectionate sympathy[2]:

O that it were within my power to be with you myself instead of
my letter. The Lectures I could give up; but the rehearsal of my
Play commences this week, and upon this depends my best hopes of
leaving town after Christmas, and living among you as long as I
live. . . . What comfort ought I not to afford, who have given you
so much pain? . . . I am distant from you some hundred miles,
but glad I am that I am no longer distant in spirit, and have faith,
that as it has happened but once, so it never can happen again.

Of this letter, in which Coleridge humbled himself
in presence of the sorrow which had darkened his
friend's home, Prof. Knight (who does not print the
letter in full) says: 'I fancy there were phrases and
statements in it which the Wordsworths did not like,
and that no immediate reply was sent to Coleridge.'
Whatever may have been done, or left undone by the

---

[1] 'I feel my mind rather lightened,' he wrote on the subject to Stuart, 'and
am glad that I can now enjoy the sensation of sincere gratitude towards him [J.
Wedgwood] for the past, and most unfeigned esteem and affection, without the
weight that every year seemed to accumulate upon it' (Letter to Stuart in
*Letters from the Lake Poets*, p. 218).

[2] Knight's *Life of W. W.* ii. 181.

Wordsworths, it is certain that Coleridge felt himself deeply wounded, for when he was free to go north he did not go. On March 10, Mrs. Clarkson wrote to Robinson [1] :—

> C., as I told you, wrote to them [the Wordsworths] several times after the death of little Tom, and said that he would . . . certainly go were it [the play] successful. William and Dorothy have both written to him to say that nothing would do W. so much good as his company and conversation. He has taken no notice whatever of these letters ; . . . and they have heard by a letter from Mr. Morgan to Southey or Mrs. C., that C. is going out of town to the seaside ! ! !  Imagine them in the depths of sorrow, receiving this cutting intelligence. . . . The account of the state of the family at Grasmere would make your heart ache—supposing myself to have been deeply injured, would one wish for a more noble triumph than to fly to the succour of the friend who had inflicted the wound ?

It was at the request, expressed or implied, of the Wordsworths that Mrs. Clarkson was endeavouring to soften Coleridge's heart. She saw him at Morgan's, but he seems to have been obdurate. Mary Lamb took Coleridge's side, and 'after all,' acknowledged Mrs. Clarkson on March 29th, ' I do incline to think with M. L[amb] [2] that there is something amongst

---

[1] Knight's *Life of W. W.* ii. 182-184.

[2] It will be remembered that Coleridge was in Malta when John Wordsworth was drowned at sea. Mary Lamb, in her letter of condolence to Dorothy Wordsworth, sent some lines expressing the feeling which now possessed Mrs. Clarkson :—

> Why is he wandering on the sea ?
> Coleridge should now with Wordsworth be.
> By slow degrees he'd steal away
> Their woe and gently bring a ray
> (So happily he'd time relief)
> Of comfort from their very grief.
> He'd tell them that their brother dead,
> When years have passéd o'er their head,
> Will be remembered with such holy,
> True, and perfect melancholy,
> That ever their lost brother John
> Will be their hearts' companion.
> His voice they'll always hear,
> His face they'll always see ;
> There's nought in life so sweet
> As such a memory.

But Mary Lamb, who was one of the wisest and shrewdest as well as one of

them which makes it perhaps better that they should
not meet just now. I am, however, quite sure that
. . . it rests with him [Coleridge] entirely to recover
all that he has lost in their hearts.' I have no doubt
Mrs. Clarkson correctly interpreted the Wordsworths'
feelings, and that it would have been better for both
parties had Coleridge forgiven and forgotten the
offence, whatever it may have been, when the Wordsworths had in their turn humbled themselves to him—
but the documents which might enable us to judge
quite confidently are not before us. A bond, such as
had existed between Coleridge and Wordsworth, once
broken may be mended, but it cannot be welded. It
was broken by Wordsworth in an unguarded moment ;
soon after it had been mended, Wordsworth, under
stress of sorrow, seems to have been driven to break
it afresh ; and one must regret that when he became
conscious of what he had done, his appeals proved
unavailing. But our regret must be even greater on
Coleridge's account than on Wordsworth's, for, in the
conduct of life, it was Wordsworth who was strong—
'strong in himself and powerful to give strength.'
One feels, too, that with Coleridge it could not have
been hardness of heart which held him in London
when he was needed at Grasmere ; but rather
paralysis of will. Whatever the cause, the effects
were disastrous. Coleridge had learned by more than
one cruel experience that in natures like his own, the
breath of whose life is sympathy, 'to be wroth with
one we love, doth work like madness in the brain.'
Between himself and every member of the Grasmere

the best of women, recognised that 'circumstances alter cases.' Her own
relations with all the parties had undergone no change, except in as far as time
had deepened and strengthened them, and she was probably better acquainted
than Mrs. Clarkson with Coleridge's reasons for the attitude he had taken up.

household there had grown up a union of true hearts, exalted and strengthened in Wordsworth's case by the sympathy of equal minds ; and if the ' year-long difference,' closed but a few months before, had so deeply affected Coleridge, with what feelings of despair must he have contemplated this fresh rupture ! It lasted until the spring of 1815 :[1] is it surprising that in the interval, Coleridge, deprived of the friendships which were his chief solace and support, sank into lower depths than he had ever touched before ? But for this new difference with the Wordsworths, Coleridge's impulse to return to the Lake country as a resident might have been reinforced and the current of his life turned into a smoother channel.

He seems to have remained in London, doing nothing, until October. Southey came up to town in September and saw him several times. On the 4th October he took Coleridge to Madame de Staël's drawing-room, 'and left him there in the full spring-tide of his discourse.'[2] (It was that clever lady's first experience of his greatness in monologue.) Southey adds that Coleridge's 'time of departure seems still uncertain,' and that ' Mrs. C. will not be sorry to hear that he is selling his German books.' This evidently last desperate effort to raise money is also mentioned to Stuart of Sep. 27. In the same letter he asks Stuart to look at that day's *Morning Chronicle* for what ' he should have called a masterly essay on the

---

[1] Even then, intercourse was only temporarily renewed in a somewhat constrained correspondence respecting the publication of Coleridge's lines on hearing the *Prelude ;* and on the respective merits of the *Prelude* and the *Excursion*— Coleridge holding the former to be the better poem. (See Knight's *Life of Wordsworth,* ii. 255-260, for Coleridge's very interesting letter ; and *Mem. of Coleorton,* ii. 175.) In 1816 came the *Biographia Literaria,* and Wordsworth's displeasure with the criticism of his poems it contained. Friendly relations were not fully re-established until the end of 1817.

[2] *Letters of R. S.* ii. 332.

cause of the downfall of the Comic Drama, if he were
not perplexed by the distinct recollection of having
*conversed* the greater part of it at Lamb's.'    Coleridge
does not say that Hazlitt was present when the article
was 'conversed,' but he implies it, for Stuart must
have known that Hazlitt was then contributing
dramatic articles to the *Chronicle*.

Coleridge had not written to his wife since March,
but when Southey was in town, proposed to go to
Greta Hall with him.    Then came the invitation or
proposal—from which side, I know not — to lecture
at Bristol; but Coleridge assured Southey that as
soon as the course was finished he would set out
direct for Keswick.    But Keswick never saw Coleridge again.    The separation arranged between husband and wife had drifted into informality, but it
proved none the less permanent.

# CHAPTER XI

## BRISTOL AND CALNE

### A.D. 1813–1816

SOME time in October Coleridge left London for Bristol by coach. It was on the morning of the day preceding that which had been announced for his first lecture at the Great Room of the 'White Lion.' He 'talked incessantly for thirty miles out of London, . . . and afterwards with little intermission till the coach reached Marlborough, when he discovered' that among his fellow-passengers was the sister of a particular friend. She was on her way to North Wales. At Bath Coleridge took a chaise, and gallantly escorted the lady to her destination, arriving at Bristol two or three days behind time.[1] He came as the guest of his faithful old friend Josiah Wade, and a fresh day was appointed for the opening lecture. It was Oct. 28, and after some difficulty the person of the lecturer was secured and deposited on the platform 'just one hour' (says Cottle) 'after all the company had impatiently awaited him.' After that evening 'no other important delay arose, and the lectures gave great satisfaction.' The course of six was completed

---

[1] Cottle's *Rem.* p. 353.

on Nov. 16,[1] the last being extra and gratuitous, 'on account of the diffuseness he unavoidably fell into in his introductory discourse.' On Nov. 17 he appears to have delivered a seventh lecture on Education, but of this no report has been found. The same fate, unfortunately, has attended a second and similarly successful course[2] of six lectures—two on Shakespeare and four on Milton—announced on Dec. 30, 1813.[3] This was followed by a third of four lectures on Milton, delivered between April 5 and 14, 1814,[4] which Cottle[5] says 'were but indifferently attended.' He adds that Coleridge announced four lectures on Homer, hoping to 'attract the many,' but that 'only a few of his old and staunch friends attended.' All these Bristol lectures, Cottle tells us, were 'of a conversational character,' such as those with which he delighted his friends in private. 'The attention of his hearers [of the lectures] never flagged, and his large dark eyes, and his countenance, in an excited state, glowing with intellect, predisposed his audience in his favour.'

I have thought it best to keep together the records of the various courses of Bristol lectures, but the narrative must needs go back to October 1813. C. R. Leslie, the painter, then a promising Academy student of twenty, was at Bristol on a short visit to his compatriots, the Allstons, and heard three of the first course of lectures. They gave him, he wrote at the time, 'a much more distinct and satisfactory view of the nature and ends of poetry, and of painting, than

---

[1] The lectures, which were on Shakespeare and Milton, were briefly reported in the Bristol papers, and from them transcribed by the pious efforts of Mr. George, the well-known Bristol bookseller. These reports are printed in Mr. Ashe's *Lectures*, etc., previously mentioned.

[2] Cottle's *Rem.* p. 354.          [3] ASHE, p. 456.
[4] *Ib.* p. 457.               [5] *Rem.* p. 354.

I ever had before.'[1]   It will be seen that Coleridge
did not fulfil his promise to return to Keswick at the
close of his lecture engagement.   He did not even
write to Keswick—at all events up to Feb. 1814.
His family had not then seen him for two years, and
it was nearly one since they had received a letter
from him.

In December 1813 I find him sending back to
Robinson two borrowed volumes of Spinoza's works,
and anxious to procure some of the writings of Jean
Paul Richter, Fichte, and Schelling.   He has just
returned to Bristol from a visit to the Morgans, who
had followed him to the west country, and were now
living in reduced circumstances, and as regards both
ladies of the family, with impaired health, near Bath.
For the spring and summer of 1814, Cottle is almost
the only authority,[2] and unreliable as he is, the best
has to be made of him.   At some uncertain time
previous to April, Coleridge borrowed of him ten
pounds to pay off ' a dirty fellow' who had threatened
arrest.

About the same time every one, save Cottle himself, had noticed in Coleridge's 'look and deportment'
'something unusual and strange'; and, soon after,
while both men were calling on Hannah More, Cottle
observed that Coleridge's hand shook so that he
spilled wine from a glass he was raising to his lips.
On mentioning this to a friend next day, it was
explained to him.   'That,' said the friend, 'arises
from the immoderate quantity of opium he takes.'

---

[1] Leslie had accompanied the Allstons from London to Bristol.   Mr.
Allston fell ill on the way, at Salt Hill, and Coleridge was sent for from town.
Leslie says (*Mem.* i. 35): 'At Salt Hill and on some other occasions, I
witnessed his [Coleridge's] performance of the duties of a friendship in a manner
which few men of his constitutional indolence could have roused themselves to
equal.'                                   [2] *Rem.* pp. 352-386.

It is remarkable (adds Cottle) that this was the first time the melancholy fact of Mr. Coleridge's excessive indulgence in opium had come to my knowledge. It astonished and afflicted me. Now, the cause of his ailments became manifest. On this subject Mr. C. may have been communicative to others, but to me he was silent. I now saw it was mistaken kindness to give him money, as I had learned that he indulged in his potations according to the extent of his means, so that to be temperate, it was expedient that he should be poor.

Cottle's phrase, 'giving him money,' refers to a movement he had kindly set afoot for Coleridge's benefit. He had aimed at getting together an annuity of a hundred and fifty pounds, 'that Coleridge might pursue his literary objects without pecuniary distractions.' The scheme appears to have been checked by opposition from Southey, who justly pointed out that Coleridge's 'distractions' were not primarily 'pecuniary,' but narcotic.

After receiving this counsel from Southey, Cottle sent to the unhappy Coleridge a lengthy communication, the tone and purport of which are sufficiently indicated by its opening sentence[1]: 'I am conscious of being influenced by the purest motives in addressing you the following letter.' Next day Coleridge replied: 'You have poured oil into the raw and festering wound of an old friend's conscience, Cottle! but it is *oil of vitriol!* I but barely glanced at the middle of the first page of your letter, and have seen no more of it—not from resentment, God forbid! but from the state of my bodily and mental sufferings, that scarcely permitted human fortitude to let in a new visitor of affliction. The object of my present reply is to state the case just as it is.'—First, he goes

---

[1] The date given is 'April 25th, 1814.' *Early Recoll*. ii. 150; and *Rem.* p. 361. Cottle evidently could not refrain from garbling his own letter, as he garbled the rest of the correspondence, for the text is not identical in the two books.

on to say, the consciousness of his guilt towards his
Maker has been his greatest anguish these ten years;
secondly, he has never concealed the cause of his
direful infirmity—and has warned two young men,
inclined to laudanum, of the consequences, as exhibited in his own case; thirdly, he can say that he
was ignorantly seduced into the habit, by bodily pain,
and not by desire of pleasurable sensations.  His
'case is a species of madness, only that it is a
derangement, an utter impotence of the volition, and
not of the intellectual faculties.  You bid me rouse
myself; go bid a man paralytic in both arms, to rub
them briskly together, and that will cure him.  "Alas!"
he would reply, "that I cannot move my arms, is my
complaint and my misery!"'  Had he 'but £200—half
to send to Mrs. Coleridge, and half to place himself in
a private madhouse where he could procure nothing but
what a physician thought proper . . . for two or three
months, there might be hope.'  He would 'willingly
place himself under Dr. Fox, in his establishment.'

On the same day Cottle replied, counselling him
to pray, and asking pardon if his 'former letter'
appeared unkind; to which Coleridge instantly responded, assuring Cottle that he 'thanked' him, that
he did endeavour to pray, but that Cottle had no con-
ception of the dreadful hell of his mind and conscience
and body.  Soon after, probably on the day following,
Coleridge wrote to Cottle a letter in which he en-
larged, very calmly, on the reasonable expectations a
Christian may entertain on the subject of sincere prayer,
quoting and recommending Archbishop Leighton, and
going on to express his resolve to put himself under Dr.
Fox if money enough can be procured.  Will Cottle
see W. Hood and Le Breton and Wade as to this?

Does he know Fox?—ending: 'I have not yet read your former letter, for I have to prepare my lecture. Oh! with how blank a spirit!—S. T. COLERIDGE.'[1] Unfortunately Cottle did not comply with Coleridge's request, or if he did, nothing resulted. Coleridge's plan of putting himself under restraint was the wisest which could have been adopted under the circumstances. Cottle wrote to Southey, and sent him a copy of his correspondence with Coleridge. Southey was shocked, but not surprised. He knew, as did 'all with whom Coleridge has lived,' that after every possible allowance is made for 'morbid bodily causes' the habit of opium-eating is 'for infinitely the greater part' motived by 'inclination and indulgence.'

The Morgans, with great difficulty and perseverance, *did* break him off the habit, at a time when his ordinary consumption of laudanum was from two quarts a week to a pint a day! He suffered dreadfully during the first abstinence, so much so as to say it was better to die than to endure his present sufferings. Mrs. Morgan resolutely replied, it was indeed better that he should die than that he should continue to live on as he had been living. It angered him at the time, but the effort was persevered in. . . . This, too, I ought to say, that all the medical men to whom Coleridge has made his confession have uniformly ascribed the evil, not to bodily ailment, but to indulgence.

Regular work is the one cure, and Southey sees nothing so advisable for Coleridge as a return to that and to Greta Hall, after a refreshing visit to Poole, and a few lectures at Birmingham and Liverpool, to put him in funds.

But whether he can do this or not (continues Southey), here it is that he ought to be. He knows in what manner he will be received; by his children with joy; by his wife, not with tears, if she can controul them—certainly not with reproaches; by me only with encouragement. He has sources of direct emolument open to him

---

[1] Contrast this, taken from the original document, with Cottle, *Rem.* p. 371. The 'former letter' was evidently Cottle's first, of April 25. Coleridge probably never summoned courage enough to read it through.

in the *Courier* and in the *Eclectic Review.*—These for his immediate wants, and for everything else, his pen is more rapid than mine,
and would be paid as well.   If you agree with me, you had better
write to Poole, that he may press him to make a visit, which I know
he has promised.   His great object should be to get out a play and
appropriate the whole produce to supporting Hartley at college.
Three months' pleasurable exertion would effect this.   Of some such
fit of industry I by no means despair; of anything more than fits, I
am afraid I *do*.   But this of course I shall never say to him.
From me he shall never hear anything but cheerful encouragement
and the language of hope. . . . I have communicated none of your
letters to Mrs. Coleridge—her spirits and health are beginning to
sink under it.[1]

It is in justice to Southey that I quote so fully
from a letter which is not only wise and kind, but
which must have been written in a spirit of no ordinary
self-sacrifice.   That its counsels came from him did
not, I fear, recommend them to Coleridge; the cup,
however, might perhaps have been tolerated, had its
contents been inviting.   But how uninviting must the
draught have seemed!   It was proposed to him to
return to companionship and a mode of life which had
been abandoned after trial, and to return under conditions and circumstances which in Coleridge's eyes
must have seemed vastly less favourable.   To present
himself at Greta Hall in his wrecked condition would
be a confession of failure altogether too abject—a confession not in mere words (which came easily enough
to this publican) but in deed, and having to be made

---

[1] *Rem.* pp. 373-375.   This letter Cottle has treated with an unusual amount
of respect, meddling more with the style than the sense.

In a letter dated a week or two before (April 17) Southey had said much the
same, adding that he could obtain employment for Coleridge on the *Quarterly.*
Should Cottle proceed in his intention to raise an annuity, the amount would not
suffice to pay for Coleridge's laudanum, and could but induce more strenuous
idleness.   At all events, says Southey, 'my name must not be mentioned.   His
wife and daughter are living with me, and here he may employ himself without
any disquietude about immediate subsistence.'   Cottle has treated this letter more
recklessly than almost any other.   Southey is made to say : 'My name must not
be mentioned.   *I subscribe enough.*   Here he may employ himself,' etc.   The
words italicised (they are italicised also by Cottle) form only one of the more
scandalous of his alterations.

to his wife and to Southey! Then there were the
Wordsworths. Dorothy's heart, and perhaps Mrs.
Wordsworth's also, was accustomed to beat inde-
pendently of her brother's when Coleridge was concerned—the friendship of these 'beloved women' might
be counted on to almost any extent, but whatever
relations might be established with the family as a
whole, they could not possibly be the old ones;
Wordsworth's house could never again be all that it
had been, an ever-open shelter and a fountain of
unquestioning sympathy.—These, I doubt not, were
the considerations which weighed with Coleridge, if
he gave Southey's proposals any serious thought.
It is far more probable, I fear, that he listened to
them only with impatience, knowing well that his
enfeebled will was unequal to the adoption of any plan,
or even to the exertion of taking the initial step.

And so he seems to have drifted on at Bristol
until the autumn, doing nothing save pretending to
give up opium under the care of Dr. Daniel and
'a respectable old decayed tradesman,' who was
hired to go about with the poet when he took his
walks abroad. Coleridge had other amusements
besides the daily one of circumventing his simple
guardian—he wrote mottoes for Proclamation-Day
transparencies, painted by Allston; he sat to
Allston for the almost superhumanly respectable-
looking portrait painted for Mr. Josiah Wade[1]; he
corrected (for a fee of ten pounds) and laughed at
Cottle's new epic, 'Messiah'; he laughed, too, at
several prolix letters addressed to him by Cottle,
ascribing all his (Coleridge's) ills, not to opium, but to

---

[1] Now in the National Portrait Gallery. It has been engraved by Sam.
Cousens.

Satanic possession.   These delights were tempered
only by the intense boredom produced by the presence
of hypochondriacal Mrs. Fermor, Lady. Beaumont's
sister, who had come to Bristol expressly for the
benefit of his society.[1]

But in spite of the seeming gaiety exhibited in
the unprinted letter of which the foregoing passage
is a summary, Coleridge was conscience-stricken and
bowed down.    It was probably on quitting kind
Wade's roof for that of the equally kind Morgan, that
he wrote the saddest of all the letters of his which
have come down to us,[2] one of the saddest, perhaps,
which any man ever penned :—

DEAR SIR,
             For I am unworthy to call any good man friend—
much less you, whose hospitality and love I have abused ; accept,
however, my intreaties for your forgiveness, and for your prayers.

Conceive a poor miserable wretch, who for many years has been
attempting to beat off pain, by a constant recurrence to the vice that
reproduces it.    Conceive a spirit in hell employed in tracing out for
others the road to that heaven from which his crimes exclude him.
In short, conceive whatever is most wretched, helpless, and hopeless, and you will form as tolerable a notion of my state, as it is possible for a good man to have.

I used to think the text in St. James that 'he who offended in
one point, offends in all,' very harsh ; but I now feel the awful, the
tremendous truth of it.    In the one crime of OPIUM, what crime
have I not made myself guilty of !—Ingratitude to my Maker ! and
to my benefactors—injustice ! and unnatural cruelty to my poor
children !—self-contempt for my repeated promise—breach, nay, too
often, actual falsehood !

After my death, I earnestly entreat, that a full and unqualified narra-
tion of my wretchedness and of its guilty cause, may be made public,
that at least some little good may be effected by the direful example.

May God Almighty bless you, and have mercy on your still
affectionate, and in his heart, grateful—       S. T. COLERIDGE.

---

[1] See Coleridge's polite statement of Mrs. Fermor's case in a letter to her
sister (*Mem. of Coleorton*, ii. 171-174).

[2] To Josiah Wade.    'Bristol, June 26th, 1814' (Cottle's *Rem.* p. 394).    I
have not seen the original document.

Before the middle of September, Coleridge was able to inform his friends that his Bristol physician being persuaded that nothing remained 'but to super-induce *positive* health on a system from which disease and its *removable* causes had been driven out,' had recommended country air. He has therefore rejoined the Morgans in a cottage at Ashley, half a mile from Box, on the Bath road. His day he represents as being laid out in the most methodical manner—he 'breakfasts before nine, works till one, walks and reads till three,' etc. etc. His morning hours are devoted to a great work now printing at Bristol, at the risk of two friends.

The title is 'Christianity, the one true Philosophy; or, Five Treatises on the Logos, or Communicative Intelligence, natural, human, and divine,' to which is prefixed a prefatory essay on the laws and limits of toleration and liberality, illustrated by fragments of Auto-biography.

A syllabus, in the author's best style, of the Five Treatises, follows, and a statement that 'the purpose of the whole is a philosophical defence of the Articles of the Church, so far as they respect doctrine, as points of faith.'[1] The work is to be 'comprised in two portly octavos.' This I believe to be the first mention of 'the *magnum opus*,' of which much will be heard here-after.

The evenings (proceeds the admirably methodical Coleridge) I have employed in composing a series of Essays on the Principles of General Criticism concerning the Fine Arts, especially those of Statuary and Painting, and of these four in title, but six or more in

---

[1] Coleridge's orthodoxy seems now to have been complete. In one of his Bristol lectures of April 1814, he said that Milton's Satan was a 'sceptical Socinian.' The phrase cost him the friendship of Dr. Estlin, and probably that of other Unitarian friends, in spite of a humble but highly argumentative apology. To Cottle he quoted *Paradise Regained*, iv. l. 196 *et seq.*, and l. 500 *et seq.* See also, *Estlin Letters*, pp. 112-117.

size, have been published in *Felix 'Farley's Bristol Journal*[1]—a
strange place for such a publication, but my motive was originally
to serve poor Allston, who is now exhibiting his pictures in Bristol.

He concludes by assuring Stuart that the essays are
the best things he has ever written, and asks if, revised
and extended to sixteen or twenty, they would suit
the *Courier.* He would supply two a week and one
political essay.[2] The offer of political contributions
was accepted, for six ' Letters to Judge Fletcher concerning his "Charge to the Grand Jury of the County
of Wexford at the Summer Assizes in 1814"'[3] were
printed in the *Courier* between September 20 and
December 10.[4]

The great folks of the neighbourhood soon found
out that a notable man had taken up his residence
among them. His first discoverers seem to have been
the Methuen[5] family of Corsham House ; the next,
Moore's Marquis of Lansdowne. His *quondam* 'idol,'
Bowles, was not far off, at Bremhill, and the two poets
foregathered. About the middle of October, Coleridge was driven to apply to Stuart for a small
advance, the reason assigned being that ' the bookseller has treated me in a strange way about a translation of Goethe's *Faust.* But it is not worth mentioning,
except that I employed some weeks unprofitably.'[6]

[1] The essays have been reprinted in Cottle's *Early Recollections* (Appendix),
1837 ; and again in *Miscellanies, Æsthetic and Literary*, by S. T. Coleridge ;
edited by T. Ashe, 1885.

[2] *Letters from the Lake Poets*, pp. 221-233. Letter dated from 'Mr. Smith's,
Ashley, Box, near Bath. 12 Sep. 1814.'

[3] The ' Charge ' was published as a pamphlet in 1814. London : Sherwood.
Pp. ii. ; 48.

[4] Reprinted in *Essays on his own Times*, pp. 677-733. The letters were
signed ' Irish Protestant ' !

[5] Some interesting reminiscences of Coleridge at this period were contributed
to the *Christian Observer* for 1845, by the Rev. T. A. Methuen, Rector of All
Cannings, Wilts. They are signed ' Πλστις.'

[6] John Murray (the second) was ' the bookseller.' Coleridge was offered
£100 for a translation and analysis of *Faust*, to be completed in two or three
months. He accepted, although he says he thinks the terms ' humiliatingly low.'

On November 23, Coleridge informs Stuart that on 'Monday after next he expects, as far as so perplexed a being dare expect anything, to remove to Calne, Wilts, at a Mr. Page's, surgeon.' He proposes further contributions to the *Courier*, and asks Stuart to see a publisher as to a collection of his scattered political essays, similar to one which had been announced as forthcoming, in the first number of *The Friend*, five years before. The Morgans accompanied him to Calne.

All this time Coleridge's wife and the other inmates of Greta Hall heard nothing from him. On October 17, Southey wrote to Cottle :—

Can you tell us anything of Coleridge? A few lines of introduction to a son of Mr. Biddulph of St. James's [Bristol] are all that we have received from him since I saw him last September twelvemonth in town. The children being thus entirely left to chance, I have applied to his brothers at Ottery concerning them, and am in hopes, through these means and the aid of other friends, of sending Hartley to college. Lady Beaumont has promised £30 annually for this purpose, Poole £10. I wrote to Coleridge three or four months ago, telling him that unless he took some steps towards providing for this object I must make the application, and required his answer within a given term of three weeks. He received the letter, and in his note by Mr. Biddulph promised to answer, but he has never taken any further notice of it. I have acted with the advice of Wordsworth. The brothers, as I expected, promise their concurrence, and I daily expect a letter stating to what amount they will contribute. What is to become of Coleridge himself! He may continue to find men who will give him board and lodging for the sake of his conversation, but who will pay his other expenses? I cannot but apprehend some shameful and dreadful end to this deplorable course.[1]

---

It came to nothing. See *Memoirs of John Murray* (1891), i. 297 *et seq.* ; also *Athenæum*, April 18, 1891, and *Table Talk* for February 16, 1833. Coleridge's disrelish for Goethe gave Crabb Robinson great concern.

[1] This letter, the original of which is now in the Fonthill Collection, is incorrectly and incompletely printed in *Life and Corr. of R. S.* iv. 81 ; and still more incorrectly and incompletely in Cottle's *Rem.* p. 386. Cottle has interpolated passages from a letter written by Southey on 2nd March 1815. *Per contra*, let it be known that Cottle, unsolicited, joined in the subscription for sending Hartley to Oxford.

On December 12, Southey informs Cottle that he
knows nothing of Coleridge save that he is writing in
the *Courier* under the name of 'An Irish Protestant,'
and that it is settled that Hartley goes to Oxford in
the spring.[1]   There seems to be something cruel, and
therefore unlike Coleridge, in the persistent silence
maintained towards his family and the friends who
were exerting themselves to promote the interests of
his darling Hartley.   When at Ashley, he delighted
to speak to his landlady about his children, and told
her that his eldest son was going to college.[2]

Early in March, after a long silence, Coleridge
renewed communication with Cottle in a mournful
letter.[3]   His health is no worse than when he left
Bristol, but it fluctuates; he is unhappy, and 'poor
indeed.'   He has collected his scattered poems, and
wishes to publish them, but he must begin the volume
with a series of Odes on the sentences of the Lord's
Prayer, a series 'which has never been seen by any'
—a statement equally true to-day.   A desire even
more urgent, is to finish his 'greater work on " Christianity, considered as Philosophy, and as the only
Philosophy."'   It is nearly finished (!) but his poverty
compels him constantly to turn aside to 'some mean
subject for the newspapers'—distressing interruptions
which deprive him of the power of executing either
task.   After his recent experience in Bristol he would
rather die than appeal to 'a club of subscribers to his
poverty'—will Cottle lend him thirty or forty pounds,
on the security of his MSS. ?   His conscience is not
easy, but he can truly say that his embarrassments are

---

[1] *Letters of R. S.* ii. 386.
[2] Wordsworth to Poole, March 13, 1815.   Knight's *Life of W. W.* ii. 247.
[3] Calne, March 17, 1815.   *Rem.* p. 386.

not caused by selfish indulgence. He is £25 in
arrear, his expenses being £2 : 10s. per week. If
Cottle think he ought to live on less, he should remember that this would be to cut himself off from 'all
social affections and from all conversation with persons
of the same education.' 'Heaven knows!' he exclaims, 'of the £300 received through you, what went
to myself.' To this Cottle replied with 'a friendly
letter,' declining the loan, but enclosing £5, having
convinced himself that the larger sum was needed, not
for board, but for opium. His letter was crossed by a
second from Coleridge, who said his 'distresses are
impatient rather than himself.' The Morgans would
gladly do all for him, but this is out of their power.
So he has written to William Hood asking him to see
four or five friends—the scorned 'club of subscribers
to his poverty' of a few days before, doubtless—who
might make up the sum he requires among them, if
Cottle will not. If relief come from neither hand—
even £20 would keep the wolf at bay for a week—
he must instantly dispose of all his MSS. to the first
bookseller who will give anything, and then try to live
by taking pupils, if not at Calne, then at Bristol. To
this second letter Cottle replied as to the first, and with
a second £5. He also urged him to come to Bristol
and consult the friends there; but from Coleridge
came no reply. Cottle had received his last letter
from that pen. The Bristol friends came to the
rescue. In some old accounts I find that in April,
Hood (in association with others) lent Coleridge £45,
besides advancing £27 : 5 : 6 for the payment of the
premium on his life-policy. These friends accepted
the security of Coleridge's MSS. for their loans.

While this distressful correspondence was going on,

Coleridge was busying himself energetically with the local agitation against the Government Bill for excluding foreign corn until the average price of·wheat should reach eighty shillings per quarter. He drew up the Calne petition to the Prince Regent, and, in support of it, 'mounted on the butcher's table, made a butcherly sort of speech of an hour long to a very ragged but not butcherly audience' in the market-place. 'Loud were the huzzas, and if it depended on the inhabitants at large, I believe they would send me up to Parliament.' So he wrote to Dr. Brabant, the eminent physician of Devizes, and excused himself from attending a meeting to be held in that town, in support of the Government measure. Meantime, he asks Dr. Brabant to buy him 'a quarter of a pound of the best plain rappee at Anstey's,' and (but in a separate paper) 'an ounce of maccabau'; and further, to recommend to ʟim a good table-beer, unlike the Calne brew, which alternates between syrup and vinegar.[1]

In June, a travelling theatrical company came to Calne and acted *Remorse*,—not for the first time in the town, for it seems to have been given there in 1813. When the company moved on to Devizes, the gratified Coleridge gave the manager, Mr. Falkner, a flaming testimonial to Dr. Brabant. On July 29 he wrote to the same friend :—

The necessity of extending what I first intended as a preface[2]

---

[1] 'Unpublished Letters written by S. T. Coleridge,' communicated by Dr. Brabant's son-in-law, the late Mr. W. M. Call, to the *Westminster Review* for April and July 1870.

[2] In the unprinted correspondence of this period I see indications which lead me to believe that the only prose contemplated at first was to take the form of a preface to the poems; and that this preface grew into a literary autobiography. In July we see that a preface to the autobiography had been begun and 'extended.' This was the second stage. A little later this 'preface' had assumed proportions so formidable that it was decided to incorporate it in the work. When the MS. was sent to the printers, two volumes were intended—Vol. I. to

to an 'Autobiographia Literaria, Sketches of my Literary Life and Opinions,' as far as poetry and poetical criticisms are concerned, has confined me to my study from eleven to four and from six to ten since I last left you. I have just finished it, having only the correction of the MS. to go through. I have given a full account (*raisonné*) of the controversy concerning Wordsworth's Poems and Theory, in which my name has been so constantly included. I have no doubt that Wordsworth will be displeased, but I have done my duty to myself and to the public, in, as I believe, completely subverting the theory, and in proving that the poet himself has never acted on it except in particular stanzas, which are the blots of his composition.

He then goes on to tell his correspondent that he has elaborated a 'disquisition on the powers of association . . . and on the generic difference between the faculties of Fancy and Imagination,' not entirely for insertion, but for Dr. Brabant's perusal. Then he apologises for 'running on as usual' past the object of his letter, which is to beg Mrs. Brabant to get him a pair of black silk stockings, costing 'from 17s. to 20s.,' to enable him to dine respectably with the Marquis and Marchioness of Lansdowne; and further, to procure for him another 'quarter of a pound of plain rappee, with half an ounce of maccabau, intermixed.'

On August 10 the first instalment of the 'copy' of the *Biographia Literaria* and a second of that of the poems were sent to the printer — or rather to Hood, to whom the MSS. had been secured. They were sent with a letter from Morgan, who says that if Coleridge goes on even half as well as he has during the previous six weeks, wonders will have been accomplished by Christmas. The good Morgan was now

contain the *Biographia*, Vol. II. the Poems (*Sibylline Leaves*). While the two were being printed concurrently, the *Biographia* outgrew the capacity of a single volume, and the Poems (the 'signature' of which is 'Vol. II.') are called in the accounts 'Vol. III.' When the whole of Volumes I. and III. and half of Vol. II. had been printed, the author quarrelled with the printers. Ultimately Vol. II. was completed by another printer, and the 'work' issued in 1817, in two separate parts—the *Biographia* (2 vols.) and the 'Sibylline Leaves' (1 vol.)

acting the part which had been taken by Miss Sarah
Hutchinson in the days of *The Friend*, — keeping
Coleridge at his task, and writing to his dictation.
Indeed, both *The Friend* and the *Biographia* represent Coleridge's talk, and (to adopt Carlyle's phrase)
these friends were the passive buckets into which he
pumped — most other listeners having been mere
sieves.   Before the end of August, Hood passed on
the 'copy' to Gutch,[1] Morgan having given his undertaking that regular supplies should be forthcoming.
The printers, however, at the end of 1816, had put in
type only about one-third of the *Sibylline Leaves*, and
of the *Biographia* nothing at all.

At the end of the Easter term Hartley (who had
been taken up to Oxford by the Wordsworths) came
to Calne on a visit to his father—a visit which was
prolonged until the end of the long vacation, and which
was greatly enjoyed both by father and son.   Hartley
cheered his mother with accounts of his father's good
health and industry, of the successful performance of
*Remorse* by the travelling company, and of a Bible
Society meeting, at which his father made an eloquent speech of three-quarters of an hour.   When
Hartley returned to Oxford, his father sped him on
his way with a ten pound note.[2]

In October Coleridge tells Stuart[3] that he has been

---

[1] John Mathew Gutch, an old schoolfellow of Coleridge and Lamb, and a
correspondent of the latter.   He was then proprietor of *Felix Farley's Journal*
at Bristol.   The actual printing of Coleridge's work was done by John Evans
& Co., but to Gutch's order.

[2] Southey had expressed to Lamb his fears for the effect which this visit might
have on Hartley, to which Lamb replied (Aug. 9, 1815, *Letters* i. 293): 'Your
fear for Hartley's intellectuals is just and rational.   Could not the Chancellor be
petitioned to remove him?   His Lordship took Mr. Betty from under the paternal
wing.   I think at least he should go through a course of matter-of-fact with some
sober man, after the mysteries.   Could he not spend a week at Poole's before he
goes back to Oxford?'

[3] Oct. 7, 1815.   *Letters from the Lake Poets*, p. 242.

busy writing for the stage—re-writing Shakespeare's
*Richard II.*, and also Beaumont and Fletcher's
*Pilgrim* and *Beggar's Bush.* He has 'unwisely
mentioned this to —— and some others connected
with the two theatres,' and, possibly by mere coin-
cidence, these three plays are announced as about
to be produced — by others! It cannot be helped,
but his work on the last-mentioned is so nearly
finished,[1] that he begs Stuart to see the Drury Lane
people about it. He has sent to the Bristol printers
the MSS. of the *Biographia Literaria* and *Sibylline
Leaves.* For the last four months he has never
worked less than six hours each day, and cannot do
more if he is to have any time for reading and
reflection. He is now at work on a tragedy and a
dramatic entertainment, giving half his time to these,
and the other half to the *magnum opus*, the title of
which is to be ' Logosophia ; or, On the Logos, human
and divine, in six Treatises '—and then there follows,
in the letter, another of Coleridge's inimitably comprehensive syllabuses and the customary statement that
the work is to occupy ' two large octavo volumes, six
hundred pages each.' He only wishes to work hard,
but what can he do, he exclaims, ' if he is to starve
while he is working!' He fears that, unless something
can be done, he must sink ; for as to politics, he can
write only on principles, and where, he asks the proprietor of the *Courier*, is the newspaper which will
admit such writings? ' I have tried (he says) ' to
negotiate with the booksellers for a translation of the
works of Cervantes (*Don Quixote* excluded) and
of Boccaccio, and Mr. Rogers [the once despised
Rogers !] promised to use his influence, but all in

---

[1] So far as I am aware, no trace of any of these re-writings has been found.

vain.'[1]   The letter concludes with the gratifying news
that his health is better than he has known it for
the last twelve years.   About this time Stuart was
again asked to make arrangements for the publication
of Coleridge's political essays, and the volume would
probably have been published had he not decided to
'complete' the book by freshly-composed additions.
Awaiting these, the negotiations apparently died out.

On March 31, 1815, we find Lord Byron[2] replying
to a letter he had received from Coleridge, requesting
(apparently) an introduction to a publisher.   Byron
says it will give him great pleasure to comply with the
request, and adds : ' If I may be permitted, I would
suggest that there never was such an opening for
tragedy. . . . I should think that the reception of
[*Remorse*] was sufficient to encourage the highest hopes
of author and audience.'   On Oct. 28th,[3] Byron wrote to
Moore : ' You have also written to Perry, who intimates
hopes of an opera from you.   Coleridge has promised
a tragedy.   Now if you keep Perry's word and Coleridge keeps his own, Drury Lane will be set up.'

Eighteen hundred and sixteen opens with a letter
in which Coleridge informs Dr. Brabant that he
'goes on pretty well,' and is ' decently industrious.'
He has finished three acts of a play in verse, but it is
not ' the tragedy he promised to Drury Lane.'   ' Lord
Byron has behaved very *politely*, but never answered
the most important part of my letter.'   The omission,
whatever it may have been, seems to have acted as
a discouragement to work on the tragedy.   For some
time after this dates fail us.   It was in April of this

---

[1] A letter respecting this business—S. T. C. to Rogers, ' Calne, May 26,
1815 '—is printed in *Rogers and his Contemporaries*, by P. W. Clayden, 1889, i. 191.
[2] Moore's *Life of Byron*, one-vol. ed. p. 278.
[3] *Ib.* p. 286.

year that Coleridge left Calne for London and Highgate, but previous to this, opium seems to have
regained the upper hand. He had received professional advice from Dr. Brabant, and informs him
that 'his plan' has succeeded, and that he confines
himself to 'the smallest dose of poison that will suffice
to keep him tranquil and capable of literary labour.'
But for thorough emancipation from 'the most pitiable
slavery, the fetters of which do indeed eat into the
soul,' he feels that he must needs have six months of
absolute repose. He is full of 'disquieting uncer-
tainty' as to the place of his residence. If he has
to part from Morgan it will be 'a sore heart-wasting,'
for no man could have 'a more faithful, zealous, and
disinterested friend.' And then the letter goes on
with a tragical account of an absurd little comedy
which had been amusing the neighbourhood. Coleridge was reported to have been 'imprudent enough,
and, in the second place, indelicate enough, to send
out a gentleman's servant in his own house to a
public-house for a bottle of brandy!' It is all
nonsense, he explains. He had been grossly mis-
understood. 'I turn' (he adds) 'from what is always
wearisome to me, and on these subjects disgusting,
namely, writing concerning my worser self,' to a
scientific excursus on two books he has been reading
—Gale and Spurzheim's *Physiognomical System* and
Bailey's *Morbid Anatomy*. The former work he thinks
beneath criticism; the latter inspires him with a wish
to examine the original authorities for some of the
theories put forward. 'I should like, if I had time, to
examine Morgagni and Lieutaud for myself.'[1]

Towards the close of March, Coleridge went up

[1] *Westminster Review*, July 1870, pp. 10, 11.

to London carrying with him the MS. of *Zapolya*, which no doubt was the play, *not* for Drury Lane, of which by the middle of January he had finished three acts. The tragedy promised for Drury Lane was never written.

Coleridge has been here about a fortnight (wrote Lamb to Wordsworth on April 9th). His health is tolerable at present, though beset with temptations. In the first place, the Covent Garden manager has declined accepting his tragedy, though (having read it) I see no reason upon earth why it might not have run a very fair chance, though it certainly wants a prominent part for a Miss O'Neil or a Mr. Kean. However, he is going to-day to write to Lord Byron to get it to Drury. Should you see Mrs. C., who has just written to C. a letter which I have given him, it will be as well to say nothing about its fate till some answer is shaped from Drury. . . . Nature, who conducts every creature by instinct to its best end, has skilfully directed C. to take up his abode at a Chemist's Laboratory in [43] Norfolk Street [Strand]. She might as well have sent a *Helluo Librorum* for cure to the Vatican. God keep him inviolate among the traps and pitfalls. He has done pretty well as yet. . . . [*P.S.*] A longer letter when C. is gone back into the country. . . . I am scarce quiet enough while he stays.[1]

A few weeks later (April 26) Lamb writes again to Wordsworth :—

Coleridge is printing *Christabel*, by Lord Byron's recommendation to Murray, with what he calls a vision, *Kubla Khan* . . . [and] has sent his tragedy to D[rury] L[ane] T[heatre]. It cannot be acted this season; and by their manner of receiving, I hope he will be able to alter it to make them accept it for the next. He is at present under the medical care of a Mr. Gillman (Killman?), a Highgate apothecary, where he plays at leaving off laud—m. I think his essentials not touched; he is very bad; but then he wonderfully picks up another day, and his face, when he repeats his verses, hath its ancient glory; an archangel a little damaged. Will Miss H[utchinson] pardon our not replying at length to her kind letter? We are not quiet enough; Morgan is with us every day, going betwixt Highgate and the Temple. Coleridge is absent but four miles, and the neighbourhood of such a man is as exciting as the presence of fifty ordinary persons. 'Tis enough to be within the whiff and wind of his genius for us not to possess our souls in quiet.

---

1 *Letters*, i. 303.

On April 9—the date of Lamb's first letter—
Coleridge consulted Dr. Adams, then an eminent
physician living in Hatton Garden. Judging by
Dr. Adams's letter to Mr. Gillman, Coleridge appears
to have stated his case with little or no reserve. For
years he has been taking large quantities of opium ;
recently he has been trying in vain to break off the
habit ; he fears his friends have not been firm enough,
and now he seeks a physician who will be not only
firm but severe in his regimen. 'As he is desirous of
retirement, and a garden,' writes Dr. Adams, 'I could
think of no one so readily as yourself.' Mr. Gillman
'had no intention of receiving an inmate,' but on
April 11 he called at Hatton Garden, when it was
arranged that Dr. Adams should drive Coleridge out
to Highgate on the following day. Coleridge, however, came alone—he came and talked and conquered,
for before the visit was over it was settled that he
should begin residence on the next day. 'I looked
with impatience,' writes Gillman, 'for the morrow. . . .
I felt indeed almost spellbound, without the desire
of release.' The morrow (Saturday) did not bring
Coleridge, of course, but it brought from him a proposal to arrive on Monday, and on the evening
appointed he came, 'bringing in his hand the proof-
sheets of *Christabel.*'

# CHAPTER XII

COLERIDGE's arrival at Highgate marked a turning-point in his life, the importance of which is only to be measured by the fact that it proved to be the last. He was then in his forty-fourth year, but he looked, and probably felt, much older. His health was broken, and he was still under the slavery of opium, but his enfeebled will had once more roused itself into an effort towards freedom. His outward circumstances had not recently undergone any material change, but it was in their nature that they should grow more and more intolerable. He was poor, and weighed down by pecuniary debts and by other unfulfilled obligations; he was alienated from his brothers, and from some friends, such as the Wordsworths, and Poole, and the Bristol group, who had been to him more than his brothers; he had a wife and three children, but the house which sheltered them had long ceased to be a home to himself. From his ninth year he had been a wanderer and a sojourner, finding 'no city to dwell in,' and now, when he was at his wits' end, tossed in a sea of troubles, the waves suddenly stilled, and he felt that he had reached his desired haven. His first sight of the Gillmans seems to have convinced him of this, and his prescience was justified, for during the eighteen years of life that remained to him, their house was his home.

He began his residence at the Grove simply as a temporary patient, but before three months had passed he was inspired to write thus to a recent acquaintance who had done him a kindness :—

If I omitted this due acknowledgment, I should think myself less deserving of the fortunate state of convalescence, and tranquil yet active impulses, which, under Providence, I owe to the unrelaxed attention, the professional skill, and above all to the continued firmness and affectionateness of the medical friend whose housemate I have been for the last three months, *and shall, I trust, continue to be indefinitely.*[1]

I am not aware of the terms on which he continued to live under Gillman's roof, but there are indications in Coleridge's later correspondence that he never ceased to contribute to the household expenses. However that may have been, it is certain that the relations throughout were entirely honourable to both parties.

*Christabel,* with its attendant *Kubla Khan* and *The Pains of Sleep,* was published in the early days of June.[2]  For the copyright of *Christabel,* Murray seems to have paid seventy guineas, with the understanding that if it were subsequently completed the copyright should revert to the poet.[3]  Murray also paid £20 for

[1] Letter to John Gale, 'Monday, 8th July, 1816.  J. Gillman's, Esq., Highgate.'  *Lippincott's Mag.* June 1874, p. 698.

[2] CHRISTABEL: KUBLA KHAN, a Vision; THE PAINS OF SLEEP.  By S. T. Coleridge, Esq.  LONDON: Printed for John Murray, Albemarle Street, by William Bulmer and Co., Cleveland Row, St. James's.  1816.  Octavo, pp. vii.; 64.

The 'second edition' differs from the first, only in respect of the title-page.

[3] The Agreements are not very clearly presented in the Murray *Memoirs* (i. 303, etc.)  Other particulars were given by Coleridge in 1825, in a letter written to his nephew, John Taylor (afterwards Mr. Justice) Coleridge, printed in BRANDL, pp. 351-354.  It is a letter of recollections, but they are manifestly drawn from

the use of *Kubla Khan*, Coleridge reserving the
copyright.   Although the pamphlet met with a
large sale and immediately went into a second
edition, its reception by the critics was disappointing.
The *Edinburgh Review*, by the hand of Hazlitt (as
Coleridge asserted), made bitter fun of it through nine
pages, the article winding up with the declaration
that ' the thing now before us is utterly destitute of
value.   It exhibits from beginning to end not a ray of
genius.'   No wonder that Coleridge, disgusted and
disheartened, thus relieved his feelings in the closing
chapter of the *Biographia Literaria* :—

> During the many years which intervened between the composi-
> tion and the publication of the *Christabel*, it became almost as well
> known among literary men as if it had been on common sale ; the
> same references were made to it, and the same liberties taken
> with it, even to the very names of the imaginary persons in the
> poem.   From almost all of our most celebrated poets, and from
> some with whom I had no personal acquaintance, I either received
> or heard of expressions of admiration that (I can truly say) appeared
> to myself utterly disproportionate to a work, that pretended to be
> nothing more than a common Faëry Tale.   Many, who had allowed
> no merit to my other poems, whether printed or manuscript, and
> who have frankly told me as much, uniformly made an exception in
> favour of the *Christabel* and the poem entitled *Love*. . . . This before
> the publication.   And since then, with very few exceptions, I have
> heard nothing but abuse, and this too in a spirit of bitterness. . . . In
> the *Edinburgh Review*, it was assailed with a malignity and a spirit
> of personal hatred that ought to have injured only the work in which
> such a tirade was suffered to appear : and this review was generally
> attributed (whether rightly or no I know not) to a man, who both in
> my presence and in my absence has repeatedly pronounced it the
> finest poem of its kind in the language.

As soon as Coleridge had settled down at Highgate, Morgan busied himself in supplying the Bristol
printers with ' copy ' for the *Sibylline Leaves*, which

a defective memory.   The most important statements in this letter are inconsistent with facts recorded at the time of their occurrence, and especially with
Coleridge's own letters of the period, printed in *Lippincott's Magazine* for June
1874.

Coleridge meant to preface with an essay of forty pages 'On the Imaginative in Poetry'—a project unfortunately never realised. It was at the same time arranged that the *Biographia* should appear in two volumes. At the beginning of May, Morgan was also negotiating with Lord Essex and Mr. Douglas Kinnaird (representing the Drury Lane Theatre Committee) with regard to *Zapolya*. The 'Second Part' was decided upon for performance during the next season, provided certain alterations were made and some songs added. Coleridge agreed, but instead of setting about the alterations at once, he gave way to a fit of despondency, and went to bed for three weeks. Nothing more was heard of *Zapolya* as a stage-play,[1] but Murray agreed to publish it complete as a poem, and made an advance of £50 on the MS. Something interfered, however, and it was not published until the following year, and then by Fenner.

Notwithstanding his strange failure to carry out the agreement to adapt *Zapolya* to the stage, and his fitful preoccupation with the completion of the two works already so long in the hands of the Bristol printers, Coleridge was full of new projects during the summer of 1816. To Murray[2] he suggested the establishment of a Review of old books, British and foreign, on the plan realised four years after, and by other hands, in the *Retrospective Review* (1820-1826). Nothing came

---

[1] In its place, Maturin's *Bertram* was accepted for Drury Lane. It was played in August, and was attacked in the *Courier*, the pen being either wielded or guided by Coleridge. Another attack on the play, which was quite unworthy of such heavy metal, was written, and used to fill up the second volume of *Biog. Lit.* In the *Edinburgh* review of the *Biog. Lit.* it is stated that the article is reprinted from the *Courier*. I have not been able to verify this statement. Maturin was desirous of replying to Coleridge, but was dissuaded by Scott (Lockhart's *Life* (1837), iv. 132).

[2] *Memoirs of John Murray*, i. 304, S. T. C. to J. M. 'Highgate, July 4, 1816.' A scheme for a retrospective review was suggested by Southey in 1809, and discussed with Scott and Ballantyne. See Southey's *Life and Corr.* iii. 236, 240.

of this proposal, but another was made and accepted. Murray promised two hundred guineas for 'a small volume of Specimens of Rabbinical Wisdom,'[1] but it was abandoned on the ground that all his time was due to the completion of the *Biographia Literaria*. In August, Coleridge proposed to Boosey & Co., the foreign booksellers of Broad Street, to begin a kind of periodical to appear monthly or fortnightly.[2] It was to be in the form of 'a letter to his literary friends in London and elsewhere concerning the real state and value of the German Literature from Gellert and Klopstock to the present year.' He adds that he has been invited by Mr. J. Hookham Frere—a new and important acquaintance, made probably through Mr. Murray—to contribute an article on Goethe's *Dichtung und Wahrheit* to the *Quarterly*, but he feels great reluctance to write in any review. Before he can undertake anything, however, he must take a holiday at the seaside to recover from the effects of overwork and anxieties. Both are described in great detail in a letter to Dr. Brabant, written from ' Muddiford, Christchurch, Hampshire, 21st September 1816.'[3] Coleridge had undertaken, at the solicitation of his new publishers, Gale & Fenner, to write 'a small tract on the present distresses, in the form of a lay sermon,' and it was advertised. He wrote and wrote until the MS. grew into a volume, and then he had to cut it down, and then it was abandoned in an unfinished

---

[1] *Lippincott's Mag.* June 1874, p. 704. S. T. C. to Rest Fenner, Sept. 22, 1816, and letter to Murray cited in preceding footnote. For sundry 'Specimens of Rabbinical Wisdom, selected from the Mishna,' see No. XI. (and some copies of No. XII.) of the original issue of *The Friend*.

[2] Unprinted letter of 31st August 1816, in the Fonthill Collection. It contains a detailed prospectus of the projected periodical in the usual comprehensive style. Nothing more was heard of it.

[3] *Westminster Rev.* July 1870, p. 17.

state.[1]  This was the overwork.  One anxiety was
caused by a calumnious report connected (I suspect)
with the ruin which about this period overtook the
Morgans' fortunes ; the other by the illness of Miss
Eliza Fricker, his favourite sister-in-law.  Absolute
seclusion seemed to him to be the only remedy, and
he went down to Muddiford, meaning, as soon as he
was strong enough and rich enough, to get a horse and
travel about on its back.

Muddiford afforded Coleridge the most delightful
of solitudes, that à deux, for he found there Scott's
friend, William Stewart Rose, living in his queer
little retreat called 'Gundimore.'  In some verses he
named after the cottage, and printed privately at
Brighton in 1837, Rose recalled how

> On these ribbed sands was Coleridge pleased to pace,
> While ebbing seas have hummed a rolling base
>        To his rapt talk.

To Rose's well-known servant and friend David Hinves
(who to some extent was the prototype of Scott's Davie
Gellatley) Coleridge presented a copy of Christabel,
'as a small token of regard,' and promised copies of
the rest of his works.[2]  The inscription is dated ' 11th

---

[1] The final outcome was the tract entitled The Statesman's Manual.  Gale &
Fenner, 1816, pp. 1-65 ; and an Appendix, i.-xlvii.—generally known as 'the
first Lay Sermon.'  It was first advertised as 'A Lay Sermon on the Distresses of
the Country, addressed to the Middle and Higher Orders,' and in the Examiner
(Sep. 8, 1816) Hazlitt wrote a cruel article, pretending to be a review of the
unpublished pamphlet.  He said one could tell what anything by Coleridge
would be as well before as after publication.  Again, when the pamphlet
appeared as The Statesman's Manual ; or the Bible the best Guide to Political
Skill and Foresight : A Lay Sermon [etc.], Hazlitt reviewed it scoffingly in the
Examiner (Dec. 29, 1816).  This he followed up by a letter to the editor (Jan.
12, 1817) contrasting the Lay Sermon with that which he heard Coleridge preach
in January 1798.  The account of the latter was embodied in the article contributed five years later to The Liberal, ' My first Acquaintance with Poets' (see
p. 81 supra).  Coleridge believed Hazlitt to be the Edinburgh reviewer of
The Statesman's Manual (Dec. 1816) ; and the ascription, as in the case of
Christabel, is probably, though not certainly, correct.

[2] Journal of Sir W. Scott, 1890, ii. 186.  See also Lockhart's Life (1837),
ii. 119.

November 1816,' and the book was probably a parting gift. At all events, Coleridge was back at Gillman's before December 5, on which day he·wrote, with a copy of the *Statesman's Manual*, to Dr. Brabant.[1] The sea-air, he says, has done him good. He works from nine till four, and from seven till twelve—sometimes later, and expects that 'next week' will appear 'the two other Lay Sermons—to the middle and labouring classes.' 'My Biographical Sketches, so long printed' (he adds), 'will then be published, and I proceed to republish *The Friend*, but as a complete Rifacimento.' He is very angry with Hazlitt. 'The man who has so grossly calumniated me in the *Examiner* and in the *Edinburgh Review* is a William Hazlitt—one who owes more to me than to his own parents. . . . All good I had done him of every kind, and never ceased to do so. The only *wrong* I have done him has been to decline his acquaintance. . . . How I feel, you may see at page xxi. of the appendix to my sermon,' and the curious reader will do well to refer to the passage, which is too long, and perhaps too strong in expression, for quotation here.

Robinson saw Coleridge on December 21, 1816,[2] and found him looking ill. But Gillman was able to give the visitor a good account of his patient's submission to discipline. He drinks only three glasses of wine daily, no spirits, and no opium beyond what is prescribed. 'Coleridge' (adds Robinson) 'has been able to work a great deal of late and with success. . . . These exertions have been too great, Mr. Gillman says. Coleridge talked easily and well, with less of his usual declamation.'

During his stay at Muddiford, Coleridge was

---

[1] *West. Rev.* July 1870, p. 21.      [2] *Diaries*, etc., i. 286.

carrying on an acrimonious correspondence with his Bristol friends, especially with Gutch, in connection with the printing of the *Sibylline Leaves* and the *Biographia*. It resulted in the transference of the printed sheets[1] to Gale & Fenner, on repayment of the cost of the printing and paper. The bulk of the advances made on the security of the MSS. by Coleridge's friends was forgiven him, but so contentious were the negotiations that the transfer was accomplished only in May 1817. By that time Coleridge had quarrelled with his new publishers over entanglements with Gutch, Murray, and Longman which it would serve no good purpose to unravel.[2] The relations between Coleridge on the one hand, and Fenner and the printer, Curtis, on the other fluctuated. From time to time they were strained almost to breaking-point, and when a peace was proclaimed, it was no better than an armed truce. •During one of these truces the scheme of the *Encyclopædia Metropolitana* was drawn out for behoof of Curtis and Fenner. A kind of committee meeting took place on April 7, 1817, and was opened by Coleridge reading his own sketch of the prospectus and plan for this 'History of Human Knowledge'—a supremely congenial task which had been entrusted to him.

Coleridge also undertook to furnish large contributions at fixed dates, and to give 'one entire day in each fortnight' to the general superintendence of the work, in consideration of receiving £500 a year. When, however, he demanded an advance in promissory notes to the amount of £300, on the security of *Biographia Literaria, Sibylline Leaves*, and the new

---

[1] The whole of the *S. L.*, and the *B. L.* up to vol. ii. p. 128.

[2] See *Lippincott's Mag.* for June 1870—Art. 'Some unpublished Letters of S. T. Coleridge'; and *Memoirs of John Murray*, i. 305-307.

edition of *The Friend*, the arrangements broke down,
and he contributed only the 'Preliminary Treatise on
Method' which formed the 'General Introduction' to
the *Encyclopædia*, and which has been often reprinted.[1]
In the middle of this *imbroglio* the second *Lay Sermon*
was published, and later on (about March) the *Biographia Literaria*.[2] The latter was a miscellany, and
as such could never have been 'completed' in any
proper sense of the word. But the second volume
had been printed up to p. 128, and it was necessary to
provide as much matter as would bring up its bulk to
something like that of the first. This was managed
by adding fifty-four pages to the critique on Wordsworth, and by inserting 'Satyrane's Letters' (which
already had served a similar purpose for *The Friend*);
a critique of Maturin's tragedy of *Bertram*, and a
rambling but very interesting autobiographic and
apologetic concluding chapter. The book was savagely
reviewed by Hazlitt in the *Edinburgh* for August
1817, and to the article Jeffrey added a footnote nearly
five pages long, signed with his initials, defending himself from certain charges[3] which Coleridge had made
against the Review and its editor. The controversy,
as conducted on both sides, is too personal, and too
trivial, to be worth reviving. In October, *Blackwood's
Magazine* contained an article on the *Biographia* and
its author. It was quite as savage, but by no means

---

[1] In the 'Cabinet Edition' of the *E. M.*

[2] '*Blessed are ye that sow beside all waters!*' A LAY SERMON, addressed to
the Higher and Middle Classes, on the existing Distresses and Discontents. By
S. T. Coleridge, Esq. [Motto, with translation, from Heraclitus.] London:
Printed for Gale & Fenner [etc.], 1817. 8vo. pp. i.-xxxi.; 1-134.

BIOGRAPHIA LITERARIA; Or Biographical Sketches of my Literary Life
and Opinions. By S. T. Coleridge, Esq. 2 vols. London: Rest Fenner, 23
Paternoster Row. 1817. 8vo., Vol. I., pp. 1-296. Vol. II., pp. 1-309.

[3] *Biog. Lit.* ed. 1817, i. 52 *n.* The passage was omitted from the second
edition (1847), but the quarrel is commented on at some length in the editorial
'Introduction.'

as witty as those from Hazlitt's pen, but it stung
Coleridge as the others had not, for it renewed the
old *Anti-Jacobin* charge [1] of abandoning his wife and
children.   He consulted Crabb Robinson [2] as to the
practicability of bringing an action for libel, but no
proceedings were taken.   In his letter to Robinson,
Coleridge says :—

> I can prove by positive evidence, by the written bargains made
> with my booksellers, etc., that I have refused every offer, however
> convenient to myself, that did not leave two-thirds of the property
> sacred to Mrs. Coleridge, [3] and that I have given up all I had in the
> world to her [4]—have continued to pay yearly £30 [5] to assure her
> what, if I live to the year 1820, will be nearly £2000 ; that beyond
> my absolute necessities . . . I have held myself accountable to her
> for every shilling ; that Hartley is with me, with all his expenses
> paid during his vacation ; and that I have been for the last six
> months, and now am, labouring hard to procure the means of
> having Derwent with me. . . . I work like a *slave* from morn to night,
> and receive as the reward less than a mechanic's wages, imposition,
> and ingratitude. [6]

He had also renewed his connection with the
*Courier*—indeed, his industry at this period, though
not always applied to the business most urgently required, appears to have been prodigious.   In March
he supplied the *Courier* with a review of his second
*Lay Sermon* which had been 'written by a friend' [7] ;
in the same month he came to the rescue of Southey

---

[1] The charge appeared in a note by the editor of *The Beauties of the Anti-
Jacobin* (London : 1799, p. 306) to *The New Morality*.  It was replied to by
Coleridge in *The Friend*, No. I. (1809), and again in the *Biog. Lit.* (1817, i. 71),
(1847, i. 65).  See *Athenæum* for May 31, 1890 ; Art. ' Coleridge and " The
Anti-Jacobin." '

[2] The letter is printed only in Brandl's *Life of Coleridge* (pp. 354-357), but
very inaccurately.

[3] I do not understand this.

[4] Referring doubtless to the Wedgwood annuity.

[5] The exact amount was £27, 5s. 6d.  When Coleridge died in 1834,
upwards of £2500 was paid on the policy.

[6] Referring to the new edition of *The Friend* (3 vols. 1818), and to its
printer and publisher, Curtis and Fenner.

[7] *Letters from the Lake Poets*, p. 270.

with two letters[1] vindicating his old friend from the
aspersions cast upon him in consequence of the
piratical publication of the absurd *Wat Tyler*, which
the future Laureate had written (but not printed) in
1794 ; and on March 26 he informed John Murray[2] that
'the article in Tuesday's *Courier* was by him ; and
two other articles on Apostacy and Renegadism[3]
which will appear next week.'   These are not included
in the *Essays on his own Times*, and it is not improbable that other contributions have been overlooked,
for in a letter to Stuart of this period Coleridge begs
that his articles 'until Street's return' may be remunerated at the rate of two guineas per column, and
proposes a succession of papers for three or four
months.   I cannot find in Southey's letters any
expression of gratitude for Coleridge's warm and
chivalrous defence of him against the attacks of the
enemy on the subject of *Wat Tyler*, and the charges
of 'apostacy' arising out of it.   Of course Hazlitt took
the fullest advantage of the opportunity, and his tirades
directed against Coleridge, Southey, and Wordsworth,
contributed to Leigh Hunt's *Examiner*, may still be
read in the volume entitled *Political Essays* published
by Hone in 1819.

In June 1817, Ludwig Tieck was in London, and
Coleridge renewed an acquaintance begun at Rome
eleven years before.   The first occasion on which
they met was at the house of Joseph Henry Green,
then a rising young surgeon, who was as deeply
interested in philosophy as in his own profession.

---

[1] *Essays on his own Times*, pp. 939-950.   Two other vindicatory letters
were written for, but not printed in, the *Westminster Review*.   They are given
n the *Essays*, pp. 950-962.

[2] *Memoirs of John Murray*, i. 306.

[3] See also *Letters from the Lake Poets*, p. 280.

Green had long been desirous of taking the waters of German philosophy at the fountain-head, and Tieck recommended a course with Professor Solger of Berlin, a scheme no doubt heartily encouraged by Coleridge. It was immediately carried out, and on Green's return from Berlin, the intimacy with Coleridge began,[1] an intimacy which proved the chief stimulus and the chief comfort of the last seventeen years of Coleridge's life.

In August, Southey came up to town. He saw Stuart, who complained of Coleridge's statements about him and his newspapers in the *Biographia*;[2] and he also saw Coleridge.

> I shall go to Highgate to-morrow (wrote Southey to his wife[3]). I gather from his [Coleridge's] note which I received this morning that he looks towards Keswick as if he meant to live there. At present this cannot be for want of room—the Rickmans being our guests—if he meant to live with his family it must be upon a separate establishment. I shall neither speak harshly nor unkindly, but at my time of life, with my occupations [the thing is impossible]. This is a hateful visit and I wish it were over. He will begin as he did when last I saw him, about Animal Magnetism[4] or some equally congruous subject, and go on from Dan to Beersheba in his endless loquacity.

And Southey, evidently quite soured by this time, goes on to say that Coleridge, if he gets an advance from the publishers of the *Encyclopædia*, will pay it

---

[1] Green's biographer, Sir John Simon, does not feel quite certain as to the date of the beginning of the intimacy, but his suggestion of 1817 is confirmed by an unprinted letter which I have seen.

[2] 'When the book appeared I was extremely angry, and went to him at Mr. Gillman's, where I too warmly reproached him' (Stuart in *Gent. Mag.* June 1838, p. 578). The controversy has been already treated at sufficient length— see p. 107 *supra*.

[3] Streatham, August 13, 1817—an unprinted letter.

[4] Coleridge was at the time deeply interested in this subject. In June he proposed to write a popular book on it, a proposal which he renewed (to Curtis) eighteen months later, when his old teacher, Blumenbach, had recanted his disbelief in Animal Magnetism. He offered to contribute an historical treatise to the *Encyc. Metrop.* The letter, which is extremely interesting, is printed in *Lippincott's Mag.* for June 1874.

away, and then abandon the whole thing.   It is highly
improbable that Coleridge had any intention of settling
at Keswick again ; but he may have said something
vague either about a visit, or a settlement, with
the view of sounding the disposition of the master
of Greta Hall.

September was passed at Littlehampton, and there
Coleridge made acquaintance with two men with whom
he was afterwards on very friendly terms.   One was a
man of fortune with an uncommon taste for philosophical speculation, Charles Augustus Tulk,[1] afterwards
M.P. for Sudbury, and a devoted friend of Flaxman.
The other was ' Dante ' Cary, to whom Coleridge introduced himself[2] while both were walking by the
shore.   He then first heard of Cary's translation of
Dante, which up to that time had received little attention from the public.   Coleridge was greatly pleased
with it, and promised to recommend it in the lectures
which he contemplated delivering in the following
winter.   He did not fail of performance, and the consequences for Cary's book were the immediate sale of
a thousand copies, a new edition, and the position of
⌐n English classic.[3]

*Zapolya*, which had been promised to Fenner for
August, was delivered somewhat late, but in time for
publication as ' A Christmas Tale,' and two thousand
copies were sold.   The essay on *Method*, which was

[1] Coleridge supplied Tulk with an account of his system in a series of twenty-
two long letters, which, bound together in a volume, were sold at Sotheby's
auction rooms, June 13, 1882.   The lot has since been broken up, but could
probably be gathered together again, and might be found to be worth printing as
a connected whole.

[2] *Memoirs of the Rev. H. F. Cary*, 1848, ii. 18.   *Athenæum* for Jan. 7,
1888—Art. ' Coleridge on Cary's *Dante*.'

[3] Such is the story as told by Cary's son and biographer (ii. 28).   Another,
unsupported, however, by any reference to authorities, appears in *Rogers and his
Contemporaries*, ii. 171.

promised for October, was delivered late in December. It was printed in January, and Coleridge received for it sixty guineas. To his friends, he complained bitterly of the way in which the essay had been treated by the editors of the *Encyclopædia*—' bedeviled, interpolated, and topsy-turvied'[1]—and he asked permission to reprint it in *The Friend*, then at press. The permission was granted on condition that it was acknowledged, with the rider, that the essay as written had not been 'approved by the committee.' This condition Coleridge could not accept, but in February 1818, being hard pressed for matter with which to fill up the third volume of *The Friend*, he seems to have taken the enemy in flank, by inserting the substance of the essay without mention of its source.[2] *The Friend* was completed sadly behind time, for it had been put to press more than a year before, on the author's assurance that only the customary 'three weeks' were required to put the whole in order. On January 5th, 1818, Coleridge wrote to Morgan[3]:—

From 10 in the morning till 4 in the afternoon, with one hour only for exercise, I shall fag from to-morrow at the third volume of *The Friend*. I hope to send off the whole by the 1st of February. [It was incomplete on Feb. 18.] As I cannot starve, and yet cannot with ease to my own feelings engage in any work that would interfere with my day's work till the MS. of the third volume of

---

[1] The expression occurs in a letter to J. P. Collier, the original of which is now in the MSS. Department of the British Museum. It was printed in *Notes and Queries*, 1st Ser. x. 22.

[2] 'Coleridge seems to have valued highly certain essays in *The Friend* in which he professed to have reconciled Plato with Bacon' (Prof. Hort in *Cambriage Essays* for 1856 (p. 334), Art. 'Coleridge'). To this passage is appended the following footnote: 'In iii. 108-216, but especially essays viii. and ix. pp. 157-175 [of *The Friend*, ed. 1844]. The same matter in nearly the same words occurs in his treatise on *Method* prefixed to the *Encycl. Metropolitana.*'

[3] Letter in Brit. Museum, *MSS. Addit.* 25612. Printed incompletely and inaccurately in BRANDL, p. 357

*The Friend* is out of my hands, I have been able to hit on [no] mode of reconciling the difficulties but by attempting a course of lectures, of which I very much wish to talk with you.'[1]

At the close of 1817, Wordsworth came up to London, and although he had been displeased[2] with Coleridge's magnificent criticism in the *Biographia*, the two old friends had much intercourse, and before returning to his fastnesses, Wordsworth wrote a most kindly letter to J. P. Collier[3] begging him to do what he could to further the success of Coleridge's projected course of lectures. To Collier, Lamb also wrote on the same subject,[4] describing Coleridge as 'in bad health and worse mind,' and needing encouragement. The recurrence to lecturing as a means of livelihood, which, as we have seen, had been planned as far back as September, took more definite shape in December, and the letter to Morgan shows that by the beginning of the new year it had become a matter of prime necessity. It was then, probably, that the prospectus[5] was issued. How unwillingly and with how keen a sense of humiliation, may be gathered from his letter to Mudford, then assistant editor of the *Courier*.

Woe is me! that at 46 I am under the necessity of appearing as a lecturer, and obliged to regard every hour given to the PERMANENT, whether as poet or philosopher, an hour stolen from others as well as from my own maintenance.[6]

---

[1] Coleridge goes on to threaten his enemies (his publishers and their printers). with a ' vigorous and harmonious' satire, to be called ' Puff and Slander,' but it probably remained unwritten.

[2] 'I recollect hearing Hazlitt say that W. would not forgive a single censure, mingled with however a great mass of eulogy.' H. C. Robinson, *loq*. (Dec. 4, 1817) ; quoted in Knight's *Life of W. W.* ii. 288.

[3] *Seven Lectures on Shakespeare and Milton* [1811]. PREFACE, p. lv.

[4] December 10, 1817. *Letters*, ii. 8.

[5] Printed in Gillman's *Life*; in *Lit. Rem.* vol. i. ; in Ashe's collection, and elsewhere.

[6] *Canterbury Magazine* for September 1834, p. 125.

The prospectus promised fourteen lectures on Shake-speare and on Poetical Literature, native and foreign. From Crabb Robinson's *Diaries* we learn that the first was delivered, at a hall in Flower-de-Luce Court, Fetter Lane, on its appointed day, Jan. 27, 1818, and that, up to the tenth, due dates (Tuesdays and Fridays) had been observed. After the tenth Robin-son went on circuit, not to return until March 26, by which date the course must have been finished.

Hazlitt was lecturing on Poetry at the same time, sometimes on the same evenings, at the Surrey Institution, a competition which cannot have con-tributed to the success of either course. On the evi-dence of Allsop—that Coleridge's lectures were ' con-stantly thronged by the most attentive and intelligent auditory I have ever seen '—it has been believed that the course was very successful pecuniarily, but neither Robinson's nor Coleridge's own account fully bears this out. The audiences fluctuated, and, even more, the quality of the lectures.[1] Robinson was far from being satisfied with most of Coleridge's appearances, feeling that as a rule he was repeating himself—which is not very surprising seeing that he had lectured on the same subjects so often before, and that if there had been any preparation at all, it must have taken place amid the distractions of finishing *The Friend.*[2]

Coleridge forgot to send a ticket for these lectures

[1] The record is scanty. A few preparatory notes, mostly marginalia, on a copy of Warburton's *Shakespeare*, with a few jottings taken down by friends, were piously collected in *Lit. Rem.* (i. 61-241) under the heading ' Course of Lectures, 1818.' A slight addition was made by the publication in *Notes and Queries* (1870, series iv. vol. v. 335, 336) of some memoranda made by a Mr. H. H. Carwardine ; and I have reprinted from Leigh Hunt's *Tatler* some notes of the ninth and fourteenth lectures (*Athenæum*, March 1889).

[2] I suppose the new edition of *The Friend* had been published before June, but have failed to discover the exact date. ' THE FRIEND : A Series of Essays, in Three Volumes (etc.) By S. T. Coleridge. A new edition. London : Printed for Rest Fenner, Paternoster Row, 1818.'

to Lamb, but there was no cessation of intercourse, and when Lamb brought out his collected 'Works' in June 1818, the volumes were dedicated to Coleridge in a letter conceived in terms both reverent and affectionate. After a passage recalling the smoky suppers at the 'Salutation and Cat,' nearly a quarter of a century before, Lamb proceeds :—

> The world has given you many a shrewd nip and gird since that time, but either my eyes are grown dimmer, or my old friend is still the *same* who stood before me three-and-twenty years ago—his hair a little confessing the hand of time, but still shrouding the same capacious brain,—his heart not altered, scarcely where it 'alteration finds.'

The old feeling had suffered no change, but opportunities of free companionship were wanting. In October, Lamb told Southey [1] that he does not now see Coleridge as often as he could wish. 'He never comes to me, and though his host and hostess are very friendly, it puts me out of my way to see one person at another person's house. It was the same when he resided at Morgan's.'

A new friendship was about to begin, and to brighten Coleridge's life. An enthusiastic young man named Thomas Allsop had introduced himself after the first lecture at Flower-de-Luce Court. By September, he was sending Coleridge presents of game, which were repaid by an invitation to 'The Grove,' and before the end of the year Coleridge addressed to him the first of a long series of friendly letters, the publication [2] of which a year or two after Coleridge's death gave offence to the poet's family. These

---

[1] October 26, 1818. *Letters,* ii. 16.

[2] *Letters, Conversations, and Recollections of S. T. Coleridge* (2 vols. Moxon, 1836). My references are to the third edition, with a Preface by the 'Editor,' 'Thomas Allsop, late of Nutfield, in the County of Surrey, and formerly of the Stock Exchange, and Royal Exchange Buildings.' Farrah, 1864. There is a notice of Allsop in the *Dictionary of National Biography.*

letters give almost its sole value to Allsop's book, and make it our main authority for the details of Coleridge's life from 1820 to 1826. Allsop's admiration for the poet and philosopher was unbounded, and his affection was expressed not only in words but in unceasing acts of practical kindness. The affection was abundantly repaid in kind by Coleridge, who almost from the first treated Allsop as a son and as a confidential friend from whom he had no secrets. To Allsop alone in those days Coleridge felt that he could pour out his mind unreservedly, and the third of the printed letters gives expression in a striking passage to his wounded feelings towards Wordsworth—feelings he would hardly have cared to betray to Lamb. The letter is dated Dec. 2, 1818; and Wordsworth is clearly intended though not named. He declares that he has never admitted '*faults* in a work of genius to those who denied or were incapable of feeling and understanding the *beauties*.'

If (he continues), in one instance, in my literary life, I have appeared to deviate from this rule first, it was not till the fame of the writer (which I had been for fourteen years successively toiling like a second Ali to build up [1]) had been established; and, secondly and chiefly, with the purpose, and, I may safely add, with the *effect*, of rescuing the necessary task from malignant defamers, and in order to set forth the excellencies, and the trifling proportion which the defects bore to the excellencies. But this, my dear sir, is a mistake to which affectionate natures are too liable, though I do not remember to have ever seen it noticed—the mistaking *those who are desirous and well pleased to be loved by you, for those who love you.*

---

[1] 'Mr. Wordsworth, for whose fame I had felt and fought with an ardour that amounted to self-oblivion, and to which I owe mainly the rancour of the *Edinburgh* clan, and (far more injurious to me) the coldness, neglect, and equivocal compliments of the *Quarterly Review*, has affirmed *in print* that a German critic *first* taught us to think correctly concerning Shakespeare' (S. T. C. to Mudford, 1818; *Canterbury Mag.* Sep. 1834, p. 126). If Coleridge here referred to the passage in the 'Essay, supplementary to the Preface' to Wordsworth's *Poems*, 1815 (i. 352), his deduction seems to be unwarranted.

He doubts if the open abuse of himself in the *Edinburgh* is worse than the cold compliments and warm 'regrets' of the *Quarterly*, but his own single regret is the old one, that pressing need of bread and cheese diverts him from 'the completion of the great work, the form and materials of which it has been the employment of the best and most genial hours of the last twenty years to mature and collect.' If only he could have a tolerably numerous audience to his first, or first and second lectures on the History of Philosophy, he should entertain a strong hope of success, for the course will be more entertaining than any he has yet delivered.

On Nov. 26, Coleridge had sent to Allsop a prospectus of two sets of lectures to be delivered at the 'Crown and Anchor' tavern, in the Strand,—one of fourteen on the History of Philosophy, the other on six select plays of Shakespeare—*Tempest, Richard II.* (and other dramatic Histories), *Hamlet, Macbeth, Othello,* and *Lear.* The two sets were to be delivered concurrently—the former on Mondays, the latter on Thursdays—intermitting the Christmas week—beginning with Monday, Dec. 7.[1] The commencement, however, was postponed for a week, the first philosophical lecture taking place on Dec. 14, and the first on Shakespeare three days later. Besides the prospectus, there was issued 'An Historical and Chronological Guide to this [Philosophical] Course, price Sixpence,'

[1] Allsop prints the body of the prospectus of the Philosophical Course (p. 240); but makes no mention of the other. Mr. E. H. Coleridge has kindly permitted me to see his unique complete copy of the original. There are other references (pp. 85, 187, 205) to these lectures in Allsop's book, but they have been overlooked by all Coleridge's editors and biographers, who uniformly write of the Flower-de-Luce Court Series (Jan.-March 1818) as the last. No adequate record of either course is known to exist—the few fragments I have been able to discover in the journals of the day will be found gathered together in the *Athenæum* for Dec. 26, 1891, and Jan. 2, 1892—Art. 'Some Lectures delivered by Coleridge in the winter of 1818-19.'

and it is no doubt a portion of this lost pamphlet which Allsop has printed at page 187. A ticket was presented to Lamb, who writes on Dec. 24 [1]:

> Thank you kindly for your ticket, though the mournful prognostic which accompanies it certainly renders its permanent pretensions less marketable; but I trust to hear many a course yet. . . . We are sorry it never lies in your way to come to us, but, dear Mahomet, we will come to you. Will it be convenient to all the good people at Highgate if we take a stage up, *not next Sunday*, but the following, viz. 3rd January 1819. Shall we be too late to catch a skirt [2] of the old out-goer? How the years crumble from under us!

If all the lectures promised in the prospectus were given, the delivery must have been carried into the beginning of April, for there was a break of a week, on account of indisposition. From Coleridge's letter to Mudford (*Canterbury Magazine*), we learn that the lectures attracted but scanty audiences.

> When I tell you that yester-evening's receipts were somewhat better than many of the preceding; and that these did not equal one-half of the costs of the room, and of the stage and hackney coach (the advertisements in the *Times* and *Morning Chronicle*, and the printer's prospectus-bill, not included), you will find no difficulty in understanding the warmth with which I express my sense of your kindness. . . . The *Romeo and Juliet* [3] pleased even beyond my anticipation: but alas! scanty are my audiences! But poverty and I have been such old cronies, that I ought not to be angry with her for sticking close to my skirts.

About the same time Coleridge wrote, also to Mudford:—

> Ah! dear Sir! that week's break was indeed unfortunate; but, I imagine, that my ill-health and despondency that barely enable me to give the lectures themselves respectably, but utterly unfit me for

---

[1] *Letters*, ii. 16.

[2] When lo! far onwards waving on the wind
     I saw the skirts of the DEPARTING YEAR!
         —Original editions of the *Ode*, ll. 7, 8.

[3] *Romeo and Juliet* was not among the six plays announced, but in a letter to Britton (Feb. 28, 1819), a portion of which is printed in the *Lit. Rem.* ii. 2, Coleridge mentions a lecture on *R. and J.* at the 'Crown and Anchor.'

all awkward [outward?] exertion and canvassing, that these joined
with my solitariness, and unconnection with parties of any kind,
literary, religious, or political, are the main causes of my failure.

In another letter he exclaims : 'Alas! dear sir,
these lectures are my only resource. I have worked
hard, very hard, for the last years of my life, but from
Literature I cannot gain even *bread*.' It is impossible
to doubt the perfect sincerity with which Coleridge
so touchingly made his moan ; and it is not surprising
that he never again attempted to lecture at his own
charges. That the vein, however, was not entirely
worked out, appears by the letter to Britton already
mentioned (p. 239, *note* '3 '). From that letter we
gather that Coleridge had been asked to re-deliver, at
the Russell Institution, the course of lectures given at
the Surrey Institution. He replies that he possesses
no MS. or record, even in his memory, of these
or any other lectures he has delivered. 'I should
greatly prefer' (he writes) 'your committee making
their own choice of the subjects from English,
Italian, or German Literature ; and even of the Fine
Arts, as far as the philosophy of the same is alone
concerned.' He goes on to say that he feels himself,
from experience, so utterly unfit to discuss pecuniary
matters, that if the committee will mention the sum it
would be disposed to give, he will consult a friend and
instantly decide. Whether anything came of these
negotiations, I am not aware. Robinson makes no
mention of hearing lectures at the Russell Institution,
but this affords no presumption against the delivery,
for he makes no mention of either of the 'Crown and
Anchor' series.

# CHAPTER XIII

## HIGHGATE—(continued)

### A.D. 1819–1825

In March 1819, Coleridge had an interview with Mr. Blackwood, who had called at the Grove to solicit contributions to his *Magazine*. Surely Coleridge's poverty and not his will consented even to receive the owner of a periodical which, only eighteen months before, had so grossly outraged him. To Mudford, Coleridge wrote[1]: 'I have had an interview with Mr. Blackwood, and it seems not impossible that we may form some connection, on condition that the *Magazine* is to be conducted henceforward,—first, pure from private slander and public malignity; second, on principles the direct opposite to those which have been hitherto supported by the *Edinburgh Review*, moral, political, and religious.' Perhaps Coleridge waited a little to see whether his conditions would be fulfilled, for, with the exception of the famous sonnet 'Fancy *in nubibus*,' nothing of his appeared in *Blackwood* until seventeen months had passed away.[2]

[1] *Canterbury Magazine* for January 1835, p. 31.
[2] With reference to this connection, from which Coleridge evidently shrank, Lamb wrote to S. T. C. (January 10, 1820; *Letters*, ii. 31): 'Why you should refuse twenty guineas per sheet for *Blackwood's* or any other magazine, passes my poor comprehension,—But, as Strap says, "you know best."' Besides the sonnet another exception may perhaps be mentioned, though it was an involun-

And yet in this spring of 1819 he must have been in desperate need of money, for he had been unable to make any remittance to his wife · out of the net proceeds of his lectures, and the fund for sending Derwent to college was still incomplete.    Next, in the summer time, came the bankruptcy of Rest Fenner.

All the profits from the sale of my writings (writes Coleridge to Allsop) which I should have had, and which, in spite of the accumulated disadvantages under which the works were published, would have been considerable, 'I have lost ; and not only so, but have been obliged, at a sum larger than all the profits of my lectures, to purchase myself my own books and the half copyrights. . . . I have withdrawn them from sale.'[1]

It was in April of this year that Coleridge met Keats in a Highgate lane, and is said to have 'felt death in the touch of his hand.'    When, thirteen years later, he related the incident to his nephew (*Table Talk*, Aug. 14, 1832) he had forgotten that the interview had lasted more than 'a minute or so' ; but Keats's own account, only recently given to the world,[2] was contemporary :—

Last Sunday I took a walk towards Highgate, and in the lane that winds by the side of Lord Mansfield's park, I met Mr. Green, our demonstrator at Guy's, in conversation with Coleridge.    I

---

tary contribution.    In August or September 1820, Coleridge wrote a rather effusive private letter to John Gibson Lockhart, who printed it (or a portion of it) in *Blackwood* for September 1820—calling it a ' Letter to Peter Morris, M.D.'—the pseudonym under which *Peter's Letters to his Kinsfolk* was published.    This abuse of his confidence was resented by Coleridge.

[1] *Letters*, etc., pp. 8, 9.    'I lost £1100 *clear*, and was forced to borrow £150 in order to buy up my own books and half copyrights, a shock which has embarrassed me in debt (thank God, to one person only) even to this amount [? moment].'    S. T. C. 8th May 1825 (BRANDL, p. 353).    I have already expressed my estimate of this letter (p. 221 *supra*).    The loss of such a sum as £1100 must have been purely imaginary.    The failure was no doubt both a pecuniary loss and a discouragement, but these were assuaged to some extent by a gift of money, accepted as a loan, from Allsop, who, however, makes no mention of this in his book.

[2] Keats's *Works*, ed. by H. Buxton Forman.    Supp. vol. 1890, p. 147 ; and *Letters of J. K.*, ed. by S. Colvin, 1891, p. 244.

joined them after inquiring by a look whether it would be agreeable. I walked with him, at his alderman-after-dinner pace, for near
two miles, I suppose. In those two miles he broached a thousand
things. Let me see if I can give you a list—nightingales—poetry
—on poetical sensation—metaphysics—different genera and species
of dreams—nightmare—a dream accompanied with a sense of
touch—single and double touch—a dream related—first and second
consciousness—the difference explained between will and volition—
so say metaphysicians from a want of smoking the second consciousness—monsters—the Kraken—mermaids—Southey believes in them
—Southey's belief too much diluted—a ghost story—Good morning
—I heard his voice as he came towards me—I heard it as he moved
away—I had heard it all the interval—if it may be called so. He
was civil enough to ask me to call on him at Highgate.

One cannot but regret that Keats failed to take
advantage of Coleridge's invitation. He was never at
any time in greater need of direction, and the elder poet
had much to teach the younger. Coleridge, in his turn,
would have been cheered and revived in the society
of a youth in whom and in whose rich achievement he
would have discerned a promise almost infinite; while
Keats might have found escape from associates whom
he had outgrown, and from influences which even
then were proving disastrous. Is it worth noting that
this same April was the month of one of Keats's most
perfect poems—*La Belle Dame sans merci*—in which
one seems to hear an echo of the voice which had discoursed to him of unearthly things but a few days
before during that walk on the skirts of Caen wood?

In spring of 1820 Coleridge was gladdened by a
visit from his sons, Hartley and Derwent. 'Would to
Heaven' (he wrote to Allsop, April 10th) 'their dear
sister were with us—the cup of paternal joy would be
full to the brim'; and he cites 'the rapture' with which
both brothers speak of Sara, who had had time to
grow almost into womanhood since her father had last
seen her in the spring of 1813. Coleridge was just

then in urgent need of something to cheer him. The
friendship with Wordsworth, once his most valued
treasure, lay bruised if not broken behind an ever-
thickening veil of misunderstandings; lecturing seemed
to be no longer a resource ; he was depressed by the
failure of his publisher ; and there were other circumstances which combined with these to cause him to
feel that he had been hopelessly distanced in the race
by some men whom he felt were no more than his
equals, and by others whom he knew to be his in-
feriors. This pervading sense of dissatisfaction comes
out strongly in a letter written to Allsop about this
time. Coleridge had been invited by a flattering note
from his neighbour, Charles Mathews, to meet Scott,
and he seems to have forced himself to accept the
encounter only by fear that refusal would cause him
to appear childish in the eyes of men of the world
such as Frere and Stewart Rose. The affair of
*Christabel* still rankled, but one may suppose also that
Coleridge's conscience was pricked when he remembered the rough treatment he had dealt out to Sir
Walter's protége, Maturin, the author of *Bertram.*

> I seem to feel (wrote Coleridge) that I *ought* to feel more desire
> to see an extraordinary man than I really do feel, and I do not wish
> to appear to two or three persons (as the Mr. Freres, William Rose,
> etc.) as if I cherished any dislike to Scott respecting the *Christabel*,
> and generally to appear out of the common and natural mode of
> thinking and acting. All this, I own, is sad weakness, but I am
> weary of *dyspathy*.[1]

Before Coleridge had had time to recover from his
fit of depression, one of the keenest sorrows of his life
came to deepen it. In 1819, Hartley had gained a

---

[1] April 10, 1820. *Letters*, etc., p. 23. Unfortunately no record of this
meeting has come down to us. It is not mentioned by Lockhart. A very interesting criticism of Scott (as an author) was written in a letter to Allsop on
April 8 [?] 1820 (*Letters*, etc., pp. 24-29).

Fellowship at Oriel. 'At the close of his proba-
tionary year he was judged to have forfeited his Oriel
Fellowship, on the ground, mainly, of intemperance.
Great efforts were made to reverse the decision. He
wrote letters to many of the Fellows. His father
went to Oxford to see and expostulate with the Provost. It was in vain. . . . The sentence might be
considered severe, it could not be said to be unjust.'
So writes Hartley's brother[1] of this painful business.
To Allsop, Coleridge wrote of it, July 31, 1820: 'Before I opened your letter . . . a heavy, a very heavy
affliction came upon me with all the aggravations of
surprise, sudden as a peal of thunder from a cloud-
less sky.' The father's conscience smote him. 'This'
(he says of Hartley) 'was the sin of his nature, and
this has been fostered by the culpable indulgence, at
least non-interference, on my part,'[2] and then he asks
Allsop to pray for him that he 'may not pass such
another night as the last.' The grief appears to have
tempted Coleridge into a resort to an extra consumption
of laudanum, with the consequence that the horrors
described in *The Pains of Sleep* were revived. In
August poor Hartley was settled in London under the
fostering care of the Basil Montagus—some reconciliation with whom must have been effected—and set
agoing by his father on some literary tasks. In
October, Coleridge, accompanied by Allsop, went
to Oxford, and had an interview with the Provost of
Oriel—Copleston, afterwards Bishop of Llandaff—on
Hartley's behalf. The 'compensation' of £300 subsequently paid to Hartley may have been an effect of

---

[1] Memoir prefixed to *Poems by H. C.* 1851, i. lxxiv.
[2] *Letters*, etc., p. 40. See *Table Talk* for Jan. 2, 1833: 'Can anything be
more dreadful than the thought that an innocent child has inherited from you a
disease or a weakness, the penalty in yourself of sin, or want of caution.'

the interview. 'Of this journey to Oxford' (says Allsop) 'I have a very painful recollection; perhaps the most painful recollection (one excepted) connected with the memory of Coleridge.'

The shock produced by Hartley's misadventure would seem to have roused Coleridge. In one of the most interesting letters [1] he ever wrote, he attempts to comfort Allsop, who was dissatisfied with his circumstances, by assuring him that he is needed as a hope and promise and impulse 'in my present efforts to realise my past labours.' In the same letter he writes :—

> I at least am as well as I ever am, and my regular employment, in which Mr. [J. H.] Green is weekly my amanuensis, the work on the books of the Old and New Testaments. . . . Would to Heaven, I were with you [in the country]! In a few days you should see that the spirit of the mountaineer is not yet utterly extinct in me.

A few days after his return from Oxford, Coleridge was still hankering after the publication of a pamphlet on the affairs of Queen Caroline,[2] from which he had been twice over dissuaded by Gillman. A month later he has been more than usually unwell, and disheartened by finding Hartley in process of developing some of his own morbid weaknesses—procrastination, shrinking from the performance of duties which are surrounded by painful associations—stimulant motives acting on both as narcotics, 'in exact proportion to their strength.' For himself, he is anxious to get forward with his *Logic* and with his *Assertion of Religion.* In an immensely long letter of January 1821,[3] begun with assurances that if Allsop were a son by nature he could not hold him dearer, Coleridge states that his purpose is to 'open himself out' to his correspondent

---

[1] August 8, 1820.  *Letters*, etc., pp. 54-60.

[2] Quarter of a century before, Coleridge had shed tears over the Princess, in the verses, *On a late connubial rupture in High Life.*

[3] *Letters*, etc., pp. 77-87.

'in detail.' Health of body is lacking, but had he the tranquillity which ease of heart alone could give, health enough might be regained for the accomplishment of his 'noblest undertaking,' the *magnum opus*, which, when completed, will revolutionise 'all that has been called *Philosophy* or Metaphysics in England and France since the era of the commencing predominance of the mechanical system at the restoration of the second Charles.' But this cannot be pursued to any advantage without a settled income. He has nothing actually ready for the booksellers, but he has four works[1] so near completion that he has 'literally nothing more to do than to *transcribe*.' The transcription, however, can only be done by his own hand, for the material exists in 'scraps and *Sibylline* leaves, including margins of books and blank pages.' Then, he owes money 'to those who will not exact it, yet who need its payment'; and, besides, he is far behindhand in the settlement of his accounts for board and lodging. These pressing needs compel him to 'abrogate the name of philosopher and poet, and scribble as fast as he can . . . for *Blackwood's Magazine*,' or (as he has been employed for the last days) 'in writing MS. Sermons for lazy clergymen, who stipulate that the composition must not be more than respectable, for fear they should be desired to publish the visitation Sermon.' 'This' (he adds) 'I have not yet had the courage to do. My soul sickens and my

---

[1] (1) *Characteristics of Shakespeare's Dramatic Works*, together with a Critique on Shakespeare's dramatic contemporaries; three volumes of 500 pages each. (2) *Philosophical Analysis of the genius and works of Dante, Spenser, etc.*; one large volume. (3) *The History of Philosophy*; two volumes. (4) *Letters on the Old and New Testament*, and on the Fathers, with advice on Preaching, etc., addressed to a candidate for Holy Orders. I have compressed the titles. Numbers 1, 2, and 3 evidently refer to notes made for the lectures he had delivered. Some part of No. 4 is extant in MS.

heart sinks. . . . Of my poetic works, I would fain
finish the *Christabel*. Alas! for the proud time
when I planned, when I had present to my mind, the
materials as well as the scheme of the Hymns entitled
Spirit, Sun, Earth, Air, Water, Fire, and Man, and the
Epic poem on—what still appears to me the one only
fit subject remaining for an Epic poem—Jerusalem besieged and destroyed by Titus.'[1] Out of the dead-lock
he can discern but one way—it is not a new one—that
a few friends 'who think respectfully and hope highly
of his powers and attainments' should subscribe for
three or four years an annuity of about £200. Two-
thirds of his time would be tranquilly devoted to the
bringing out of the four minor works, one after the
other; the remainder to the completion of the Great
Work 'and my *Christabel*, and what else the happier
hour might inspire.' Towards this scheme Mr. Green
has offered £30 to £40 yearly; another young
friend and pupil, £50; and he thinks he can rely on
£10 to £20 from another. Will Allsop advise him?
he asks, and decide if without 'moral degradation'
the statement now made, but in a compressed form,
might be circulated among the right sort of people?

Allsop tells us nothing more, and we may assume
that nothing came of the scheme, but in March, Coleridge informs his friend[2] that he has called on Murray
with a proposal that 'he should take him and his con-
cerns, past and future, for print and reprint, under his
umbrageous foliage.' 'He promises . . .' but here
the scrap of a letter ends—'*cætera desunt*,' adds
Allsop. Whatever publisher and author may have
promised to each other, no business resulted, and

---

[1] See, on this 'only fit subject,' *Table Talk*, April 28, 1832, and September
4, 1833.                                                    [2] *Letters*, etc., p. 95.

Coleridge had nothing to offer to the trade for yet three years.

In July he writes to Poole, whom he had met shortly before in London, that his health is not painfully worse, and that he is making steady progress with the *magnum opus*, and asks for copies of the letters about his childhood [1] and about the 'Brocken'— probably intending to work them up into papers for *Blackwood*. If such was the intention, it was not carried out. At last, in September, he managed to scrape together something for *Blackwood* — trifles which appeared in the magazine for the following month,[2] together with what professes to be a private letter to the proprietor.[3]

A sojourn of nearly two months at Ramsgate,[4] in company with the Gillmans, greatly improved the philosopher's health and spirits, and he was almost persuaded by Dr. Anster [5] to undertake the delivery of a course of lectures in Dublin.[6]

---

[1] Some of which are printed in the supplement to the *Biographia Literaria*, ed. 1847, and quoted from in the first chapter of this book. The 'Brocken' letter was printed in the *Amulet* for 1829. See p. 98 *supra*.

[2] 'Selections from Mr. Coleridge's Literary Correspondence with Friends and Men of Letters.'

[3] I have a copy of the real letter, which is very unlike the print. Coleridge promised 'within ten days' several papers, which, in their turn, would be followed by 'the substance of his Lectures on Shakespeare,' etc. He further promised to devote the next six weeks undividedly to the magazine, and requests an advance of £50 to enable him to go to the seaside. This advance no doubt was made, for a week later he tells Allsop (p. 130) that his circumstances are easier, and that he is about to sail for Ramsgate. Of the articles promised none appeared in *Blackwood* except *Maxilian*, a fantastic piece of mental autobiography, printed in the number for Jan. 1822, and this no doubt fully liquidated the balance of the advance of £50.

[4] The Cowden Clarkes introduced themselves to him on the East Cliff as friends of Lamb, and straightway he discoursed to them on the spot for an hour and a half. They knew Coleridge must be in the town, for a friend 'had heard an elderly gentleman in the public library, who looked like a Dissenting minister, talk as she never heard man talk' (*Recoll. of Writers*, 1878, pp. 30-32).

[5] Regius Professor of Civil Law at Trinity College, Dublin, and translator of *Faust*. I have a copy of his *Poems* (1819), the first few leaves of which were cut open and annotated by Coleridge.

[6] Allsop's *Letters*, etc., pp. 149-161.

But with the new year (1822) came a new idea—
the extension of his philosophical class.[1]  For more
than four years Green had been 'pumped·into' for the
whole of one day in each week.  A Mr. Stutfield,
with a Mr. Watson, had recently begun to come on
Thursdays, and Coleridge thought he could as easily
dictate to five or six amanuenses as to a pair,—if so
many were procurable.  In February an advertisement was inserted in the *Courier*, but Stuart—who
had forgiven or forgotten the wounds received in the
house of his friend—thought it hardly precise enough,
and in a long letter which explained the scheme,[2] Coleridge consulted him as to something more effective.

There have been three or four young men (under five-and-
twenty) who, within the last five years, have believed themselves,
and have been thought by their acquaintance, to have derived
benefit from their frequent opportunities of conversing, reading, and
occasionally corresponding with me ; the benefit consisting, not
merely, nor even principally, in the information received, but in the
improvement and accelerated growth of their faculties ; and in the
formation, or at least in the grounding, strengthening and *integra-
tion*, as it were, of their whole character.  Under this persuasion, at
least, a young man . . . has importuned me to suffer him to be
with me . . . some one day in each week from noon to four or five
o'clock ; but as what he could afford would leave it doubtful whether
it would compensate for the .expenditure of my time and the inter-
ruption of my literary pursuits (in plain English, whether I could
not get more by employing the time in writing for the Magazine, or
the booksellers) it was suggested . . . that I might form a class of five
or six men who are educating themselves for the Pulpit, the Bar, the
Senate, or any of those walks of life, in which the possession and the
display of intellect are of especial importance.

The 'course' was to occupy two years, and the class-
room might be either at Highgate or in Green's
drawing-room in Lincoln's Inn Fields.  Either then
or soon after, some such classes were formed, but I

[1] Allsop's *Letters*, etc., p. 166.
[2] *Letters from the Lake Poets*, pp. 281-286.  'Posted March 15, 1822.'

doubt if any numbered so many as five or six pupils, or lasted for two years. To *Fraser's Magazine* for 1835, one of these disciples contributed specimens of what he and his fellows took down from Coleridge's lips ; and he informs us that, although no fees were stipulated, the disciples 'gave the teacher such recompense of reward as they were able to render.'[1]

In a letter to Allsop of Dec. 26, 1822,[2] Coleridge announces that the work on Logic,—in its three main divisions, Canon, Criterion, and Organ,—is all but completed. He has no doubt that, by the end of January, the book will be 'ready for the press.' By the time this work is 'printed off,' he will be ready with another volume of *Logical Exercises*, and all this 'without interrupting the greater work on Religion, of which the first half . . . was completed on Sunday last.' Perhaps I have printed too many such passages from Coleridge's letters, but I have suppressed an immeasurably greater number — and may plead that the life of a visionary cannot be told without the inclusion of a good many examples of the visions which most persistently haunted him.[3]

---

[1] January 1835, p. 50. A second article appeared in the following November.

[2] *Letters*, etc., p. 204. See also Prefatory Memoir of Green in *Spiritual Philosophy*, i. xxxviii.

[3] In 1892, Mr. C. A. Ward of Chingford Hatch acquired 'two volumes, quarto, of MSS. bound, entitled respectively, "The History of Logic," and "The Elements of Logic"' (*Athenæum*, July 1, 1893—Art. "Coleridge's 'Logic'"). Mr. Ward has kindly informed me that these MSS. came to him indirectly from the auction sale at which the library of Coleridge's literary executor, the late Mr. Joseph Henry Green, was dispersed. Mr. Ward assumes, apparently with good reason, that the MSS. are of Coleridge's composition, though not in his handwriting, and that they represent the dictated work on Logic mentioned in his letter to Allsop quoted in the text. It may also be assumed that it was of these MSS. that Mr. Green wrote as follows in *Notes and Queries* for June 10, 1854 :—'Of the three parts mentioned [in Coleridge's letter of Dec. 26, 1822] as the components of the work [on Logic], the "Criterion" and "Organ" do not to my knowledge exist ; and with regard to the other parts of the manuscript, including the "Canon," I believe that I have exercised a sound discretion in not publishing them in their present form and unfinished state.' This formed part of

In the Christmas week of 1822, Mrs. Coleridge
and her daughter Sara arrived at the Grove on a visit
which was prolonged until the end of the following
February, after which the ladies went on to stay with
their relatives at Ottery St. Mary. It is pleasant to
read in a contemporary letter of Mrs. Coleridge that
'our visits to Highgate and Ottery have been produc-
tive of the greatest satisfaction to all parties.' 'All
parties' included Henry Nelson Coleridge, who seems
at once to have fallen in love with his cousin, whose
delicate beauty and grace charmed all beholders.
'Yes,' wrote Lamb to Barton, 'I have seen Miss
Coleridge, and wish I had just such a—daughter.
God love her! . . . Heaven send her uncle [Southey]
do not breed her up a *Quarterly Reviewer!*'[1] The
cousin's love was returned, and the girl's mother
smiled on the attachment, but there could yet be no
formal engagement. The cousins themselves, however, considered the matter as settled, and never
wavered throughout the seven years which had to
pass before marriage was practicable—the long
delay being mainly caused by the delicate health of
both.

Coleridge, though he seems to have hesitated a

---

Mr. Green's answer to a 'query' as to Coleridge's unpublished MSS. which had
been made by the late Mr. Mansfield Ingleby. See also a paper 'On the
unpublished MSS. of S. T. Coleridge,' read by C. M. Ingleby, LL.D., before
the Royal Society of Literature, June 12, 1867 (*Trans.* 2nd Ser. ix. part i.)

[1] Feb. 17, 1823. On March 11 he writes again to Barton: 'The She-
Coleridges have taken flight, to my regret. With Sara's own-made acquisitions,
her unaffectedness and no-pretensions are beautiful. You might pass an age
with her without suspecting that she knew anything but her mother tongue. . . .
Poor C., I wish he had a home to receive his daughter in; but he is but a
stranger or a visitor in this world.' On the 5th March, Lamb describes a dinner-
party at which he had been present the evening before. 'I dined in Parnassus,
with Wordsworth, Coleridge, Rogers, and Tom Moore. . . . Coleridge was in
his finest vein of talk—had all the talk; and let 'em talk as evilly as they do of
the envy of poets, I am sure not one there but was content to be nothing but a
listener.' (Moore's account of the dinner will be found in his *Journals*, iv. 51.
It is quoted in *Lamb's Letters*, ii. 320.)

good deal before sanctioning the engagement,[1] took very kindly to his nephew as a friend and companion. The first record of *Table Talk* between uncle and nephew is headed 'Dec. 29, 1822,' a date which coincides almost exactly with the arrival of the aunt and cousin. 'It was,' writes H. N. C., 'the very first evening I spent with him after my boyhood.' The renewed intercourse was destined to be cemented by mutual affection, and this led to the happy reconciliation of Coleridge with the other members of his family. On May Day of this year he dined with his nephew John Taylor Coleridge, the brother of Henry Nelson ; and, a little later, we read of his meeting, at the same house, their father, Colonel James. Various records of this and succeeding years show that Coleridge went pretty frequently into society, charming alike with his divine talk the dignified guests of Beaumont and Sotheby, the professional and philosophic friends of Green, and the equally refined but more general company brought together by Mr. and Mrs. Aders. The famous Highgate 'Thursday evening' was probably not a regular institution much, if at all, before 1824, but two or three years earlier the silver tongue had begun to attract an increasing stream of willing listeners, other than the professed disciples. Edward Irving was a sedulous and eminently receptive visitor as early as 1822.

In a letter of July, Southey mentions that Coleridge talked of publishing a work on Logic, of collecting his poems, and of adapting *Wallenstein* for

---

[1] 'If the matter were quite open, I should incline to disapprove the intermarriage of first cousins ; but the Church has decided otherwise on the authority of Augustine, and that seems enough on such a point' (*Table Talk*, June 10, 1824). Subsequently, confidence in these authorities was shaken, for on July 29, 1826, he requests Mr. and Mrs. Daniel Stuart to favour him with their opinion on the point (*Letters from the Lake Poets*, p. 299).

the stage—'Kean having taken a fancy to exhibit himself in it'[1]—but none of these projects came to anything, save the second, and that some five years later. The autumn of 1823 is remarkable for a revival of Coleridge's long dormant poetical faculty. The first draft of the exquisite *Youth and Age* is dated 'Sep. 10, 1823,' and seems to have been inspired by a day-dream of happy Quantock times.[2] Unfortunately, the faculty seems to have gone to sleep again almost immediately, and all the hours which could be spared from talk, and Green, and the *magnum opus* were given to Leighton, of whom Coleridge had said to Cottle, in 1807, that if there could be an 'intermediate space between inspired and uninspired writings' that space would be occupied by those of the Scottish Archbishop.[3] What had been at first intended as selections of 'Beauties'[4] grew into that which became the most popular of all Coleridge's prose works—*Aids to Reflection*. In January 1824 Lamb reports that the book is a 'good part printed but sticks for a little *more copy*.' It 'stuck,' alas! for more than a year—why, it is impossible to conjecture, unless his interest in Leighton palled, for in the interval Coleridge must have written[5] the bulk of a volume or two

---

[1] *Life and Corr.*, v. 142.

[2] The first draft of *Youth and Age* is printed only in *Poetical Works*, ed. 1893, p. 640.

[3] 'There is in him something that must be felt, even as the Scriptures must be felt.' *Rem.* p. 314.

[4] 'With a few notes and a biographical preface. . . . Hence the term, *Editor*, subscribed to the Notes.' See Preface to *Aids to Reflection*, 1825, p. iii.

[5] Although not published till 1840, Coleridge's *Confessions of an Enquiring Spirit* was probably composed in the latter half of 1824. 'Letter I.' begins thus : 'I employed the compelled and most unwelcome leisure of severe indisposition in reading *The Confessions of a Fair Saint* in Mr. Carlyle's recent translation of the *Wilhelm Meister*. . . . This, acting in conjunction with the concluding sentences of your letter . . . gave the immediate occasion to the following confessions,' etc. Carlyle presented Coleridge with a copy of the newly-published *Wilhelm Meister* in June 1824.

of similar *marginalia* on the books he read in the delightful new room prepared for him by his kind hosts —the one pictured in the frontispiece to the second volume of *Table Talk*.  The cage had been gilded, but the bird seems to have felt the pressure of the wires, for towards the end of March 1824, Coleridge took French leave, and established himself at Allsop's house in London.  The Gillmans probably had no difficulty in discovering the whereabouts of the truant, and in ten days they happily recovered him, never to lose him any more.[1]  Two months later we find him attending a 'dance and rout at Mr. Green's in Lincoln's Inn Fields.'  'Even in the dancing-room, notwithstanding the noise of the music, he was able to declaim very amusingly on his favourite topics' to the ever-willing Robinson, who had joined the giddy throng and who 'stayed till three.'  A week later the same diarist records: [Thursday] June 10th, 'Dined at Lamb's, and then walked with him to Highgate, self-invited.  There we found a large party.  Mr. Coleridge talked his best.'[2]

In the previous month Irving had preached a Missionary Society sermon, which, when published in the winter, bore a dedication to Coleridge that greatly took the fancy of Lamb.  'I have got acquainted with Mr. Irving, the Scotch preacher' (he writes to Leigh Hunt).  'He is a humble disciple at the foot of Gamaliel S. T. C.  Judge how his own sectarists must

---

[1] See letter of April 8, 1824, and Allsop's remarks thereon (*Letters*, etc., p. 213).  The cause of the temporary rupture is unknown to me, but there is some reason for supposing it to have been connected with the discovery that Coleridge was not strictly confining his consumption of laudanum to the quantities prescribed and supplied by Mr. Gillman.

[2] The subject was the internal evidence for Christianity.  It pleased Henry Taylor (*ætat.* 24) to play devil's advocate on behalf of Mahometanism, which impelled Lamb, when the departing guests were hunting for their hats, to ask him : 'Are you looking for your turban, sir?'

stare when I tell you he has dedicated a book to
S. T. C., acknowledging to have learnt more of the
nature of faith, Christianity, and Christian Church from
him, than from all the men he ever conversed with!'[1]
'This' (wrote Lamb to Barton) 'from him,—the great
dandled and petted sectarian—to a religious character
so equivocal in the world's eye as that of S. T. C., so
foreign to the Kirk's estimate—can this man be a
quack?'

In May or June, 1825, *Aids to Reflection*[2] struggled
into the light, but with a printed list of 'Corrections and
Amendments' as long as that which graced the *Sibylline Leaves*, while the presentation copies had as many
more added in manuscript. To Julius Hare it
appeared to crown its author as 'the true sovereign of
modern English thought'; while some younger men,
as yet unknown to the author—Maurice and Sterling
among others—felt that to this book they 'owed even
their own selves.'[3]

Theologians differing as widely as the Bishop
(Howley) of London, and Blanco White joined in
approving, but the reviewers were almost silent, and
the sale was slow.[4] The author's natural disappoint-

---

[1] *Letters*, ii. 121, 127.    Lamb repeated this in a letter to Wordsworth,
April 6, 1825 (*Ib.* ii. 129).

[2] *Aids to Reflection in the formation of a manly character, on the several
grounds of Prudence, Morality, and Religion: illustrated by select passages from
our elder Divines, especially from Archbishop Leighton.*  By S. T. Coleridge.

> This makes that whatsoever here befalls,
> You in the region of yourself remain,
> Neighb'ring on Heaven : and that no foreign land.
>                                        *Daniel.*

London : Printed for Taylor & Hessey, 93 Fleet Street ; and 13 Waterloo Place,
Pall Mall.    1825.    8vo, pp. xvi.; 404.    Frequently reprinted.

[3] Prefatory Memoir of John Sterling in *Essays and Tales*, by J. S., 2 vols.
1848, i. xiv.

[4] S. T. C. to Stuart (*Letters from the Lake Poets*, p. 287).    He adds that
the comment on Aph. vi. p. 147 'contains the aim and object of the whole
book'; and draws particular attention to the notes at pp. 204-207 and 218; to
the last 12 lines of p. 252 ; and to the 'Conclusion, p. 377.'

ment was somewhat solaced by his nomination to one of the ten Royal Associateships of the newly-chartered 'Royal Society of Literature,' each of which carried an annuity of a hundred guineas from the King's Privy Purse. This appointment was probably obtained through the exertions of Basil Montagu, aided by the powerful influence of John Hookham Frere, who for some years past had been one of Coleridge's kindest and most highly-valued friends. It would seem that each Associate had to go through the formality of delivering an essay before the Society, and accordingly Coleridge, on May 18, 1825, read a paper on the *Prometheus* of Æschylus, which has been printed in his *Literary Remains*. It was stated to be 'preparatory to a series of disquisitions,' which, however, did not follow.

About this time appeared Hazlitt's *Spirit of the Age*, with a flamboyant sketch of Coleridge for one of its most notable chapters. The high lights, as usual, are very high, and the shadows very black, but the middle tints, also as usual, are laid on with an unsteady hand—in this particular instance, perhaps, owing to some remorseful desire to be simply just and fair. The presence of an attempt in this direction is as apparent as its want of success, for though the essay bristles with barbed home-truths, they are not, as usual, poisoned. Coleridge is charged, of course, with political apostasy, but only to the extent of having 'turned on the pivot of a subtle casuistry to the unclean side'; he has not declined to the utter profligacy of becoming a poet-laureate or a stamp-distributer—only into 'torpid uneasy repose, tantalised by useless resources, haunted by vain imaginings, his lips idly moving, but his heart for ever still.'   Coleridge took it all very complacently, expressing his own view of his past and present in the good-humoured doggerel which he called *A Trifle* and the editors of his poems, *A Character.*

# CHAPTER XIV

## LAST YEARS AT HIGHGATE

### A.D. 1825–1834

THE receipt of the annuity from the Privy Purse doubtless eased Coleridge's mind, and the minds of those about him, and I think that from this time he must have given up the struggle which, hitherto, and with varying energy and varying success, he had endeavoured in some fashion to keep up with the outer world. After the publication of *Aids to Reflection*, he seems to have assumed, and to have been permitted to keep for the rest of his life, the unique position which Carlyle so picturesquely describes: 'Coleridge sat on the brow of Highgate Hill in those years, looking down on London and its smoke-tumult, like a sage escaped from the inanity of life's battle, attracting towards him the thoughts of innumerable brave souls engaged there.'[1] Carlyle was himself one of the first of the brave souls who were attracted to the pool—led thither in June 1824 by his friend Irving; but unlike that friend, he came away sorrowing, having found no healing in its waters. The well-known, full-length portrait of Coleridge, elaborated with all the resources of an art in which Carlyle was supreme, in

[1] *Life of Sterling*, chap. viii.

the *Life of John Sterling*, though placed there in a
setting of 1828-30, was painted exclusively from
studies made between June 1824 and March 1825.
Here is the first rough sketch :—

I have seen many curiosities ; not the least of them I reckon
Coleridge, the Kantian metaphysician and quondam Lake poet. I
will tell you all about our interview when we meet. Figure a fat,
flabby, incurvated personage, at once short, rotund, and relaxed,
with a watery mouth, a snuffy nose, a pair of strange brown, timid,
yet earnest-looking eyes, a high tapering brow, and a great bush of
grey hair ; and you have some faint idea of Coleridge. He is a
kind, good soul, full of religion and affection, and poetry and animal
magnetism. His cardinal sin is that he wants *will*. He has no
resolution. He shrinks from pain or labour in any of its shapes.
His very attitude bespeaks this. He never straightens his knee-
joints. He stoops with his fat, ill-shapen shoulders, and in walking
he deos not tread, but shovel [shuffle?] and slide. My father
would call it 'skluiffing.' He is also always busied to keep, by
strong and frequent inhalations, the water of his mouth from overflowing, and his eyes have a look of anxious impotence. He
*would* do all with his heart, but he knows he dares not. The conversation of the man is much as I anticipated—a forest of thoughts,
some true, many false, more *part* dubious, all of them ingenious
in some degree, often in a high degree. But there is nó method in
his talk ; he wanders like a man sailing among many currents,
whithersoever his lazy mind directs him ; and what is more
unpleasant, he preaches, or rather soliloquises. He cannot speak,
he can only *tal-k* (so he names it). Hence I found him unprofit-
able, even tedious, but we parted very good friends, and promising
to go back, and see him some evening—a promise which I fully
intend to keep. I sent him a copy of *Meister* about which we had
some friendly talk. I reckon him a man of great and useless
genius, a strange, not at all a great man.[1]

Further intercourse led Carlyle to describe Coleridge as 'sunk inextricably in putrescent indolence';

[1] T. C. to his brother John, June 24, 1824 (Froude's *T. Carlyle*, 1795-1835,
i. 222). In the *Reminiscences* (i. 231) Carlyle says : 'Early in 1825 was my
last sight of "Coleridge." Another great Scotchman, also a friend of Irving,
Dr. Chalmers, a man assuredly deficient neither in sympathy nor imagination,
heard Coleridge talk for three hours without getting more than occasional
glimpses of "what he would be at"' (Hanna's *Life*, iii. 160). Chalmers's little
daughter (afterwards Mrs. Hanna) accompanied him, and used to relate how
she sate literally entranced by the mellifluous flow of the discourse of which
she did not understand a word. When its music ceased, the child's overwrought
feelings found relief in tears.

and, enamoured of the pretty metaphor, he repeats and expands it in a letter of January 22, 1825 : 'Coleridge is a mass of richest spices putrefied into a dunghill. I never hear him *tawlk* without feeling ready to worship him, and toss him in a blanket.'[1]

Intercourse with Lamb was kept up intermittently. In March 1826, one finds him preparing for a Thursday evening 'that he may not appear unclassic,' but a private undraped Wednesday, such as we read of two months later, was probably more to his taste. In the summer of this year Coleridge paid a visit to the Lambs' cottage at Islington, meeting Thomas Hood and praising his now forgotten Hogarth-like etching, *The Progress of Cant* and some little drawings the silent young man had brought with him. An anonymous member of the party relates that when the evening was far spent Coleridge walked back alone to Highgate—a distance of three or four miles—and describes the affectionate leave-taking of the friends 'as if they had been boys,' and how Coleridge gave Mary a parting kiss.[2] In March, Coleridge had thoughts of varying his employments by writing a pantomime, possibly to be founded on Decker's *Old Fortunatus*, as Lamb, who was consulted, offered to lend one of that dramatist's plays, if Coleridge 'thought he could filch something out of it.'[3]

---

[1] FROUDE, i. 292. One should try to enjoy all this full-flavoured language without taking it too seriously. Even in 1824-25 Carlyle confesses that the 'sad hag, Dyspepsia, had got him bitted and bridled, and was ever striving to make his waking living day a thing of ghastly nightmares (*Rem.* i. 241). He called the then literary world of London 'this rascal rout, this dirty rabble, destitute . . . even of common honesty' (FROUDE, i. 264). How much he knew of it may be gauged, possibly, by the statement that 'the *gin-shops* and pawnbrokers bewail Hazlitt's absence'—Hazlitt, who drank only tea ! Besides, one must not forget that Carlyle was, by nature and practice, Coleridge's rival in monologue, and ill-suited for the part of 'passive bucket' assigned to him at Highgate.

[2] *Monthly Repository* for 1835, pp. 162-169.

[3] C. L. to S. T. C. March 22, 1826 (*Letters*, ii. 144).

About this time, Coleridge informed Stuart [1] that his mind during the past two years, and particularly during the last, had been undergoing a change as regards personal religion.   He finds himself thinking and reasoning on all religious subjects with a more cheerful sense of freedom, because he is secure of his faith in a personal God, a resurrection and a Redeemer, and further, and practically for the first time, 'confident in the efficacy of prayer.' [2]   This spring saw the publication of Henry Nelson Coleridge's delightfully vivacious *Six Months in the West Indies*, a record of his travels in search of health during the winter of 1825-26.   Some of its vivacities displeased the author's uncle and prospective father-in-law, as we gather from a letter of Lamb: 'Your finding out my style in your nephew's pleasant book is surprising to me.   I want eyes to descry it.   You are a little too hard on his morality, though I confess he has more of Sterne about him than of Sternhold.   But he saddens into excellent sense before the conclusion.' [3] The nephew does not seem to have been taken into favour again until the beginning of 1827, when his sweetheart arrived on a second and longer visit to her father.

An attempt was then being made to procure some sinecure place for Coleridge.   Frere had obtained from the Prime Minister, Lord Liverpool, a promise,

---

[1] April 19, 1826 (*Letters from the Lake Poets*, p. 294).

[2] See *Table Talk*, June 1, 1830, *note ;* also Cottle's *Rem.* pp. 370, 382.

[3] C. L. to S. T. C. March 22, 1826 (*Letters*, ii. 144).   I fear that Coleridge was making things hard for the lovers.   Uncle and nephew appear to have held no *Table Talk* between June 10, 1824, and February 24, 1827.   Of this long period H. N. C.'s voyage only accounts for December 1824 to September 1825; and it was in July 1826 that Coleridge had the renewed doubts as to the propriety of marriage between first cousins (see p. 253 *supra*, footnote 1).   There is another great gap in the *Table Talk*—August 30, 1827, to April 13, 1830.   The marriage took place at Keswick in September 1829.

apparently, of the Paymastership of the Gentleman Pensioners—vacant by the death of William Gifford!—but the negotiations, unfortunately, dragged on until the autumn, when the death of Canning, who had accepted the legacy of his predecessor's promise, put an end to Coleridge's hopes.[1]  On February 24 he informs Stuart that ' Mr. Gillman, with Mr. Jameson, has undertaken to superintend an edition of all his poems, to be brought out by Pickering : that is to say, I have given all the poems, as far as this edition is concerned, to Mr. Gillman.'[2]  This was the edition in three volumes (it had been advertised to appear in four) which was published in 1828.[3]  Three hundred copies only were printed, and before October all had been sold, and another edition was prepared—to appear, after much revision, in 1829.[4]

The earliest glimpse one gets of the poet in 1828 is in Scott's *Journal* for April 22 :—

Lockhart and I dined with Sotheby, where we met a large dining party, the orator of which was that extraordinary man Coleridge. After eating a hearty dinner, during which he spoke not a word, he began a most learned harangue on the Samothracian Mysteries, which he considered as affording the germs of all tales about fairies past, present, and to come.  He then diverged to Homer, whose *Iliad*

---

[1] *Letters from the Lake Poets*, pp. 301-307, February and October 1827.

[2] *Ibid.* p. 306.  Jameson was a friend of Hartley, and the husband of Mrs. Jameson, the well-known writer on Art.

[3] THE POETICAL WORKS OF S. T. COLERIDGE, including the Dramas of *Wallenstein*, *Remorse*, and *Zapolya*.  In three Volumes.  London : William Pickering.  MDCCCXXVIII.
Octavo, Vol. I. pp. x., 253; II. 370; III. 428.

[4] *Letters from the Lake Poets*, p. 319—THE POETICAL WORKS OF S. T. COLERIDGE, including the Dramas of *Wallenstein*, *Remorse*, and *Zapolya*. In three Volumes.  [The publisher's device of Aldine anchor and dolphin.] London : William Pickering.  MDCCCXXIX.
Octavo, Vol. I. pp. x., 353; II. 394; III. 428.
The last edition on which Coleridge was able to bestow personal care and attention.  That of 1834 was arranged mainly, if not entirely, at the discretion of H. N. Coleridge.  The editions of 1828 and 1829 differ materially.  See *Poet. Works*, 1893, Appendix K, pp. 552-555.

he considered a collection of poems by different authors, at different times during a century.[1] There was, he said, the individuality of an age, but not of a country. Morritt, a zealous worshipper of the old bard, was incensed at a system which would turn·him into a polytheist, gave battle with keenness, and was joined by Sotheby, our host. Mr. Coleridge behaved with the utmost complaisance and temper, but relaxed not from his exertions. 'Zounds, I was never so bethumped with words.' Morritt's impatience must have cost him an extra sixpence worth of snuff.[2]

In June and July, Coleridge, accompanied by Wordsworth and his daughter Dora, spent six pleasant weeks on the Rhine. Fortunately, two not inconsiderable records of portions of the tour have been preserved by outside observers. T. Colley Grattan, then resident in Brussels, acted as the helpful and intelligent guide of the party to Waterloo and other places in the neighbourhood, and in his *Beaten Paths*[3] he gives a pleasant account of the time. When the tourists moved up to Godesberg to stay with the Aderses at their villa, they found a fellow-guest in the much-reminiscent Julian Young, then a giddy but observant youth just escaped from Oxford. In his

[1] Coleridge was a Wolfian (without having read Wolf), and the creed is vigorously expressed in *Table Talk* for May 12, 1830, and July 9, 1832. Coleridge professed to have received his first hint from Vico's *Scienza Nuova*.

[2] *The Journal of Sir Walter Scott, from the original at Abbotsford*, 1890, ii. 164. (The passage in an abbreviated form is in Lockhart's *Life* (1837), vii. 126).
   Mr. Douglas quotes in a footnote a passage from Lockhart's *Theodore Hook* (1853, pp. 23-4) in which an account is given of a dinner-party of a highly bacchanalian description, at which Lockhart met Coleridge, probably about this period. A more detailed account will be found in Jerdan's *Autobiography* (1853, iv. 233-4). The party was given by F. M. Reynolds in a summer cottage at Highgate. Theodore Hook entertained the company with a string of impromptu verses on Coleridge, who greatly enjoyed the feat. Coleridge seems to have taken an active part in all the revels of the evening. 'In walking home' (writes Lockhart) 'with Mr. Coleridge, he entertained —— and me with a most excellent lecture on the distinction between talent and genius, and declared that Hook was as true a genius as Dante—*that* was his example.' What appears to be Coleridge's letter to Reynolds, accepting his invitation to this party, is printed in the *Athenæum* for Jan. 17, 1835, but neither this letter nor either of the chronicles is dated. The party took place, probably, in the autumn of 1828 or 1829.

[3] *Beaten Paths, and those who trod them*, by Thomas Colley Grattan, 2 vols. 1865, ii. 107-145.

*Journal*[1] Young gives a lively account of his intercourse with the poets. Their fame, he tells us, 'soon
attracted to Mrs. Aders's house all the "illuminati" of
Bonn—Niebuhr, Becker, Augustus Schlegel, and many
others,' and copious talk ensued—in German. Little of
it, however, could have been for edification, for Wordsworth had probably forgotten most of his slender Goslar
attainment, while Coleridge's pronunciation of German
was so unintelligible that Schlegel, the only one of the
'illuminati' who understood English, had to beg him
to use his native tongue. When the two poets were
together, Wordsworth 'as a rule allowed Coleridge to
have all the talk to himself,' and Young 'never saw
any manifestations of small jealousy' between the
friends—being good enough to add an expression of
his pleased surprise, 'considering the vanity possessed
by each.' Both diarists describe Coleridge's general
appearance as suggesting 'a dissenting minister.'
Grattan was glad to find him unlike his 'engraved
portrait'—(he evidently means Northcote's scowling
counterfeit)—face extremely handsome, mouth particularly pleasing, grey eyes 'full of intelligent softness,'
cheeks unfurrowed and lit with a healthy bloom, figure
'full and lazy, but not actually stout,' black coat with
shorts and silk stockings. Young's portrait is, in
essentials, not inconsistent, but in some details is
(naturally perhaps) less flattering—build uncouth, hair
long and neglected, 'stockings of lavender-coloured
worsted,' white starchless neck-cloth tied in a limp
bow, shabby suit of dusky black.

It was on his way home that Coleridge sniffed the
two-and-seventy stenches of Cologne—at their worst,

[1] *A Memoir of Charles Mayne Young, Tragedian, with Extracts from his
Son's Journal.* By Julian Charles Young. 2nd ed. 1871, pp. 115-123.

probably, in a hot July—but he thoroughly enjoyed his tour, and reported himself to Stuart as improved by it in health, spirits, and mental activity. This was written in October, when he took another pleasant outing in a week's visit to the Lambs at Enfield Chase. Here he describes himself as 'living temperately and taking a good deal of exercise,' but, unfortunately, the visit wound itself up in a twelve-mile walk in tight shoes. Poets enjoy no immunity from the penalities of such follies, and the consequent confinement to the sofa brought on 'an indescribable depression of spirits' and 'a succession of disturbed nights'—nights which prompted him to quote illustratively from *The Pains of Sleep.* A smart attack of erysipelas followed, which he 'strongly suspected to be, in his constitution, a substitute for the gout, to which his father was subject'—an unguarded and consequently a significant remark, showing how he had forgotten that a quarter of a century before he had attributed a good many things to the gout in his own system. He is going to recruit by spending the month of November at Ramsgate, when he will 'do nothing but write verses and finish the correction of the last part of his work *On the Power and Use of Words.*'[1]

Whether either of these duties occupied his sea-side leisure, or whether the 'work' ever existed, I am unaware. This and the previous year (1827) saw the production of a few verses not unworthy of a place in his 'Tribuna,' or 'Salon carré'—*The Two Founts, Duty surviving Self-Love, The Improvisatore, Work without Hope,* and *The Garden of Boccaccio.* The beautiful lines, *Love, Hope, and Patience in Education,* belong to the following year.

[1] *Letters from the Lake Poets,* pp. 324-328.

These later poems lack in great measure the jewel tints which glow in the *Ancient Mariner* and *Christabel*, and exhibit little of the sweep of brush which distinguishes the early odes ; but, although now 'a common greyness silvers everything,' the old magic still mingles with the colours on the palette. Coleridge's attitude as he now looked over the wide landscape where all nature seemed at work, himself, held in the bondage of a spell of his own creating, "the sole unbusy thing," recalls Browning's picture of Andrea del Sarto watching the lights of Fiesole die out one by one, like his own hopes and ambitions. Coleridge also remembered days when he could leave the ground and 'put on the glory, Rafael's daily wear'—now he, himself a very Rafael, asks only to 'sit the grey remainder of his evening out,' and 'muse perfectly how he could paint—were he but back in France.'

> All Nature seems at work.    Slugs leave their lair—
> The bees are stirring—birds are on the wing—
> And Winter slumbering in the open air,
> Wears on his smiling face a dream of Spring !
> And I the while, the sole unbusy thing,
> Nor honey make, nor pair, nor build, nor sing.
>
>     Yet well I ken the banks where amaranths blow,
> Have traced the fount whence streams of nectar flow
> Bloom, O ye amaranths ! bloom for whom ye may,
> For me ye bloom not !    Glide, rich streams, away !
> With lips unbrightened, wreathless brow, I stroll :
> And would you learn the spells that drowse my soul ?
> Work without Hope draws nectar in a sieve,
> And Hope without an object cannot live.[1]

---

[1] '*Work without Hope*.   Lines composed 21st February 1827.'   The poem seems to have been composed in 1825, but as Coleridge added the date in the *Poet. Works* of 1828, his feelings were probably unchanged.   In March 18, 1826, he wrote thus to Lady Beaumont :   'Though I am at present sadly below even *my* par of health, or rather unhealth, and am the more depressed thereby from the consciousness that in this yearly resurrection of Nature from her winter sleep, amid young leaves and blossoms and twittering nest-building birds, the sun so gladsome, the breezes with such healing on their wings, all good and lovely things are beneath me, above me, and everywhere around me, and all from God,

In the winter of 1827-28 the Highgate 'Thursdays' began to be attended by a clever and enthusiastic young man, who, like Coleridge himself, had
left Cambridge without taking a degree.    Their
reasons    were    probably    the    same,    though the
divergencies between tests and beliefs were, in John
Sterling's case, much narrower than they had been in
that of Coleridge.   Like his college tutor, Julius Hare,
and his chief undergraduate friend, F. D. Maurice,[1]
Sterling had been steeped in the philosophy of the
*Biographia, The Friend*, and *Aids to Reflection*, and
until Coleridge's death he was one of the most assiduous
of the Highgate disciples.   Unfortunately, he took
notes of none but his first conversation with the
master, whose manner and address struck him as
'formally courteous,' and in keeping with his rather
'old-fashioned' appearance.   'He always speaks in
the tone and in the gesture of common conversation,
and laughs a good deal, but gently. . . . He speaks
perhaps rather slowly, but never stops, and seldom
even hesitates.'   On this first occasion Sterling
was 'in his company about three hours; and of
that time he spoke during two and three-quarters.'[2]
In 1834 Sterling entered the Church and worked
as Hare's curate for six months.   'This clerical aber-
ration,' writes Carlyle (p. 138), 'we have ascribed to
Coleridge; and do clearly think that had there been

---

while my incapability of enjoying, or, at best, languor in receiving them, is directly
or indirectly from myself, from past procrastination, and cowardly impatience of
pain' (*Coleorton Letters*, ii. 246).   See *Poetical Works*, ed. 1893, p. 643.

   [1] It is commonly assumed that Maurice, who, perhaps, did more than any
other man to spread the influence of Coleridge's teaching, went much to Highgate, but I am assured that he never even saw Coleridge.

   [2] *Essays and Tales by John Sterling* . . . with a Memoir of his Life, by J.
C. Hare, M.A. (2 vols. 1848), i. xxiv.   The memoir is not encumbered by over-
precision, either in the matter of dates, or otherwise.   In common with its
subject, its final cause seems to have been *The Life of John Sterling*, by T.
Carlyle.   London, 1851.

no Coleridge, neither had this been—nor had English
Puseyism, or some other strange portents been.'
Carlyle, it may be noted, did not make Sterling's
acquaintance until the beginning of 1835.    His
speculation may be true enough as respects Sterling.
As to the wider issues, it is probably a good deal
too sweeping.   Coleridge's teaching helped, if not to
originate, at least to develop both the High Church
and Broad Church revivals.    The movements have
since coalesced to a great extent, but students find
no difficulty in tracing historically the influence which
Coleridge exerted—an influence not the less powerful,
perhaps, because it was strictly indirect.

Early in 1829, Carlyle, who was himself a prophet
yet without honour, published in the *Foreign Review*
an essay on Novalis which opened with a kindly, almost
an enthusiastic appreciation of Coleridge.    It must
have cheered the heart of the elder philosopher, the
sheets of whose *Friend* and *Biographia Literaria* lay
mouldering in Mr. Gillman's cellar.

They are but a slight business (wrote Carlyle) compared with
Novalis's *Schriften* . . . yet Coleridge's works were triumphantly
condemned by the whole reviewing world, as clearly unintelligible,
and among readers they have still but an unseen circulation ; like
living brooks, hidden for the present under mountains of froth
and theatrical snow-paper, and which only at a distant day, when
these mountains shall have decomposed themselves into gas and
earthly residuum, may roll forth in their true limpid shape to
gladden the general eye with what beauty and everlasting freshness
does reside in them.    It is admitted too on all hands, that
Mr. Coleridge is a man of 'genius,' that is, a man having more
intellectual insight than other men ; and strangely enough, it is
taken for granted, at the same time, that he has less intellectual
insight than any other.    For why else are his doctrines to be thrown
out of doors without examination as false and worthless, simply because they are obscure?

In the autumn of 1827, Coleridge wrote some

fatherly verses to the bride of his son Derwent.[1]   Two
years later a similar occasion arose, but if any poetical
tribute was paid, it has not come down to us.   On
September 3, 1829, his daughter Sara was married to
her cousin Henry Nelson Coleridge, but the ceremony
took place at Crosthwaite church, near Greta Hall,
and although the young people settled at Hampstead,
the record of *Table Talk*, suspended on Aug. 30,
1827, was not resumed until April 30, 1830.   From
that date, however, it continues, almost without break,
until the end of Coleridge's life.   He seems to have
had a long illness in the summer of 1829, for Lamb in
answering a letter of that period says : 'How you
frighted me !   Never write again "Coleridge is dead"
at the end of a line, and tamely come in with "to his
friends" at the beginning of another.   Love is quicker,
and fear from love, than the transition ocular from line
to line.'[2]   On October 26, Lamb writes to Gillman[3]
of his grief at hearing of Coleridge's 'indifferent
health—and he not to know it!'   'A little school-
divinity,' he thinks, 'well applied, may be healing.
I send him honest Tom of Aquin . . . rescued
t'other day from a stall in Barbican.'   In November,
Mary Lamb is driven over to Highgate to fetch back
'*Him of Aquinum*,' and to borrow 'the golden works
of the dear fine silly old angel,' Fuller, which the
Lambs returned a month later, with a promise to
spend the first fine day at the Grove, trusting to the
Gate-House for beds.   In the May following, Lamb
reports of Coleridge[4] that he has had some severe
attack, not paralytic ; 'but if I had not heard of it,' he

[1] *To Mary Pridham, Poet. Works*, ed. 1893, p. 203.
[2] To Allsop (Lamb's *Letters*, ii. 226).
[3] *Ib*. ii. 232.
[4] May 10, 1830 (*Ib*. ii. 254).

adds, ' I should not have found it out.   He looks and especially speaks strong.'

It was doubtless of this illness that in a letter of July Coleridge writes that it had 'brought him to the brink of the grave.'   The letter was addressed to Thomas Poole, and accompanied a presentation copy of the writer's *Constitution of Church and State*,[1] in the course of which is drawn a fascinating picture of his old friend, the presentee.   In the preface to this pamphlet, the last of his works printed during his lifetime, Coleridge explains at considerable length that, while he is not unfriendly to Catholic Emancipation, he has scruples regarding the means proposed for its attainment.   He says the work is 'transcribed for the greater part from a paper drawn up by him some years ago at the request of J. Hookham Frere,' and which paper, had it been finished before he [Frere] left England, it was his intention to have laid before the late Lord Liverpool.'   He 'begs he may not be suspected of predilection for any particular sect or party; for wherever he looks, in religion or politics, he seems to see a world of power and talent wasted on the support of half-truths.'   His convictions on this subject, though revised from year to year, have been steadfast, and the pain of differing from men he has loved and revered, is 'aggravated by the reflection that in receding from the Burkes, Cannings, and Lansdownes, he did not move a step nearer to the feelings and opinions of their antagonists.'   The pamphlet, however, procured for Coleridge the name

---

[1] *On the Constitution of the Church and State, according to the idea of each ; with and toward a right judgment on the late Catholic Bill.*  By S. T. Coleridge, Esq., R.A., R.S.L.   London : Hurst, Chance, & Co. 1830, pp. viii. ; **227.**   A ' second edition,' with alterations and additions, soon followed—pp. viii. ; **241.** The sketch of Poole is at p. 102 of the first, and p. 115 of the second edition.

of High-churchman and Tory, and it is this work
which has often been credited with giving the first
impulse to the influences which, a few years later,
brought about the 'Oxford Movement.'

On June 26, 1830, died George IV., and with him
died the pensions of the Royal Associates. Apparently
they did not find this out until the following year. In
the *Englishman's Magazine* for June 1831, attention
was directed to the fact that 'intimation had been
given to Mr. Coleridge and his brother Associates
that they must expect their allowances "very shortly"
to cease'—the allowances having been a personal
bounty of the late King. On June 3, 1831, Gillman
wrote a letter to the *Times*, 'in consequence of a paragraph which appeared in the *Times* of this day.' He
states that on the sudden suppression of the honorarium,
representations on Coleridge's behalf were made to
Lord Brougham, with the result that the Treasury
(Lord Grey) offered a private grant of £200, which
Coleridge 'had felt it his duty most respectfully to
decline.' Stuart, however, wrote to King William's
son, the Earl of Munster, pointing out the hardship
entailed on Coleridge, whom he describes as old and
infirm, and without other means of subsistence. He
begs the Earl to lay the matter before his royal father.
To this a prompt reply came, excusing the King on
account of his 'very reduced income,' but promising
that the matter shall be submitted to His Majesty. To
these letters, which are printed in *Letters from the
Lake Poets* (pp. 319-322), the following note is appended: 'The annuity . . . was not renewed, but a
sum of £300 was ultimately handed over to Coleridge
by the Treasury.' Even apart from this bounty,
Coleridge was not a sufferer by the withdrawal of

the King's pension, for Frere made it up to him annually.[1]

The record of Coleridge's life after 1830 is summed up in a sentence written by him within a fortnight of his death : 'For the last three or four years I have, with few and brief intervals, been confined to a sick-room.'[2] In January 1831, Wordsworth saw his old friend several times and had long conversations with him, being grieved to observe that 'his constitution seems much broken up.' 'I have heard' (he adds) 'that he has been worse since I saw him. His mind has lost none of its vigour.'[3] In April 1832, Lamb writes to remove some mistaken sick-man's fancy :—

Not an unkind thought has passed in my brain concerning you ; but I have been wofully neglectful of you ; so that if I do not hear from you before then, I will set out on Wednesday morning to take you by the hand. I would do it this moment, but an unexpected visit might flurry you. I shall take silence for acquiescence, and come. I am glad you could write so long a letter. . . . If you ever [he adds in a *P.S.*] thought an offence, much more wrote it, against me, it must have been in the times of Noah, and the great waters have swept it away. Mary's most kind love. . . . Here she is crying for mere love over your letter. I wring out less, but not sincerer showers.[4]

In the same week Crabb Robinson 'saw Coleridge in bed. He looked beautifully—his eye remarkably brilliant—and he talked as eloquently as ever. His declamation was against the [Reform] Bill,' which, he considered, was being passed merely from fear of re-sisting popular opinion.[5] At the end of September, Robinson took Landor out to see him. They found him 'horribly bent and looking seventy years of age,' and disposed to talk principally of the loss of his

[1] Sir Walter Scott's *Journal*, 1890, ii. 449.
[2] Letter to Adam S. Kinnaird, July 13, 1834 (last page of *Table Talk*).
[3] Jan. 24, 1831, Knight's *Life*, iii. 189.
[4] Enfield, April 14, 1832 (*Letters*, ii. 278).
[5] *Diaries*, etc., ii. 128.

pension.   'Landor spoke in his dashing way, which Coleridge could understand.'[1]

A few weeks before this he had been able to go over to Hampstead to attend the christening of his grandchild Edith, the daughter of the second Sara. In conveying this news to Poole, the elder Mrs. Coleridge added that her husband 'talked a great deal of you, as he always does when he speaks of his early days.'[2]   And it was of those early days that Wordsworth too was thinking when, during this summer, he wrote to Rowan Hamilton[3] : 'He [S. T. C.] and my beloved sister are the two beings to whom my intellect is most indebted, and they are now proceeding as it were *pari passu*, along the path of sickness—I will not say towards the grave, but I trust towards a blessed immortality.'

Coleridge's health must have improved considerably in the summer of 1833, for in June he visited Cambridge on the occasion of the third meeting of the British Association.

My emotions (he said), at revisiting the University were at first overwhelming.   I could not speak for an hour ; yet my feelings were, upon the whole, pleasurable, and I have not passed, of late years at least, three days of such great enjoyment and healthful excitement of mind and body.   The bed on which I slept—and slept soundly too—was, as near as I can describe it, a couple of sacks full of potatoes tied together.   Truly I lay down at night a man, and arose in the morning a bruise.

'The two persons' (says H. N. Coleridge) 'of whom he spoke with the greatest interest were Mr. Faraday and Mr. Thirlwall.'[4]   Of this visit, Mrs. Clarkson

---

[1] *Diaries*, etc., ii. 132.
[2] *T. Poole and his Friends*, ii. 280.
[3] June 25, 1832, Knight's *Life*, iii. 213.
[4] *Table Talk*. Note to June 29, 1833. In *Conversations at Cambridge* (1836) Coleridge's old schoolfellow C. V. Le Grice professes to give specimens of his table-talk on one of these June evenings at Thirlwall's rooms in Trinity— in which college the old poet seems to have been put up.

heard through Rydal Mount that Coleridge, 'though not able to rise till the afternoon, had a crowded *levée* at his bedside.'[1] It was in July of this year that he declared he could write as good verses as ever 'if perfectly free from vexations, and in the *ad libitum* hearing of good music'; and that his reason for not finishing *Christabel* was not the want of a plan, but the seemingly inevitable failure of continuations.[2]

It must have been about this time that Harriet Martineau paid that visit to Coleridge, of which she has given a characteristic account.

> He looked very old with his rounded shoulders, and drooping head, and excessively thin limbs. His eyes were as wonderful as they were ever represented to be—light grey, extremely prominent, and actually glittering. . . . He told me that he read my [Political Economy] tales as they came out, and . . . avowed that there were some points in which we differed. . . . For instance, said he, 'You appear to consider that society is an aggregate of individuals.' I replied, I certainly did, whereupon he went off . . . on a long flight in survey of society from his own balloon in his own current. He came down again to some considerations of individuals, and at length to some special biographical topics, ending with criticisms on old biographers, whose venerable works he brought down from the shelf. . . . I am glad to have seen his weird face, and heard his dreamy voice; and my notion of possession, prophecy,—of involuntary speech from involuntary brain action has been clearer since.[3]

What Coleridge thought of 'modern Political Economy' is stated in very plain language in *Table Talk* for March 17, 1833, and June 23, 1834. It is a 'solemn humbug'; without theorems, presenting only problems; 'the direct tendency of every rule of which is to denationalise, to make the love of our country a foolish superstition.'

On Aug. 5, Emerson, then a young man of thirty, on his first pilgrimage to Europe, called on

---

[1] H. C. R.'s *Diaries*, etc., ii. 143.   [2] *Table Talk*, July 6, 1833.
[3] *Autobiography*, i. 396-9.

Coleridge.[1]    He saw 'a short, thick old man, with
bright blue [*sic*] eyes, and fine clear complexion,' who
'took snuff freely, which presently soiled his cravat
and neat black suit'—the Coleridge whom Maclise
in that same year drew for the *Fraser* Gallery.[2]   The
visit was a failure, for an unhappy mention of Dr.
Channing caused the champion of orthodoxy to 'burst
into a declamation on the folly and ignorance of
Unitarianism,—its high unreasonableness,'—a declama
tion which gained fresh impetus from Emerson's inter-
jected avowal that he himself 'had been born and bred
a Unitarian.'   When at the end of an hour the visitor
rose to go, Coleridge changed the note from negative
to positive, reciting the lately-composed lines on his
*Baptismal Birthday;* and Emerson when he left, felt
that nothing had been satisfied but his curiosity.

Coleridge had then barely another year to live, and
though it was one of ever-increasing bodily pain and
weakness, all witnesses testify that the spirit remained
strong and willing to the very end.   In the winter he
took leave of himself in the well-known *Epitaph*,[3] but
his eyes were yet to be gladdened by another spring
and summer.   Within two months of the end, Poole
found his old friend with 'a mind as strong as ever,
seemingly impatient to take leave of its encumbrance.'[4]

[1] *English Traits*, chap. i. (*Works*, 1883, iv. 6-10).

[2] *Fraser's Mag.* viii. 632.   Reprinted in *A Gallery of Illustrious Literary
Characters*, ed. by W. Bates, 1873.

> [3] Stop, Christian passer-by !—Stop, child of God,
> And read with gentle breast.   Beneath this sod
> A poet lies, or that which once seem'd he.—
> O, 'lift one thought in prayer for S. T. C. ;
> That he who many a year with toil of breath
> Found death in life, may here find life in death
> Mercy for praise—to be forgiven for fame
> He ask'd, and hop'd, through Christ.
>         Do thou the same !
> *9th November* 1833.

[4] *T. Poole and his Friends*, ii. 294.

A month later another visitor, unnamed, observed that Coleridge's 'countenance was pervaded by a most remarkable serenity,' which, as the conversation showed, was a true reflection of his mind. In this atmosphere of peace, he assured his visitor, all things were seen by him 'reconciled and harmonised.'[1] On July 20th, dangerous symptoms appeared, and for several days his sufferings were great, but they abated during the final thirty-six hours. The only account of the closing scenes which has come down to us is contained in a letter written by his daughter Sara, Mrs. H. N. Coleridge :—

Henry saw him for the last time on Sunday [July 20], and conveyed his blessing to my mother and myself; but we made no attempt to see him, and my brothers were not sent for, because the medical men apprehended that the agitation of such interviews would be more than he ought to encounter. Not many hours before his death, he was raised in his bed and wrote a precious faintly-scrawled scrap, which we shall ever preserve, recommending his faithful nurse, Harriet, to the care of his family. Mr. Green, who had been so long the partner of his literary labours, was with him at the last, and to him on the last evening of his life, he repeated a certain part of his religious philosophy, which he was especially anxious to have accurately recorded. He articulated with the utmost difficulty, but his mind was clear and powerful, and so continued till he fell into a state of coma, which lasted till he ceased to breathe, about six o'clock in the morning [Friday, July 25]. . . . A few out of his many deeply attached and revering friends attended his remains to the grave, together with my husband and [his brother, the poet's nephew] Edward, and that body which did him such 'grievous wrong' was laid in its final resting-place in Highgate churchyard.[2]

None of Coleridge's oldest friends stood by the grave. Poole was far in the west, Wordsworth and Southey as far in the north, and Morgan was dead.

---

[1] Knight's *Life of Wordsworth*, iii. 236.

[2] *Mem. of Sara* [Mrs. H. N.] *Coleridge*, i. 109, 111. The funeral took place on August 2. In the same letter Mrs. Coleridge mentions that her father's body ' was opened, according to her own earnest request. The causes of his death were sufficiently manifest in the state of the vital parts ; but that internal pain from which he suffered more or less during his whole life was not to be explained, or only by that which medical men call nervous sympathy.'

Lamb was near, but his feelings would not permit him to join the sorrowing company. During the few months of life which remained to him, he never recovered from his sense of loss. 'Coleridge is dead,' was the abiding thought in his mind and on his lips. ' His great and dear spirit haunts me,' he wrote, five weeks before his own death—' never saw I his likeness, nor probably the world can see again. I seem to love the house he died in more passionately than when he lived. What was his mansion is consecrated to me a chapel.'[1] When Wordsworth read the news his voice faltered and then broke, but he seems to have said little except of his friend's genius, calling him ' the most *wonderful* man that he had ever known.[2] What Southey said has not been recorded. What he wrote[3] is better forgotten. Doubtless he had the rights which his wrongs gave him, but he remembered both at an inappropriate moment. He had been, so to speak, a father to the fatherless and a husband to the widow, and it detracts nothing from the credit due to him, that in many ways, perhaps even in a pecuniary sense, he had been repaid to an extent larger than is generally supposed. But surely, just then, a sense of his inestimable indebtedness to his dead comrade of forty years, for friendship, for inspiration, and for intellectual stimulus, should have been uppermost in his mind.

In his will Coleridge well described the Gillmans as his 'dear friends, his more than friends, the guardians of his health, happiness, and interests' during the latter sixteen years of his life, and no one

---

[1] *New Monthly Magazine*, Feb. 1835.
[2] Knight's *Life*, iii. 235.
[3] Letter to Mrs. Hughes in *Letters*, etc., iv. 381. See also Thomas Moore's *Memoirs* (vii. 69-73) quoted in Knight's *Life of Wordsworth*, iii. 248.

who loves Coleridge, and all that he was and is to the world, can but share in his feelings of gratitude. The will, which is full of such acknowledgments, is, in other respects, thus summarised by the poet's daughter [1] :—

What little he had to bequeath (a policy of assurance worth about £2560) is my mother's for life, of course, and will come to her children equally after her time. Mr. Green has the sole power over my father's literary remains, and the philosophical part he will himself prepare for publication; some theological treatises [2] he has placed in the hands of Mr. Julius Hare of Cambridge and his curate, Mr. Sterling (both men of great ability). Henry will arrange literary and critical pieces, notes on the margins of books, or any miscellaneous productions of that kind that may be met with among his MSS., and probably some letters will appear if they can be collected.

How worthily Coleridge's nephew fulfilled his duty, so long as fading health permitted, and with what ability and filial piety the task which fell from his hands was taken up and carried on, first by the poet's daughter, and next by her brother Derwent, is well known to a grateful world. The tasks handed over by Green were possible tasks. That which was impossible he chivalrously kept for himself—the completion of the *magnum opus*.

About a year after Coleridge's death, an accession of fortune enabled Green to renounce the private practice of his profession, and in his country retirement he devoted the remaining twenty-eight years of his life to an attempt to realise his master's dream.[3] It

---

[1] *Mem. of S. Coleridge*, i. iii. Most of the will (dated Sep. 17, 1829) is given in the *Gent. Mag.* for December 1834. It is printed in full, with the codicil of July 2, 1830, in Coleridge's *Poems*. London: J. T. Cox, 1836, pp. liii.-lx.

[2] What became of the 'theological treatises'—what they were, or whether they ever reached the hands of Hare and Sterling, I know not. One may have been *Confessions of an Inquiring Spirit*, edited by H. N. Coleridge (1840); and another, certain commentaries on the Gospels and Epistles, which still remain in MS.

[3] *Spiritual Philosophy*, founded on the teaching of the late S. T. Coleridge, by the late J. H. Green, F.R.S., D.C.L., edited with a Memoir of the Author's Life, by John Simon, F.R.S., 2 vols. 1865.

was in vain.    There was no *magnum opus*—'the existence of any such work was mere matter of moonshine,' says Green's biographer and editor.

Coleridge had not left any available written materials for setting
comprehensively before the public in his own language, and in an
argued form, the philosophical system with which he wished his name
to be identified.    Instead of it there were fragments—for the most
part mutually inadaptable fragments, and beginnings, and studies of
special subjects, and numberless notes on the margins and fly leaves
of books.    True, that in unambiguous terms he had sounded the
key-note of his philosophy.    And there was the tradition of his oral
teachings.    And many of the written fragments were in the highest
degree interesting and suggestive, such as those which were successively published, under Mr. Green's authority, in the four volumes
of *Literary Remains*, and in the so-entitled *Confessions of an Inquiring
Spirit*.

In his Hunterian Orations of 1840 and 1847, Green
probably accomplished more in the setting forth of
Coleridge's philosophical views than in the *Spiritual
Philosophy*.    But of these high matters I have no
right to speak, and even were it otherwise, this would
not be the place.    Neither have I felt called on to discuss Coleridge's position as a poet.    That has been
settled, and is unlikely to be disturbed.    My sole aim
has been to supply a fairly complete and accurate
narrative of the events of his life.

I WOULD fain leave the foregoing narrative to work its own impression on the mind of the reader. If its somewhat fuller and more orderly presentment of what I believe to be the truth, be not found to tend, on the whole, to raise Coleridge in the eyes of men, I shall, I confess, feel both surprised and disappointed. It is neither by glossing over his failings, nor by fixing an exclusive eye on them, that a true estimate of any man is to be arrived at. A better way is to collect as many facts as we can, set them in the light of the circumstances in which they were born, sort them fairly into the opposing scales, and weigh them in an atmosphere as free as possible from cant and prejudice. To my own mind it seems that Coleridge's failings are too obvious to require either all the insistence or all the moralising which have been lavished on them; and that his fall is less wonderful than his recovery. His will was congenitally weak, and his habits weakened it still farther; but his conscience, which was never allowed to sleep, tortured him; and, after many days, its workings stimulated the. paralysed will, and he was saved.

A brief dawn of unsurpassed promise and achievement; 'a trouble' as of 'clouds and weeping rain'; then, a long summer evening's work done by 'the setting sun's pathetic light'—such was Coleridge's day, the after-glow of which is still in the sky. I am sure that the temple, with all the rubble which blended with its marble, must have been a grander whole than any we are able to reconstruct for ourselves from the stones which lie about the field. The living Coleridge was ever his own apology—men and women who neither shared nor ignored his shortcomings, not only loved him, but honoured and followed him. This power of attraction, which might almost be called universal, so diverse were the minds and natures attracted, is itself conclusive proof of very rare qualities. We may read and re-read his life, but we cannot know him as the Lambs, or the Wordsworths, or Poole, or Hookham Frere, or the Gillmans, or Green knew him. Hatred as well as love may be blind, but friendship has eyes, and their testimony may wisely be used in correcting our own impressions.

Mrs. Coleridge survived her husband for eleven years. In 1845 she passed away, at the house of her daughter, which had been her home since 1830. The three children who had grown up all outlived both parents. Hartley, the eldest born, was a poet and a man of letters. Not a few of his sonnets have taken a place in permanent literature, and as a critic and essayist he is remarkable for lucidity of style, and balance of thought and judgment. He was a gentle, simple, humble-minded man, but his life was marred and broken by intemperance. He lies, in death as in life, close to the heart of Wordsworth, and his name still lingers in affectionate remembrance by those 'lakes and sandy shores' beside which he was, as his father had prophesied, to 'wander like a breeze.' The career of Derwent, both as to the conduct of life and its rewards, was in marked contrast to his brother's. His bent was to be a student, but he was forced into action, partly by circumstance, partly by an honourable ambition. During a long and useful life, more than twenty years of which were spent as Principal of St. Mark's College, Chelsea, he did signal service to the cause of national education. He cannot be said to have left his mark on literature, but his chief work, *The Scriptural Character of the English Church*, won the admiration of F. D. Maurice for 'its calm scholar-like tone and careful English style.' He was appointed a Prebendary of St. Paul's in 1846, and Rector of Hanwell in 1863. The leisure of his later years was devoted to linguistic and philological studies, in which his attainments were remarkable. At rare intervals, to the inner circle of his friends, he would talk by the hour, and though in these 'conversational mono-logues' he resembled rather than approached his father, he delivered himself with a luminous wisdom all his own. He edited the works of his father, of his brother, and of his friends, Winthrop Mackworth Praed and John Moultrie. Of his sister Sara, it has been said that 'her father looked down into her eyes, and left in them the light of his own.' Her beauty and grace were as remarkable as her talents, her learning, and her accomplishments; but her chief characteristic was 'the radiant spirituality of her intellectual and imaginative being.' This, with other rare qualities of mind and spirit, is indicated in Wordsworth's affectionate appreciation in *The Triad*, and conspicuous in her fairy-tale *Phantasmion*, and in the letters which compose the bulk of her *Memoirs*.

# APPENDIX

THE ORIGINAL PROSPECTUS OF 'THE WATCHMAN'

*(See Chapter III. p.* 51)

———

That All may know the TRUTH ;
And that the TRUTH may make us FREE ! !

———

*On Friday, the* 5*th Day of February*

1796

WILL BE PUBLISHED

No. I.

(PRICE FOUR PENCE)

OF A

MISCELLANY, TO BE PUBLISHED EVERY EIGHTH DAY,

UNDER THE NAME OF

'THE WATCHMAN.'

———

BY S. T. COLERIDGE,

AUTHOR OF

ADDRESSES TO THE PEOPLE,

A PLOT DISCOVERED, etc., etc.

———

The Publishers in the different
Towns and Cities will be
specified in future Advertisements.

# PROSPECTUS

IN AN ENSLAVED STATE THE RULERS FORM AND SUPPLY THE OPINIONS OF THE PEOPLE.

This is the mark by which Despotism is distinguished: for it is the power by which Despotism is begun and continued.

—— ' *The abuses, that are rooted in all the old Governments of Europe, give such numbers of men such a direct interest in supporting, cherishing, and defending abuses, that no wonder advocates for tyranny of every species are found in every country and almost in every company. What a mass of People in every part of England are some way or other interested in the present representation of the people, in tythes, charters, corporations, monopolies, and taxation! and not merely in the things themselves, but in all the abuses attending them; and how many are there who derive their profit or their consideration in life, not merely from such institutions, but from the evils they engender!* '

ARTHUR YOUNG'S TRAVELS.

Among the most powerful advocates and auxiliaries of abuses we must class (with a few honorable exceptions) the weekly Provincial Newspapers, the Editors of which receive the Treasury Prints gratis, and in some instances *with particular paragraphs marked out for their insertion.* —— These Papers form the chief, and sometimes the only, reading of that large and important body of men, who living out of towns and cities have no opportunity of hearing calumnies exposed and false statements detected. Thus are Administrations enabled to steal away their Rights and Liberties, either so gradually as to undermine their Freedom without alarming them: or if it be necessary to carry any great point suddenly, to overthrow their Freedom by alarming them against themselves.

A PEOPLE ARE FREE IN PROPORTION AS THEY FORM THEIR OWN OPINIONS. In the strictest sense of the word KNOWLEDGE IS POWER.

Without previous illumination a change in the *forms* of Government will be of no avail. These are but the shadows, the virtue and rationality of the People at large are the substance, of Freedom : and where Corruption and Ignorance are prevalent, the best *forms* of Government are but the 'Shadows of a Shade !' We actually transfer the Sovereignty to the People, when we make them susceptible of it. In the present perilous state of our Constitution the Friends of Freedom, of Reason, and of Human Nature, must feel it their duty by every mean in their power to supply or circulate political information. We ask not their patronage : It will be obtained in proportion as we shall be found to deserve it. —— Our Miscellany will be comprised in two sheets, or thirty-two pages, closely printed, the size and type the same as of this PROSPECTUS. —— The contents will be

  I. An History of the domestic and foreign Occurrences of the preceding days.

 II. The Speeches in both Houses of Parliament : and during the Recess, select Parliamentary Speeches, from the commencement of the reign of Charles the First to the present æra, with Notes historical and biographical.

III. Original Essays and Poetry, chiefly or altogether political.

It's chief objects are to co-operate (1) with the WHIG CLUB in procuring a repeal of Lord Grenville's and Mr. Pitt's bills, now passed into laws, and (2) with the PATRIOTIC SOCIETIES for obtaining a Right of Suffrage general and frequent.

In the cities of London, Bristol, 　　　, 　　, and 　　, it will appear as regularly as a Newspaper, over which it will have these advantages :—

  I. There being no advertisements, a greater quantity of original matter must be given.

 II. From its form, it may be bound up at the end of the year, and become an Annual Register.

III. This last circumstance may induce Men of Letters to prefer this Miscellany to more perishable publications, as the vehicle of their effusions.

It remains to say, that whatever powers or acquirements the Editor possesses, he will dedicate *entirely* to this work; and (which is of more importance to the Public) he has received promises of occasional assistance from literary men of eminence and established reputation.     With such encouragement he offers himself to the Public as a faithful

### WATCHMAN,

to proclaim the State of the Political Atmosphere, and preserve Freedom and her Friends from the attacks of Robbers and Assassins!!

# INDEX

THE END